Middlemarch

Middlemarsh

The Hopkins River,
Kindred Wetlands
and Remarkable People

Rod Giblett

TRANSNATIONAL PRESS LONDON

2023

TRANSNATIONAL LIVES SERIES: 4

Middlemarsh: The Hopkins River, Kindred Wetlands and Remarkable People
By Rod Giblett

First published in 2023 by Transnational Press London in the United Kingdom, 13 Stamford Place, Sale, M33 3BT, UK.
www.tplondon.com

Transnational Press London® and the logo and its affiliated brands are registered trademarks.

Requests for permission to reproduce material from this work should be sent to: sales@tplondon.com

ISBN: 978-1-80135-199-7 (Paperback)
ISBN: 978-1-80135-213-0 (Hardcover)
ISBN: 978-1-80135-200-0 (Digital)

Cover Design: Nihal Yazgan
Cover Image: Eugene Von Guérard Mt William from Mt Dryden, Victoria 1857, oil on canvas 61.5 x 91.5 cm (sight) 76.2 x 106 x 7 cm (framed) State Art Collection, Art Gallery of Western Australia

Transnational Press London Ltd. is a company registered in England and Wales No. 8771684.

Dedicated to the People of these Places –

Past, Present and Future

ABOUT THE AUTHOR

Rod Giblett is the author of 30 books of fiction and faction ('non-fiction'). He lived by a wetland in Western Australia for 28 years that he called 'Black Swan Lake' and wrote several books about it. He now lives in Melbourne and wrote about it, its wetlands and the Yarra River in *Modern Melbourne: City and Site of Nature and Culture* (Intellect Books, 2020). He is Honorary Associate Professor of Environmental Humanities in the Writing and Literature Program of the School of Communication and Creative Arts at Deakin University.

CONTENTS

PREFACE

One book leads to another; one book grows out of another; one book flows out of others. Flowing is a fitting figure for a book about a river, creeks, wetlands and water. The present volume grew out of a brief discussion of two paintings of wetlands in mid-western Victoria by the nineteenth-century colonial landscape painter Eugene von Guérard. This discussion was part of a chapter on wetlands in Australian painting and photography (Giblett 2020a). It was included in John Ryan's and Li Chen's edited collection *Australian Wetland Cultures* (Ryan and Chen, eds 2020). I also contributed a chapter to this volume on Aboriginal wetland cultures, their sacral water beings and their refraction in Rainbow Serpent anthropology and Rainbow Spirit theology (Giblett 2020e). I take up and develop this discussion in the present volume in relation to particular Aboriginal peoples and places in mid-western Victoria, their practices of wetland cultures and their stories about and images of them, including the Rainbow Serpent.

The discussion of von Guérard's wetland paintings was combined later in a longer discussion of mid-western Victoria and some of its wetlands with a discussion of these wetlands portrayed by the contemporary environmental artist Carole Mules in a chapter of *Wetlands and Western Cultures* (Giblett 2021c, chapter 4). Carole's environmental artwork (including of these wetlands) was included in a group exhibition in the Willaura Modern gallery from December 2020 to March 2021. I was fortunate to be in Willaura for the opening of the exhibition in December 2020. In light of my recent research into Mitchell's field notes and those of his assistant, Staplyton, this chapter has been expanded and revised as chapter 3 of the present volume.

The penultimate chapter of *Wetlands and Western Cultures* (Giblett 2021c, chapter 8) discussed the life and work of the American environmental philosopher and nature writer Henry David Thoreau. This chapter grew out of an earlier, brief discussion of Thoreau as 'the patron saint of swamps' in the final chapter of *Postmodern Wetlands* (Giblett 1996, chapter 10), the first such instance of his sanctification as such. Both discussions focussed on his journal and 'Walking,' his last, great essay of nature writing published after his death. The later discussion also focussed on *Walden*, his second and most famous book, and on my visit to Walden Pond in 2019. Writing the first chapter of the present volume gave me the opportunity to reflect on the pertinence to my discussion of the Hopkins River of Thoreau's first and least famous book, *A Week on the Concord and Merrimack Rivers*. In this chapter I dub him 'a companion of a captain of conservation' on our journey along the course of the Hopkins River from source to sea. Thoreau also makes a cameo appearance in later chapters, especially in relation to birds and bird-hunting or not in chapter 4, and to fish and fishing (or angling) or not in the final chapter.

When I first started thinking about writing the present volume, I thought about trying to travel down the Hopkins River from source to sea by boat, canoe or kayak, to reproduce the Thoreauvian water-borne experience, and write a kind of *A Week on the Hopkins River*, an Australian equivalent to Thoreau's book. Unfortunately, I was unable to do so for a number reasons in different cases, including the fact that the river is obstructed and shallow in many places by all accounts, including that of Bob McKenzie (2001) who walked down the Hopkins. Where it is not, such as the nine-kilometre long estuary, a commercial boat tour of the estuary had ceased operations in 2020 due to COVID and I was unable to access a private boat in May 2021 during my visit to Warrnambool.

I also thought about trying to go on a pilgrimage along the banks of the river and to follow in the footsteps of Bob McKenzie down the Hopkins, but this also proved impossible for a number of reasons. Bob McKenzie took five weeks to walk the length of the Hopkins in 2000 and had to get permission beforehand to cross the boundary fences demarcating private property and intersecting with the river. His river pilgrimage was also supported by a logistical operation. All these factors were a bridge too far for me.

I had to settle for various road trips over several years to Ararat, Rossbridge, Lake Bolac, Wickliffe, Willaura, Mortlake, Framlingham, Allansford and Warrnambool. These enabled me to experience the river from its banks, its kindred wetlands from their margins and to fill in some of the gaps on its journey from source to sea. I was also fortunate to meet some informative locals and in some cases to have tours of some of these places guided by them (as acknowledged elsewhere in the present volume). A road trip to Wickliffe and Chatsworth booked for August 2021 and a second road trip to Mortlake booked for February 2021 were cancelled due to lockdowns in Melbourne. On both occasions I had teed up to meet with some informative locals and to have tours guided by them of their stretch of the river and their homely wetlands. My appreciation and knowledge would have been enhanced and enriched if these tours had gone ahead. No doubt the present volume is the poorer without making them. Blame COVID! On the upside, my exchanges with these informative locals were largely conducted by email. This meant their responses to my questions were considered and easily citable with their permission as acknowledged later.

In the process of researching *Middlemarsh*, I found a number of allusions in the historical record to biblical events and places, such as the renaming of the well-watered grassy plains of the region as the garden of Eden. Pursuing and unpacking these allusions developed into writing *Middlemarsh* as 'A Week *of* the Hopkins River' arranged in seven chapters and the introduction structured around, and thematized by, the biblical story of the seven days of creation in the book of *Genesis*. Parallels between the two stories are drawn by presenting verses from *Genesis* about each of the seven days of creation as an epigraph to the introduction and each of the seven chapters, and by referring to them later in the discussion in these chapters. *Middlemarsh* is a book for the contemplation and conservation of the creativity of the life-giving waters of the Hopkins, its kindred, womby wetlands and its rich, fertile plains presented in the introduction and the seven chapters that follow. It also discusses other allusions in the historical record of other stories from the bible. These stories include the latter day Noah who "came to rest" at Ararat and founded this town in Australia and the latter day Moses of Major Mitchell who led God's 'chosen people' of colonial settlers to 'the promised land' of 'Australia Felix.'

One book also grows out of contacts with likeminded people; one contact leads to another contact and another book. At the opening of the group exhibition in the Willaura Modern gallery in December 2020, I was very fortunate to meet Ayesha Burdett and Howard Brandenburg who live on their family farm on the Hopkins River called 'River Bend' near Wickliffe. They are involved in its conservation as introduced in 'the cast of characters' of the first chapter and whose life-stories are told in chapter 4 of the present volume and their work (including artwork) discussed too. Some of Howard's artworks were exhibited in the group exhibition. He is also a scientific illustrator of fish, some of which are of the fish of the Hopkins River and its tributaries. Ayesha is a freshwater ecologist and the Landcare facilitator for the Upper Hopkins whose work is discussed in this chapter too. Fortunately, I was able to visit Wickliffe in March 2022, chat with Ayesha and George Burdett and Howard Brandenburg, and have a guided tour of their section of the Hopkins River.

Chapter 5 of the present volume grew out of reading Charles Massy's discussion in *Call of the Reed Warbler* (2020) of Richard and Jenny Weatherly's regenerative farming practices on their farm, including working with wetlands, on the Hopkins River near Mortlake that I visited in December 2020. This chapter also grew out of *Forest Family* (Giblett and Ryan, eds 2018) that interweaves the environmental and conservation history of the forests of south-west Western Australia, the family history of the Gibletts who were pioneers in Balbarrup/Manjimup in these forests from 1865 and the Aboriginal history of the forests and the place. My family history is also connected with western Victoria. A great aunt of mine was made pregnant by a western district pastoralist and banished to Western Australia with £10 for her trouble. She and her sister, my grandmother, ended up in Manjimup where they started up and ran a boarding house. My grandfather and grandmother met and married in Manjimup.

Richard Weatherley's *A Brush with Birds* was published in December 2020. It weaves together his family history, memoirs of growing up by wetlands along the Hopkins River, autobiography of his training and development as an artist, stories of travelling the world and coming home to regenerate farmland and rehabilitate wetlands, accompanied by his illustrations of local and international birds and bird habitats. I bought a copy of this book from Roz Greenwood's bookshop in Dunkeld in December 2020 where it had been launched a couple of weeks before. Writing chapter five gave me the opportunity to retell the story of the prominent Aboriginal elder of this place, Kaawirn Kuunawarn (Hissing Swan) who was born there in *c*.1820 and removed from it in 1865, and to place the story of the Weatherlys who arrived in 1895 and still live there within that much longer historical view and greater cultural context. This discontinuous family history with a three decade gap between them is also a shared human history of the place over two centuries. It shows how the two cultures are intertwined in a common concern with caring for Country. The Aboriginal, colonial, environmental, family and farming histories of this place have not previously been told together in one place. Chapter 5 does so, and so does chapter 6 with another place further downstream on the Hopkins.

Chapter 6 grew out of reading Banjo Clarke's life story of living for much of his life by the Hopkins River at Framlingham Aboriginal community (formerly Mission, or 'the Mish'). This and the final chapter grew out of making contact with some very helpful people in Warrnambool in May 2021 and accessing materials held in the Deakin University library by the Hopkins River in Warrnambool. While I was in Warrnambool one of my travelling companions saw banners hanging in the streets promoting the 'Soggy Homes' interactive installation and the 'Mirteetch Meering (Sea Country)' exhibition at the Warrnambool Art Gallery held from January to June 2021. Serendipity in research is a valuable phenomenon. We had hit paydirt! Chapter 6 delivers the pay off.

Following in the recent footsteps of *Australian Wetland Cultures* (Ryan and Chen, eds 2020), *Forest Family* (Giblett and Ryan, eds 2018) and *Wetlands and Western Cultures* (Giblett 2021c) and building on previous work on people and places of nature and culture (Giblett 2011), on local and oral natural and cultural history of the people and place of a wetland in Western Australia (Giblett 2006) and nature writing about it (Giblett 2013), and on wetlands in other places and their peoples in Western Australia (Giblett and Webb 1996) and in Canada (Giblett 2014), the present volume interweaves Aboriginal, colonial, family and environmental history in an ecocultural study of people and place that is committed politically and environmentally to conservation, decolonization, justice, treaty-making, truth-telling and reconciliation.

The present volume also follows in the footsteps of the pioneering work of Raymond Williams who I have dubbed "the patron saint of ecocultural studies" (Giblett 2020c, chapter 10). Williams' work on nature ("the most complex word in the English language"), landscapes (such as 'pleasing prospects'), livelihood and socialist ecology is directly pertinent to the present study of the 'pleasing prospects' of mid-western Victoria fed and watered by the Hopkins River, its tributaries and wetlands, as well as to the livelihoods of the Aboriginal and colonial settlers who lived and still live here. It is also pertinent to the calls of the present study for re-commoning the land countering the enclosing of the commons into private property. The stories of the Hopkins River, its kindred wetlands and the remarkable people of these watery places are the narrative threads that tie *Middlemarsh* together along the course of the river from source to sea.

The three appendices to the present volume place the Hopkins River and its kindred wetlands within a larger national, transnational and transdisciplinary context by reviewing three recent books, the first book about the Murray-Darling Basin in Australia and its wetlands (O'Gorman, 2021), the second about some English wetlands (Gearey *et al*, 2020) and the third introducing the Environmental Humanities, including what it calls "the wetland humanities" (Hubbell and Ryan, 2022). They give a bigger picture and provide a greater context of wetland history and conservation elsewhere in Australia and transnationally in England. They are also situated within the greater context of the disciplines of cultural geography, environmental history, ecocultural studies and the transdisciplinary Environmental Humanities.

The wetlands discussed in the first two books highlight similar issues and challenges to those discussed in the present volume with the wetlands of the Hopkins basin. They also provide similar avenues of hope and opportunities for the conservation of wetlands around the world. The first book is about specific wetlands in the Murray-Darling Basin coming out of environmental history and ethnography published in the Weyerhauser Environmental Books series by the University of Washington Press.

The second book is about specific wetlands in England coming out of historical geography and the environmental humanities published in the Palgrave Pivot series. The first two books are part of a spate of recent books about wetlands arising out of similar approaches, such as the edited collection *Australian Wetland Cultures* (Ryan and Chen, 2020) published in the Environment and Society series by Lexington Books, and about wetlands in other countries, such as *Canadian Wetlands* published in the Cultural Studies of Natures, Landscapes and Environments series by Intellect Books (Giblett 2014), as well as a number of books about specific wetlands in the United States, Spain and Vietnam also published in the Weyerhauser Environmental Books series (Sutter 2021, x-xi). The third book places the wetland humanities within the broader transdisciplinary and transnational context of the Environmental Humanities. My review of it also places it within the context of ecocultural studies, psychoanalytic ecology and the work of Walter Benjamin. More books about wetlands have since appeared in 2022, making them the flavour of the month, or the year, such as Tom Blass's *Swamp Songs*, my *Swamp Deaths* and Annie Proulx's *Fen, Bog and Swamp*.

Middlemarsh with its appendices reviewing kindred books about wetlands and the environmental humanities invite the reader to wade into wetlands and books about them, further explore them, and contribute to their conservation. Wetland cultures live!

Coburg,

Victoria,

Australia,

2022

ACKNOWLEDGEMENTS

I begin by making an acknowledgement of country. I acknowledge the Eastern Maar Corporation, the Registered Aboriginal Party for the Djab wurrung, Pik Wurrung, Kuurn Kopan Noot and Girai Wurrung peoples, the traditional owners, users and inhabitants of the lands (dry, wet and in-between) that this book is about. This country "always was, always will be, Aboriginal country." I acknowledge especially Kaawirn Kuunawarn (hissing swan) (*c*.1820-1889) whose name is given to (or taken from, and memorialised by) Lake Connewarren, Connewarren Lane and *Connewarran* station. His story is fairly well-documented in the existing literature, a matter of public record and easily accessible online (for all of which I am grateful). His story is retold briefly in chapter 5 in relation to his place of birth of Lake Connewarren and his home of the clan estates in the bioregion of the Victorian volcanic plains and in chapter 6 in relation to his place of death at Framlingham.

I am grateful to Carole Mules for drawing my attention to the meaning of the Aboriginal name 'Connewarran' in Ian Clark's multi-voluminous and immensely invaluable work documenting Aboriginal peoples, their languages and lands in Victoria. I am also grateful to Carole for drawing my attention to, and lending me her copy of, Heather Ronald's history of the Chirnside family. I am also grateful to her for drawing my attention to the history of Mortlake and Lake Webster, to Lourandos' chapter on "swamp managers" of southwestern Victoria and for permission to reproduce a quote from her email to me of December 1, 2020. I am also grateful to Helen Miller and Warwick Mules for setting up the initial contact with Carole. Sadly Carole passed away in September 2021 while I was writing the present volume and she is sorely missed by all who knew her. She is now laid to rest in the Streatham Cemetery where her father is also buried. Her environmental artwork is introduced in chapter 1 and later reproduced and discussed in chapter 3. I am grateful to the copyright holders and current owners for permission to reproduce her artwork as indicated in the captions to these figures in chapter 3. The dedication of the present volume to 'the People of these Places – Past, Present and Future' implicitly includes Carole; the dedication of my work in progress, *Black Waters Live: Or, the Fertile Serpent,* is explicitly and directly dedicated to her memory.

I am grateful to John Charles Ryan for drawing my attention to the concept of the paludal (from the Latin for *palus* for mire or marsh) and for his helpful comments and email exchanges on the yam daisy. I am also grateful to John for his invitation to contribute to *Revista Interdisciplinar de Literatura e Ecocrítica (RILE),* where a shorter version of the introduction was published in volume 1, number 9, 2022, pages 15-35.

I am grateful to Ayesha Burdett and Howard Brandenburg for their valuable and vital input into chapter 4, especially the email exchanges of August and September 2021 when various COVID lockdowns in Melbourne meant that a planned trip to visit them had to be cancelled and I had to resort to electronic means of communication. They graciously answered my questions, corrected my mistakes and supplied important autobiographical information and family history for chapter 4. I am also grateful to both of them for permission to quote from their emails. As mentioned previously in the 'Preface,' I was able to visit Ayesha and Howard and meet George Burdett in March 2022 at 'River Bend' near Wickliffe and have a guided and informative tour of some of their section of the Hopkins River for which I am grateful too.

Mark Gubbins of *Coolana* in the Chatsworth area drew my attention to the work of John Morgan of La Trobe University on the native grasslands of south-eastern Australia. John kindly provided an electronic copy of the edited collection he and many others wrote on the topic. I am grateful to both Mark and John for their assistance.

I am grateful to Ian McNiven of Monash University for helpful archaeological advice about Lake Connewarren and Aboriginal oven mounds. I am grateful to Hamish Weatherly for his guided tour of *Connewarran* station in December 2020 and for his information about the history of his family and farm. I am also grateful to Richard Weatherly for setting up this contact and with Mark Gubbins, as well as for his informative and insightful emails about the history of this place quoted in chapter 5 of the present volume. A shorter version of this chapter was first published in the *Victorian Historical Journal*, volume 92, number 2, December 2021, pages 379-395. I am grateful to the editors, Richard Broome and Judith Smart, for their helpful comments and suggestions on earlier versions and for their permission to republish material from the article in the present volume. Craige Proctor of the Mortlake and District Historical Society kindly supplied the photo of Lake Connewarren held by the Society and information about Bob McKenzie for both of which I am grateful.

I am also grateful to Samantha Fidge, the Archaeologist and Heritage Advisor for the Eastern Maar Aboriginal Corporation, the Registered Aboriginal Party for the Country of the Djab wurrung, Pik Wurrung and Girai wurrung peoples, for drawing my attention to ACHRIS (Aboriginal Cultural Heritage Register and Information System).

I am grateful to Uncle Robert Lowe for his guided tour along the banks of the Hopkins River around Framlingham in May 2021 and to Chris Clifford of the Deakin University Library in Warrnambool for setting up the contact. Chris also assembled a number of sources from the library collection for my perusal for which I am also grateful. I am also grateful to John Sherwood, formerly of Warrnambool Institute, later Warrnambool College of Advanced Education, now the campus of Deakin University in Warrnambool and a co-editor of *Tuuram: Hopkins Estuary and Coastal Environs* for his guided tour of the lower Hopkins in May 2021 and his gift of a copy of this book. Barbara Webb lent me her copy of *Wisdom Man*, the life-story of Banjo Clarke, for which I am grateful. I am also grateful to Geoff Rollinson, the chairperson of the 'Save the Hopkins – Stop the Quarry' group for providing documentation in support of their campaign and to Amanda Boucher for permission to quote her heritage 'due diligence' assessment of the proposal for the quarry. These contacts and sources were vital for writing the present volume, especially chapters 6 and 7.

I apologise in advance to all those remarkable people whose stories of their life in their home place in the Hopkins Basin I have not retold in the present volume. As in the famous analogy of the iceberg, the stories of the home places and people I have retold are only the tip of a much bigger body of stories that I haven't retold and that could be the basis for a subsequent volume.

The three reviews of recent books about wetlands, wetland humanities and the Environmental Humanities appended to the present volume have been published previously. The review of *English Wetlands* appeared in *Cultural Geographies,* volume 29, issue 2, December 2021, pages 328-329. The review of *Wetlands in a Dry Land* about the Murray-Darling Basin appeared in *Cultural Geographies* online in September 2022. I am grateful to its book reviews editor, Amanda George, for permission to reproduce already published material in the present volume. A slightly different, more self-promotional review of *Introduction to the Environmental Humanities* was published in *Ecocene: Cappadocia Journal of Environmental Humanities,* volume 3, number 2, December 2022, pages 149–53. I am grateful to its book reviews editor, Fatma Aykanat, for permission to reproduce already published material in the present volume.

I would like to take this opportunity to acknowledge J. Andrew Hubbell, one of the co-authors of *Introduction to the Environmental Humanities,* for his warm and supportive friendship. I am grateful to him for the invitation to deliver a lecture on the theme of resilience in the Anthropocene at Susquehanna University in Pennsylvania in April 2019, for gaining funding for my airfare to and from the US and for his generous hospitality in his wonderful home overlooking the magnificent Susquehanna River. I am also grateful to John C. Ryan for sending to me a copy of their co-authored book, *Introduction to the Environmental Humanities,* and for his warm acknowledgement in it in print in both published form and in a letter, and in a handwritten inscription.

I am not an Aboriginal person and so I do not speak with any cultural authority on Aboriginal cultural matters. In the present volume, I merely cite the published sources and comment sympathetically on them. I am a white fella learning about the land and wetlands, people and place, and engaging in truth-telling and mutually respectful, cross-cultural dialogue for equitable reconciliation in caring for Country by indigenous and non-indigenous peoples. I am also inviting the reader to do so too.

I accessed online information about the Girai wurrung people and Kaawirn Kuunawarn for chapter 5 on January 26, 2021, known officially as 'Australia Day' and unofficially as 'Invasion Day.' The existing literature cited above going back to the 1980s uses the terms 'invasion' and 'occupation' to refer to the British colonization of Australia beginning on January 26, 1788. It lends weight to the unofficial naming of January 26 as 'Invasion Day' and to the campaign to "change the date" of Australia Day to a less traumatic one. The conflict on and around January 26 foregrounded my desire for truth-telling, engaging in dialogue, building bridges, protesting for social justice and gaining equitable reconciliation between the two cultures expressed in the present volume.

In another acknowledgement of Country, I acknowledge the Wurundjeri people, the traditional owners, users and inhabitants of the lands where I wrote the present volume in Coburg. The lands of the Wurundjeri and Woi Wurrung peoples of Melbourne are a place of lost wetlands as I discuss in 'City of Ghost Swamps,' the first part of *Modern Melbourne: City and Site of Nature and Culture* (Giblett 2020b, 17-84). Many wetlands in western Victoria survive and should not have to endure the same fate as their urban cousins of aquaterracide, the killing of wetlands.

INTRODUCTION TO THE HOPKINS RIVER, ITS BASIN, PEOPLE AND PLACES

> 1 In the beginning God created the heaven and the earth. 2 And the earth was without form, and void; and darkness was upon the face of the deep. And the Spirit of God moved upon the face of the waters. *Genesis 1*

The Hopkins River is the longest river in Victoria. It begins in the bioregion of the central Victorian uplands, and bisects the bioregions of the five million year-old Victorian volcanic plains and the Warrnambool plains on the coast of Bass Strait. Along its serpentine course from source to sea through fertile plains it is accompanied by kindred wetlands that flow into it and feed and water its grasslands. This book calls this area 'Middlemarsh.' The area is rich in Aboriginal culture, language, story and contentious history, including colonization, massacres and a recent proposal for a quarry adjacent to Aboriginal land. Middlemarsh is a cradle of Aboriginal civilizations, including the construction of stone houses and eel traps, and the cultivation of wetlands in paludiculture (Giblett 2021c, 4-5). It is akin to Mesopotamia, the cradle of civilizations where wetlands were cultivated too. Both places are also the sites of creation stories, specifically in Mesopotamian mythology and biblical theology and in Aboriginal mythology associated with 'the Rainbow Serpent.' The fertile crescent of Mesopotamia is regarded highly as a birthplace of western culture. The fertile serpent of Middlemarsh should be valued equally as a birthplace of Aboriginal cultures.

From the 'head' of its catchment in the hills near the town of Ararat in mid-western Victoria, the Hopkins flows roughly due south to its 'mouth' in the Bass Strait on the south coast near Warrnambool on the shores of the Southern Ocean. Rather than 'mouth,' should that be 'cloaca'? The 'head' of the catchment of a river and the 'mouth' of a river are at opposite ends of the river, but the mouth is in the head of the body of humans and other animals. The reluctance on the part of colonial explorers to name the outflow, or exit, of a river by its related part of the human body points to squeamishness about naming the excretory and reproductive organ and going up the inner digestive passage or tract of the body of the earth, but not on the part of colonial explorers and setters about penetrating the earth itself (as we will see in chapter 3 of the present volume).

Cloaca is a more precise and apt term for the outflow of a river figured in the anatomical terms of some animals, including all reptiles, such as 'the Rainbow Serpent.' Cloaca is both an excretory and reproductive organ, a fitting trope for the decomposing and regenerating elements in the water of rivers and wetlands in God's first and best work in the biblical terms of *Genesis* 1: 2. In other terms, other than biblical terms that is, swamps and other wetlands are the 'Great Mother'(*Magna Mater*) or 'Great Goddess' of creation (see Giblett 1996, 145-150, 196-198; 2011, 30).

Yet 'mouth' is a somewhat appropriate term for figuring the dynamic place on the Bass Strait where the Hopkins River meets the sea as both salt water and beach sand flow into the estuary of the river in a reverse delta. The estuary is both an artery and a vein, conveying matter back and forth from womby wetlands to watery sea. The nine kilometre-long estuary from Tooram Stones to the sea is a "salt wedge" with a layer of salt water of greater or lesser depth above an underlying layer of fresh water. The depths of these layers depends on rainfall with heavy rain upstream in the catchment creating flooding downstream reducing the top layer of saline water to virtually nothing. Estuarine water flows out through the gap in the rock bar blasted in the early part of the twentieth-century (John Sherwood, pers. comm.). The coastal zone is "ecologically very dynamic" and the estuary is a highly productive ecosystem, more productive than the open ocean (Bantow, Rashleigh and Sherwood 1995, 3, 9). Where the Hopkins River meets the sea is thus both cloaca and mouth. It is a sacred place with its rocky outcrops, beach sand and ancient middens.

The Hopkins River is Victoria's longest river measuring over 270 kilometres in length from source to sea. The ten-times longer Murray River that forms much of the Victorian border with the neighbouring state of New South Wales is located entirely within that state. The Murray River is also Australia's longest river and a national icon whose history has been told many times and in many ways, unlike the Hopkins. The Murray-Darling Basin[1] also contains internationally important wetlands, unlike the Hopkins Basin whose wetlands are regarded as locally important.

The Murray River is like the Thames River, England's longest (at 346 kilometres) and most famous river. The Thames has a polluted estuary, unlike the Hopkins estuary (as we will see in the final chapter of the present volume).

The shorter and less famous Hopkins River and the wetlands in its basin deserve to be better known and for the stories of it, the places along it and the people who have lived and still live by it to be told (as the present volume aims to do and as the story of the Thames, the places along it and its people have been told on many occasions, over many centuries, again unlike the Hopkins and unlike Victoria's most famous and much shorter river at 242 kilometres, the Yarra that flows through Melbourne[2]). The Seine and the Thames have had their bards, writers, artists, photographers and film-makers to whom Sciolino (2020) and Ackroyd (2009) devote much of their books on the two rivers, though for Ackroyd (2009, 338) "the river has no bard" in the sense that "there has been no great poem devoted to the Thames." The Concord River and Walden Pond have two great prose poems (including poetry) devoted to them: *A Week on the Concord and Merrimack Rivers* and *Walden*, both by Henry David Thoreau. The Thames has had its poets, such as Chaucer, Spenser, Milton and Blake, its prose poets, such as Kenneth Grahame, its classic realist writers, such as Joseph Conrad and Charles Dickens, and recently "the new nature writing" of Crampton (2019) and Lichtenstein (2015). The Yarra River also has its artists and its new nature writers, such as Maya Ward who relates in *The Comfort of Water: A River Pilgrimage* (2011) her walk along the river from its 'mouth' to its 'head,' from sea to source (or more precisely from bay to spring; see Giblett 2020b, chapter 8 for a discussion of the Yarra, its artists and its writers). The Hopkins is yet to find its bards and nature writers, though it has many artists as we will see on many occasions and in several chapters of the present volume.

A river is a story, with a beginning, a middle and an end. The river cannot tell its own story, so it needs a storyteller who can tell its story on its behalf without be-halving or diminishing it. The story of the river has many twists and turns, as well as some straight passages and boring bits. It has many levels above and below, some visible to the naked eye and open to observation, some invisible that require imagination. The river binds the stories of the places along it and its peoples together. The Hopkins River is no exception.

Wetlands cannot tell their own story either. They rely on others to tell their story, such as the leading intergovernmental agency on wetlands which states that:

> They are among the world's most productive environments; cradles of biological diversity that provide the water and productivity upon which countless species of plants and animals depend for survival. Wetlands are indispensable for the countless benefits or "ecosystem services" that they provide humanity, ranging from freshwater supply, food and building materials, and biodiversity, to flood control, groundwater recharge, and climate change mitigation. Yet study after study demonstrates that wetland area[s] and [their] quality continue to decline in most regions of the world. As a result, the ecosystem services that wetlands provide to people are compromised. (Ramsar Convention Bureau, online)

Yet more than the mere providers of "ecosystem services," wetlands are habitats for plants and animals, and homes for people. They are vital for life on earth, including human and non-human life, although they only make up 7% of the earth's surface. They are in the minority. Like other minorities, they need artists and writers to create in their support. Unlike other minorities, they cannot do so themselves. The kindred wetlands of the Hopkins River are no exception, hence the present volume.

The Hopkins River rises between Mt Langi Ghiran and Ararat, flows by the rugged mountain ranges of Gariwerd ('the Grampians'), then through fertile, sweeping plains dotted with life-giving wetlands, God's first and best work as indicated in *Genesis* 1: 2, before mixing with the sea and coming to rest in its estuary in the coastal city of Warrnambool located on Bass Strait between mainland Australia and the island of Tasmania.

The Hopkins River has about a dozen creeks that flow into it and many kindred wetlands accompanying it on its way, some of whose underground waters flow into it too, such as the Cockajemmy Lakes. Mt Emu Creek is the main tributary of the river, but it only joins the river near its estuary on the south coast of Victoria. It is 271km long, roughly the same length as the Hopkins River, and is the longest creek in Victoria. Its Aboriginal name of "Barriyalug" means "salty creek" (Clark 2018b, 97). The lower stretches of Barriyalug and the Hopkins River are threatened by the proposed development of a basalt ('bluestone') quarry at Panmure that will "kill the river," says Aboriginal elder Uncle Robert Lowe (pers. comm.). The proposal is resisted by many members of the local community and has prompted a campaign to 'save the Hopkins' by stopping the quarry (figure 0.1).

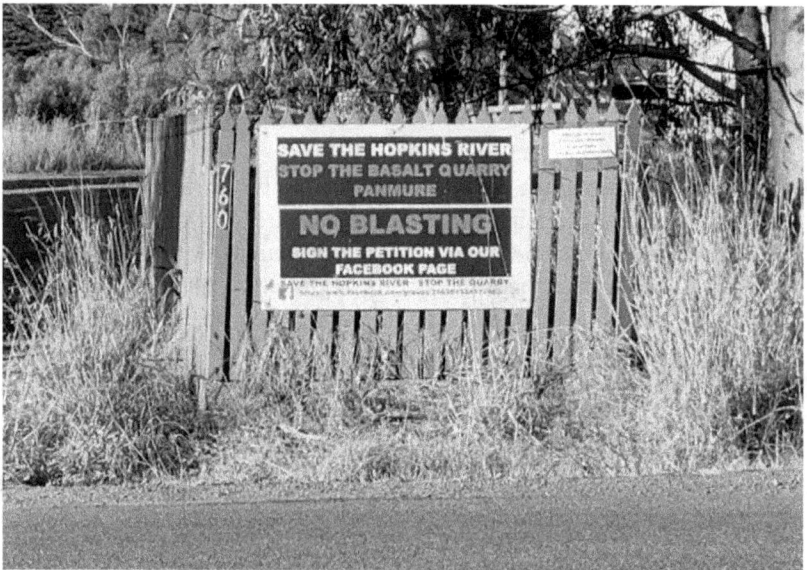

Figure 0.1 Save the Hopkins, Stop the Quarry. Photo by Rod Giblett

The campaign has resulted in a petition to the Victorian State Parliament to 'Save the Hopkins' (Parliament of Victoria, Legislative Council e-Petitions, 2020). The case for stopping the quarry and conserving the river was presented to the Victorian Civil and Administrative Tribunal in November 2022. The outcome is anticipated in early 2023. The present volume presents the conservation and cultural values of the Hopkins River, its creeks, wetlands and environs. It supports the campaign to conserve the area. The proposed quarry and the case for and against it is discussed in chapter 6 of the present volume.

The Hopkins River basin is 8,650 square kilometres in extent with approximately 40 Landcare groups working in it (Bantow, Rashleigh and Sherwood 1995, 2, 66). This area is the traditional home lands and country owned, occupied and used by the Djab Wurrung, Kuurn Kopan Noot, Girai Wurrung and Pik Wurrung peoples (Dawson, 1881, 1-2). I acknowledge them here and in the 'Acknowledgements.' In the late nineteenth century local Aboriginal people informed James Dawson about their lands, customs and languages in mid-western Victoria and he recorded this information in his book, *Australian Aborigines: The Languages and Customs of Several Tribes of Aborigines in the Western District of Victoria, Australia* (Dawson 1881).

Dawson called the Djab Wurrung people the "Hopkins tribe" and located their country from where the Hopkins River rises in the north, extending to Mt William in the west, to Salt Creek in the east and Lake Bolac in the south. Dawson located the country of the Kuurn Kopan Noot and what he later called "the Bolac Tribe" people along both sides of the Hopkins River between Caramut, Mt Napier, Dunkeld, Wickliffe, Lake Bolac, and along the western side of Salt Creek to where it joins the Hopkins near Hexham. Dawson called the Girai Wurrung people the "Mount Shadwell tribe" and located their country on the eastern side of Salt Creek and its junction with the Hopkins River and along Mt Emu Creek between Mt Fyans, Mt Elephant, Mt Noorat, Lake Keilambete and Framlingham Aboriginal station. Dawson called the Pik Wurrung people the "Port Fairy tribe" with their country including Allansford, Framlingham and down the Hopkins River to the sea (Dawson 1881, 1-2, 95). With its kindred wetlands, I call this area 'Middlemarsh.'

In the 1980s Ian Clark (1990, 108-109; 208-209) used Dawson as one source for his mapping of the Aboriginal languages and clans of western Victoria in the nineteenth century. He did not include the Kuurn Kopan Noot and the Pik Wurrung peoples. The area between the Hopkins River from Wickliffe and Lake Bolac to Salt Creek and its junction with the Hopkins is an overlapping area of Aboriginal languages and clans for both Clark and Dawson. This area is Hopkins River central, the middle of Middlemarsh. The Hopkins River flows through an area rich in Aboriginal culture, language, story and contentious history, which is hardly surprising given the record of tens of thousands years of Aboriginal possession and settlement, followed by colonial dispossession and massacres.

Clark (2009) relates later that:

> The Hopkins River rises in what is now cleared farming land between Mt Langi Ghiran and Ararat in Djab Wurrung country. The name "Hopkins" was conferred by New South Wales (NSW) Surveyor General Major T[homas] L. Mitchell in September 1836 after Sir John Paul Hopkins, a military friend.[3] The river transects three language areas (Djabwurrung, Giraiwurrung and Dhauwurdwurrung), and some 25 placenames have been documented that apply to junctions with other streams, waterholes, the confluence of the river, and other localities along its course [see Clark 2009, Table 8.1]. Three of these names are considered to be Djabwurrung, three are considered to be either Djabwurrung or Dhauwurdwurrung/Giraiwurrung, and the remaining 19 are considered to be Dhauwurdwurrung/Giraiwurrung. Of these 25 names, [George] Robinson [the Protector of Aborigines] is a primary source for 20, Dawson (1881) for four, and Smyth (1878) for the remaining name.

Places along the river are rich in names, or "microtoponymy," small place names. Mt Emu Creek, or "*Barriyalug*," is a hydronym. Numerous waterholes along the Hopkins River also have "hydronyms" (Clark 2018b, 97). Hydronyms are the names of water bodies that "are an important means by which Aboriginal people communicate the location and suitability of water sources" (Clark 2018b, 97). Until Mitchell named the river the Hopkins, the river had no name as a whole, or no name that has come down to the present. It existed in the names of the places along its course. Mitchell abstracted the river from its places in a typical colonial gesture of concern for flowing water and the lie of the land, not with Aboriginal places that were the homes of Aboriginal people along the river, nor with water bodies, such as wetlands, along the course of the river that made these places home and homely by providing water.

In the very wet season of 1836, Mitchell encountered what he later called "the Grampians" and recorded in his field notes that:

> on the 11th July, I discovered the summits of a noble mountain range of broken and picturesque outline, and by subsequent survey I found that was the predominant feature of that vast territory lying between the River Murray and the southern coast, giving birth to numerous streams of convenient width and constant current, by which the surrounding country is watered abundantly. (Andrews 1986, 135)

Assistant Surveyor Granville William Chetwynd Staplyton concurred when he described how "an isolated range standing up in the midst of a fertile pastoral country [...] serves to water the Country with fine streams" (Andrews 1986, 141). "This splendid heap of mountains," as Staplyton also describes them, known to local Aboriginal people as "Gariwerd," Mitchell initially called "the Gulielmean Mountains" after King William IV. He eventually called them "these Grampians of the south," with an obscure nod to the Scottish Highlands (as we will see in chapter 3 of the present volume) and reserved "Mt William" for "the highest and most eastern summit" (Andrews 1986, 135).

Mitchell not only saw some aspects of the Grampians as picturesque, but also regarded some of them as sublime (as we will also see in chapter 3 of the present volume), whereas Staplyton stuck to the picturesque, such as when he describes how he "emerged upon a vast grassy plain" and "the most romantic view that can be imagined" of the Grampians "here opens to the beholder. The grandest I ever saw in New Holland," as Australia was known at that time (Andrews 1986, 141; cited in part by Wilkie 2020, 44). The plain was also dotted with many wetlands (as we will also see in chapter 3 of the present volume). The Grampians "gave birth" not only to many streams, but also to many lakes and lagoons, as Mitchell also noted, including the Cockajemmy Lakes that flow into the Hopkins River and the twenty-seven lakes Stapylton observed from Mt Arapiles on 23rd July and noted in his journal (Andrews 1986, 134, 136, 143).

On September 23rd 1836 Mitchell ascended Mt Cole west of present day Ararat near the source of the Hopkins River. He wrote later in the published journal of the expedition that he found "the prospect extremely promising, the land being variegated with open plains and strips of forest, and studded with smooth green hills of the most beautiful forms." The prospect was promising both spatially and temporally. It looked pleasing in the present and boded well for the future. The work of Aboriginal people in co-creating the land in the past and present was overlooked. Mitchell later named this "vast territory" "Australia Felix" (Australia the Blessed, or Blessèd). According to one commentator on Mitchell, it was a name "chosen to describe so fertile and favourable a tract, a land blessed by fortune" (Andrews 1986, 120). "Fortune" is here the passive agent of blessing the land, whereas Aboriginal people were the active co-creators of the fortune of the fertile land that colonizing settlers stole from them.

In biblical terms and as the historian of Ararat puts its (Banfield 1986, 4), 'Australia Felix' was "the promised land" with Mitchell as a latter day Moses who led God's chosen people out of slavery on an exodus through the deserted land *to* the promised land and who saw it from Mt Pisgah. Moses did not lead God's chosen people *into* the promised land as he had not prevented them from making and worshipping idols. Mitchell led a latter day expedition of exploration for potential colonial settlers out of the desert of industrial England and wage slavery into the promised land of 'Australia Felix.' He did not get to lead them into it either, but showed them the way in his books. Rather than Mitchell as Moses leading colonial settlers to the promised land of 'Australia Felix,' the present volume proposes the American environmental philosopher, soil conservationist and "patron saint of marshes" Aldo Leopold as a new Moses leading land lovers to land and mental health.[4] Leopold is the Moses of managing lands with a set of conservation commandments (as discussed in chapter 5). Stories from the bible keep on cropping up in *Middlemarsh* and being rewritten. It is a new book of *Genesis*, a work of conservation counter-theology.[5]

In secular terms, 'Australia Felix' was "the land of hope and glory" (as the same commentator on Mitchell and Stapylton puts it; Andrews 1986, 6), alluding anachronistically to Edward Elgar's patriotic song of 1901 referring to England that still expressed jingoistic sentiments going back to at least Mitchell's time and culminating in the bellicose imperialism of the late nineteenth and early twentieth centuries and the bloodbath of the mud-hell of trench warfare in World War I. 'Australia Felix' was reminiscent of England. Or it was England transplanted to the great south land. Mitchell and Stapylton saw the fertile and well-watered grass plains of mid-western Victoria and thought that they were well-suited for sheep — which they were and still are. The Grampians for Stapylton (Andrews 1986, 141) were "properly speaking an isolated range standing up in the midst of a fertile pastoral country."

Mitchell and Stapylton also gained the impression, as the same commentator puts it, that:

> this land [...] had once been covered by an ocean [and t]hey were absolutely right [...] Thirty million years ago the sea stretched far inland to the Murray River. In the next ten million years [...] the Grampians were 'awash.' [...] The sea commenced its retreat about ten million years ago and [...], from a couple of million years ago, significant uplift and warping of the land took place[. The gradients of streams, including the Hopkins] flattened, [and] their flows either evaporated or disappeared into the watertable, or both. (Andrews 1986, 134; for Stapylton's own account see Andrews 1986, 143)

Or appeared seasonally in the "chain of lagoons" and other wetlands that flowed into rivers on and under the surface, such as Mitchell observed with the Cockajemmy Lakes and the Hopkins River (as we will see in chapter 3 of the present volume).

Both Mitchell and Stapylton also found and noted that the boggy state of the earth with the preponderance of wetlands was an impediment to wheeled vehicular transportation. Mitchell noted that 'Mt William,' "this lofty mass, so essential to water the lower country, presents no impediment [...] to the formation of roads, and the progress of colonization" (Andrews 1986, 136). Roads were an instrument for colonization for Mitchell. The "lower country," however, at the time presented an impediment to the expedition. Mitchell went on to report that "from the continued rainy weather, the earth was in a very soft state, and this at length became a most serious impediment to the progress of the expedition" (Andrews 1986, 136). When they did find "firmer ground" in 'the Grampians,' they were "still occasionally impeded by the soft and boggy state of the earth" (Andrews 1986, 137).

Mitchell's reports or field books of 1836 reproduced in Andrews (1986) differ in some substantial ways from his later elaborated and embroidered account of his travels in the same country during his three expeditions, published three years later (Mitchell 1839), not least that the former describes "the boggy state of the earth" and its impediments to transportation, whereas the latter largely ignores these aspects and talks up the pleasing aesthetic qualities of 'Australia Felix,' and so its suitability for colonization and pastoralism.[6]

According to Rod Bird (2014, 3) in his short history of wetlands in south-west Victoria, Stapylton saw the land in much more practical ways than Mitchell did as he "had the task of coping with this soft, exceedingly swampy country. His view of the landscape was not so lyrical for he was responsible for the extrication of bogged wagons and boat carriages and the management of unruly convicts." Yet Stapylton also waxed lyrical about the landscape (as we will see in chapter 3 of the present volume) and Mitchell also reported in his field notes the same transportational impediments as Stapylton did that were posed by the swampy qualities of the country (as we have just seen). Soft and boggy wetlands do not lend themselves to being easily traversed by heavy boat carriages and baggage wagons. Wetlands at least since Roman times in Britain have been denigrated (literally and figuratively 'blackened') for the transportational difficulties they pose to the imperial colonizer (Giblett 1996, 18-19 206-207; 2021c, 1).

British colonizers, such as Mitchell and Stapylton, encountered and bemoaned the same swampy or paludal conditions in Australia. Looking at the dry and wet land from the point of view of transportation (as Stapylton did and as Mitchell reported in his field notes) is different from looking at it from that of its potential for industrial agriculture and pastoralism (as Mitchell and Stapylton also did) and from that of the aesthetics of the pleasing prospect of the picturesque pastoral (as Stapylton did) and the rugged mountainous sublime (as Mitchell also did and as the colonial landscape painter Eugene von Guérard did too). Mitchell held and expressed differing views of the same country at different times for different audiences. While the picturesque and the pastoralist were compatible and mutually reinforcing, the pastoralist, the paludal and the transportational were inimical to each other. Mitchell's and Stapylton's perceptions of 'Australia Felix' are discussed in greater detail chapter 3 of the present volume.

The colonial landscape painter von Guérard travelled extensively in 'Australia Felix' in the 1850s and made many sketches that he later worked up into paintings, sometimes many years later when he had a client willing to pay for the privilege. He depicted the rugged mountain ranges of Gariwerd and the sweeping plains of 'Australia Felix' in terms of the European aesthetic conventions of the sublime, the beautiful and the pleasing pastoral picturesque (discussed in greater detail shortly). Pastoralism and landscape painting went hand-in-hand and were mutually reinforcing colonizing enterprises. The picture told the story; the story enacted the picture. He also depicted some of the extensive wetlands in the area, either in the foreground or midground, with rugged mountains rising majestically in the background.

In one painting he called 'Mount William and Part of the Grampians, West Victoria,' he depicted the sublime Mount William in the background with slimy Mount William Swamp in the foreground to provide interest and lead the eye/I of the viewer to the majestic mountain renamed from Mount Duwil by Mitchell after King William IV, the then reigning monarch of Britain and its empire including Australia (figure 3.2). In another painting he called 'Mount William from Mount Dryden,' von Guérard depicted the wetlands of Fyans Creek in the midground to convey the eye/I from the foreground with kangaroos grazing peacefully in pastoral bucolic bliss to Mount William rising imperturbably in the background (figure 3.1 and reproduced on the cover of the present volume). He left out the Aboriginal graziers who tended the mob of kangaroos and cared for the country with cool burning to make it suitable for grazing. These two paintings of von Guérard dating from 1865 and 1857 respectively are discussed in chapter 3 of the present volume.

'Australia Felix' is a kind of Australian fertile crescent among the wetlands on the volcanic plains of mid-western Victoria between Gariwerd ('the Grampians'), the Hopkins River and Bass Strait. The fertile crescent of Mesopotamia, from Greek *mesos*, 'middle' + *potamos* 'river,' lies between the Tigris and Euphrates Rivers. In the Mesopotamian myth of 'The Epic of Creation' the fertile crescent was created by Tiamat who is "salt water personified as a primeval goddess. [She is the] Mother of the first generation of gods. [She] epitomizes chaos" (Dalley 2000, 329). This creation myth is the basis for the biblical story of creation in *Genesis* 1: 2 and for the old Germanic theology of *chaoskampf* ('the war of chaos') and the creation of order out of chaos (see Giblett 2018, chapter 1). The head waters of the Tigris and Euphrates Rivers rise close to Mt Ararat in present day Türkiye where Noah's ark "came to rest" after the "Great Flood" (as related in *Genesis* 8: 4). The other Mt Ararat in Australia is where the first colonial squatters of the area "came to rest" "like the ark" near the site of the present day town of Ararat (as related in Banfield's (1986) history of the town and as discussed in the following chapter of the present volume). This is another instance of a story from *Genesis* cropping up in *Middlemarsh* and being rewritten.

The rich alluvium of Mesopotamia between the two rivers of the Tigris and Euphrates was what Scott (2017, 47, 127) calls "a [...] wetland paradise" where marshlanders practiced "an exuberant diversity of livelihoods." He argues that "the earliest large fixed settlements sprang up in wetlands" (Scott 2017, 47) in Mesopotamia. Smaller fixed settlements were built near cultivated wetlands in Australia. Drawing on the work of Jennifer Pournelle on Mesopotamian marshlands, Scott goes on to relate that these settlements "relied overwhelmingly on wetland resources [...] for their subsistence" (Scott 2017, 47). Or more precisely, they relied overwhelmingly on wetland resources for their sustenance as these wetlands were traditionally a rich source of animal and plant foods as Scott (47-57, 127-128) goes on to discuss and as they were for the Gunditjmara people. As both peoples in roughly the same period regulated the flows of water and cultivated water plants in wetlands, they were not only hunters, gatherers and foragers (as Scott calls the Mesopotamian marshlanders and as anthropologists call Aboriginal people in general), but also paludiculturalists. By using fire to manage native vegetation as a food source for themselves they were also agriculturalists, and for native animals they were also graziers and pasturalists (as distinct from pastoralists as we will see later).

Mesopotamian wetlands were the site of the civilizations of Akkad, Sumer, Babylonia, and Assyria dating back over 4000 years. The rich, volcanic plains of 'Australia Mesopalus,' or 'Middlemarsh,' from Greek *mesos* 'middle' + Latin *palus*, 'marsh' or 'mire,' were also a wetland 'paradise' where Aboriginal marshlanders also practiced an exuberant diversity of livelihoods and constructed settlements by wetlands in the area dating back over 4000 years. The mid-western districts of Victoria are more precisely 'Mesopalia' ('Middlemarshes') because of the sheer number of wetlands dotting the fertile, well-watered plains around the Hopkins River between the mountains and the sea. These wetlands were the site of the civilizations of Aboriginal peoples who constructed oven mounds, stone houses and eel and fish traps, wove baskets to catch eels and fish, and cultivated native grains and edible wetland plants. Their presence and use were documented in the Connewarren area on the Hopkins river near Mortlake from the late nineteenth century (and are discussed in chapter 5 of the present volume).

Like the biblical book of *Genesis, Middlemarsh* tells the story of the beginnings of life in wetlands and of Aboriginal people in places of mid-western Victoria. These creative places were seen by early colonial explorers and colonizers as the garden of Eden. The original garden of Eden is usually located in ancient Mesopotamia, literally between the Rivers Tigris and Euphrates, a birthplace of western civilization (rather than of civilization *per se*). Major Mitchell first called 'Australia Felix' an Eden (as we will see in chapter 3 of the present volume). Located between the wetlands and the creeks along the Hopkins River of mid-western Victoria, this area is what I am calling Middlemarshes, or 'Mesopalia.' Wetlands were the birthplace of Aboriginal civilizations in western Victoria. Wetlands were the birthplace of civilizations in both ancient Mesopotamia and Aboriginal Australia. Wetlands were also the cradle of ancient cities in Mesopotamia, China, Mexico and Africa (Wilson 2020, 15-18, 20-25), of ancient and modern cities in Europe, and of modern, colonial cities in North America and Australia (Giblett 2016 and chapter 7, n2 of the present volume). Wetlands were also the cradle of Aboriginal villages in western Victoria (as we will see in chapter 2 of the present volume).

Among the wetlands and the creeks along the Hopkins River of mid-western Victoria the Djab Wurrung, Kuurn Kopan Noot, Girai Wurrung and Pik Wurrung peoples established and sustained their civilizations in their garden of Eden for tens of thousands of years. The first fall from grace and expulsion as related in *Genesis* was from the original garden of Eden; a second fall from grace and dispossession occurred with the second Eden with the colonial invasion. Redemption and reconciliation are still coming. The messiah of conservation has come and spoken to those who have ears to hear (as will see in chapter 3 of the present volume). In keeping with rewriting stories from *Genesis* in *Middlemarsh,* a third Eden is perhaps located on a farm on the Hopkins River where Ayesha Burdett and Howard Brandenburg live and with them as a kind of latter day environmental Eve and Adam as she is a freshwater ecologist employed in facilitating local land management and he is an artist, including an illustrator of fish of the river (as we will see in chapter 4 of the present volume). *Middlemarsh* is an Australian *Genesis*, a book of beginnings, old and new.

This is no less so than with Aboriginal people and their civilizations in mid-western Victoria. Eel and fish traps and stone houses located at Lake Condah and Condah Swamp in the country of the Gunditjmara people date back over 4000 years. They are older than Stonehenge (Gunditjmara People with Wettenhall 2010) and are now a World Heritage Site (AAP 2019). These people practiced architecture with the construction of stone houses, agriculture with the cultivation of native grasses and cereals, aquaculture with the building of stone traps and weaving of baskets to catch eels and fish, aquaorniculture (from the Latin *aqua* for water and the Greek *orni* for bird) with the weaving of nets to snare water birds and paludiculture with the cultivation of edible wetland plants.[8]

More than intensive hunters, gatherers, fishers and foragers, and mere managers and manipulators of plants, animals and fish, it is well-documented that the Gunditjmara people of mid-western Victoria around Lake Condah were designers and builders of eel and fish traps (or "engineers of aquaculture"; Gunditjmara People 2010, 16-22) and cultivators of wetland plants (Gunditjmara People 2010, 7, 13-16, 67), or practitioners of paludiculture. More than mere 'swamp managers' and swamp farmers for the engineering of water in aquaculture and in irrigation for the cultivation and harvesting of edible plants and animals in paludiculture, they were paludiphytes, lovers of wetlands.

Aboriginal people endured the impact and repetition of the twin "tragedies of improvement," as Simon Winchester (2021, 171-193) calls them, of "the enclosure of the commons" in England and "the clearance of the estates" in Scotland. Both tragedies paved the way for industrial capitalism by privatizing land as a source of wealth and creating dislocated workers as a source of cheap labour for factories.[9] Both tragedies were repeated in Australia where Aboriginal people who owned drylands and wetlands in common on their estates were 'cleared' and their commons enclosed. Early colonists enclosed Aboriginal lands and wetlands into private property by squatting on them. Later the legislatures in which the squatters and their fellow colonial settlers sat legitimated their (dis)possession by law. They also cleared Aboriginal clans from their estates, physically removing them, or enslaving them, or massacring them. Early colonists largely destroyed Aboriginal triumphs of traditional improvement, such as eel traps, oven mounds, stone houses, fire management, grassland pasturalism of native animals and wetland paludiculture, to make way for their own industrial improvements of wetland drainage, dryland agriculture, stone mansions and grassland pastoralism of sheep and cattle. These so-called 'improvements' were a third tragedy of improvement inflicted on Aboriginal peoples and their lands with the ruination of wetlands, soil erosion of grasslands and fiery destruction of bushlands. The differences between Aboriginal and colonial improvements were spatial in scale, temporal in sustainability, economic in kind and environmental in impact.

Improvements are a sign of civilization in John Stuart Mill's definition (cited by Mayes 2018, 36). Aboriginal improvements are signs of their civilizations. One of their most famous improvements was through the use of fire that created "woods and lawns and marshes" that looked "like a gentleman's park," as James Cook and members of his expedition along the eastern seaboard of Australia observed in the eighteenth century (cited by Winchester 2021, 236). Aboriginal people were also owners of the land, wet and dry, as they "mixed their labour with nature" in John Locke's terms (cited by Mayes 2018, 34). This property ownership was held in common. Common ownership is the traditional form of ownership. It precedes and refuses medieval and modern 'Crown Land,' private property, public property, state ownership and native title.[10] Drylands are the environmental foundation for agricultural capitalist economies; wetlands are the environmental foundation for paludicultural common economies.

'Commoning land' and 'decolonizing nature' are urgent, contemporary political projects. Colonization is as much about the colonization of nature as it is about the colonization of 'the natives,' and the colonization of nature is just as much about the colonization of 'swamps' as the colonization of 'the bush.' Indeed, for Frantz Fanon, the pioneer theorist of decolonization, they are one and the same thing:

> hostile nature, obstinate and fundamentally rebellious, is in fact represented in the colonies by the bush, by mosquitoes [from swamps], natives and fever [from mosquito bites], and colonization is a success when all this indocile nature has finally been tamed. Railways across the bush, *the draining of swamps* and a native population which is non-existent politically and economically are in fact *one and the same thing*. (Fanon 1967, 201; my emphases)

The draining of swamps produces the flat and dry surface of the earth on which the straight lines of the railway and the rectilinear grid of the roads, streets and lots of the settler's farms and towns can be laid out (as we see in chapter 3 of the present volume). The draining of swamps is both a precondition for colonization of the earth's surface via the construction of the colonial settlement and the development of agriculture and the colonization of the earth's depth (like mining) via the reduction of depth to surface in the case of the map or the obliteration of wetlands by draining or filling.

In the era of so-called post-colonialism, it is necessary to ask the question: what process of decolonization has been carried out in relation to the colonization of spaces and places, like wetlands, by maps (from which they are absent or on which they are present, reduced to surface and frozen in time), by colonizing settlers, and by urban development? Decolonization will not be fully achieved until space and places are decolonized, and not only external, terrestrial and extra-terrestrial space and places, but also internal, corporeal space and places, especially those regions of the human body — the 'nether regions' — associated with the black waters and the dark and dank regions of the earth — the nether(wet)lands.[11]

Recognition of prior Aboriginal ownership of Australia needs to be enshrined in the Australian constitution and a voice to the Australian

Parliament established, both called for by the *Uluru Statement from the Heart,* as is truth-telling. Pastoralist private property and its practices have extinguished native title in those places where they take place and have taken Aboriginal place. The traditional means and triumphs of improvement of sustenance of hunting, gathering, foraging, agriculture (dryland cultivation of native cereals), aquaculture, paludiculture and aquaorniculture (netting of waterbirds) have not been able to continue unabated and uninterrupted in this and many other places in Australia. Dryland cultivation of native cereals is returning to some places in Australia (such as in New South Wales; see, for example, Allam 2020).

The practices of paludiculture were widespread in wetlands throughout south-eastern Australia prior to the colonial invasion. Aboriginal people still practice them today in some places, such as the Nari Nari people at Gayini in the Murray-Darling Basin (Nature Conservancy Australia 2020; Ruzicka 2020). Elsewhere in the Murray-Darling Basin industrial rice-growers proclaim on their roadside fence signs that "you can't eat a wetland." In a swift rejoinder, Emily O'Gorman (2021, 5) relates how "many Aboriginal people will tell you [that] you can eat a wetland by cultivating and harvesting plants in them, hunting animals such as duck, and catching fish."[12] In mid-western Victoria Aboriginal people caught ducks and fish using nets they wove. Using smoke from fires they ignited they also harvested plants and hunted black swans in wetlands and using stone traps they built they caught eels (as we will see in some of the following chapters of the present volume).

The fertile grasslands and wetlands of Middlemarsh in mid-western Victoria are a cradle of Aboriginal civilizations. They are also the cradle of the civilization of 'Western District' pastoralism and the western district pastoralist (as discussed in several chapters of the present volume). Like George Eliot's novel *Middlemarch* of 1871-2 that explores nearly every subject of concern to modern life, such as art, religion, science, mythology, melancholy, gender, politics, self, sexuality, society, human failings, and fraught relationships (Ashton 1994), *Middlemarsh* discusses most of these topics a century and a half later. *Middlemarsh* also explores other topics of concern to modern life, such as exploration, colonization, indigenous and colonial cultures, as well as human achievements and relationships with more-than-human plants and animals, and other environmental issues with rivers and wetlands.

The first publication of *Middlemarch* in book form was subtitled *A Study of Provincial Life. Middlemarsh* is also a study of provincial life, as well as a study of bioregional life in the Hopkins River basin of mid-western Victoria. Yet unlike *Middlemarch* that delves into the petty intrigues, love affairs, courtship rituals, disastrous marriages, dysfunctional families, personal jealousies, professional rivalries, parochial politics, divergent medical practices, thwarted ambitions, dodgy finances, human resilience and denominational doctrinal disputes of *Middlemarch, Middlemarsh* does not follow suit with the people of the places of Middlemarsh. Rather, it promotes landcare, conservation and living bio- and psycho-symbiotic livelihoods in the bioregional home habitats of the living earth in mid-western Victoria.[13] *Middlemarch* is a fictional novel, whereas *Middlemarsh* is a novel faction. Unlike the fictional stories and characters of *Middlemarch, Middlemarsh* tells the true stories of factual characters.

In the Aboriginal myth of creation of south-eastern Australia Bunjil, "the all-creator," created everything. The Bunjil is often regarded as an eagle-hawk or as a wedge-tail eagle, or "he often took the form of Werpil the Eagle so he could view his work" (Wettenhall 1999, 49; figure 0.2).

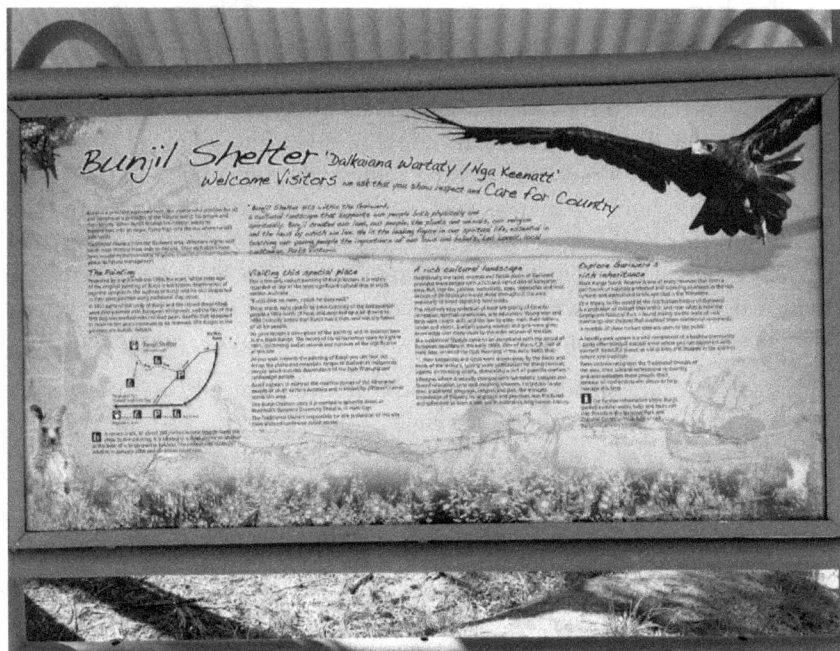

Figure 0.2: Interpretive Signage for Bunjil's Shelter, Black Range, Victoria. Photo by Rod Giblett.

As the all-creator, the Bunjil can assume many forms (Clarke 2018e, 4, 6-7; 2018f, 36; Giblett 2020b, 164). It is figured as humanoid in the only visual representation to survive in a cavern or rock shelter (Wettenhall 1999, 55-56; figure 0.3).

'Bunjil's Shelter' is located in the Black Ranges east of Gariwerd and Lake Fyans and at the northern end of Middlemarsh overlooking the fertile plains and 'good country' of 'Australia Felix,' a fitting place for the Bunjil to reside, with Gariwerd rising in the background.

Figure 0.3: Bunjil's Cave or Shelter, Black Range, Victoria. Photo by Rod Giblett (see also Massola 1968, cover photograph by John Gollings).

Bunjil created Middlemarsh and "the Rainbow Serpent of the Hopkins River" (Patricia Clarke 2008). I take 'of' to be both possessive (the Rainbow Serpent is the Hopkins River's, and vice versa) and a tautological copula (the Rainbow Serpent *is* the Hopkins River, and vice versa). The Rainbow Serpent is not in the river, nor of the river, but *is* the river and vice versa. They are tautological (the Rainbow Serpent is the river and vice versa). They are ontologically equivalent, the same being, consubstantial. The 'Rainbow Serpent' or 'Rainbow Spirit' in Australian Aboriginal myth/religion/story is water animalised and sacralised as a marsh monster mother/swamp serpent spirit (see Giblett 2020e). The Rainbow Serpent of the Hopkins River is the water of the river and kindred wetlands animalised and sacralised thus. The Hopkins River/Rainbow Serpent is the waters of the earth in the region on the surface and in the depths, above and below ground, the river, wetlands and aquifers. The River Serpent is not merely a gastro-intestinal tract draining the country, digesting nutrients and excreting wastes, but a body with the kidneys, liver, placenta and womb of wetlands and aquifers that nourish and filter water as the lifeblood of the body of the earth of Middlemarsh and the bioregions in it.

The Hopkins River for Bob McKenzie (2001, 22) "has been the lifeblood of the rural communities through which it passes." Rivers are the lifeblood of Australia for Ian Hoskins (2020) in his recent book of this title, though they are more precisely, as he points out, veins, capillaries and arteries (Hoskins 2020, 5). Moreover, fresh water, as he also points out, is "often likened to lifeblood" (Hoskins 2020, 5). It is not confined to rivers, but is found in wetlands too. Hoskins (2020, 7) acknowledges the importance of wetlands "related to river systems" in what John Lhotsky (cited by Hoskins 2020, 5) called the "vascular system" of "the organism of the globe," but Hoskins does not accord them the status of organs, such as kidneys, in the body of the earth. The lifeblood of living water flows through wetlands filtering waste from water and feeding nutrients to the land.

The Hopkins is like the Seine, which is for Sciolino (2020, 83, 257) the lifeblood of Paris and the regions along the river in France. The Hopkins is also a sacred river like the Seine (Sciolino 2020, 25-26) and the Thames (Ackroyd 2009, 77-108). The Hopkins is also serpentine like the Seine "with the path of a snake" (Sciolino 2020, 26). The nineteenth-century poet Paul Verlaine called the Seine "an aged serpent" (cited by Sciolino 2020, 208). Sciolino follows suit and describes "the Seine's serpentine curves" and places "where the river twisted back on itself live a coiling snake" (Sciolino 2020, 247, 253; see also 269, 283). The Seine is also the river of "the goddess Sequana," "the goddess of healing," from whom it, or she, takes her feminine name in defiance of the grammar police (Sciolino 2020, 10, 17, 40-49, 75, 308, 338). The Seine is also a marshy river with many wetlands along its course,[14] like the Hopkins. The Thames, or at least the upper reaches, has also been gendered as feminine, while it becomes masculine from London to the sea (Ackroyd 2009, 29). Like the Seine, the Thames is associated with a goddess, Isis, "the mother goddess," "the womb of regeneration," "the goddess of fertility" who "represents water as feminine [...] like amniotic fluid" (Ackroyd 2009, 27, 29). The Hopkins is also a womb for Aboriginal people (as we will see in the following chapter of the present volume). *Middlemarsh* places the Hopkins River within the historical, cultural, transnational and environmental contexts of the lives of other more famous rivers, such as the Thames in England, the Seine in France, the Yarra and Murray-Darling Rivers in Australia and the Tigris and Euphrates Rivers of Mesopotamia. *Middlemarsh* tells the transnational life-stories of the Hopkins River, its kindred wetlands and their remarkable people past and present.

The Hopkins has been associated with the sacral Rainbow Serpent. Viewed from above and as depicted in Aboriginal paintings of the depths of country, as surveyed in colonial cadastral maps of the surface of the land and as viewed from the air as Bob McKenzie (2001, 39) did, the Hopkins River "twists and turns as it snakes" its way through the country of Middlemarsh between the mountains and the sea with the Rainbow Serpent's head in the Telegraph Hills and its tail in the estuary near the city of Warrnambool on the south coast of Victoria. Rather than crescent-shaped, the Hopkins River is 'S'-shaped as portrayed in the serpent of Patricia Clarke's "Map of the Western District (Banjo Clarke's Country)" (Clarke 2003, inside front cover). The head of the serpent is the head of the river in the hills and its cloaca is its estuary on the coast. Rather than a fertile crescent, the watery volcanic plain between the mountains, the river and the sea is a 'Fertile Serpent.' The circles nestled in the curves of the serpent in her painting map camps dotted around kindred wetlands with oven mounds (as discussed in chapter 5 of the present volume). The lines linking these places map the 'song-lines,' storylines and dreaming tracks between them. This map is a portrait of his country; it is not a landscape to view and master from a distance; it is land to live in, own and know intimately. It does not freeze a moment in time, unlike cadastral maps; it tells a story of a place and its creation.

The Voyage in the Vessel of this Volume

Chapter 1 introduces the central characters of the story of the Hopkins River basin. These are the remarkable people who made or make a place here their home country in the past or present. Their life-stories are retold to greater or lesser extent in the following chapters of the present volume. The first chapter also brings on board the vessel of the present volume a companion of a captain of conservation, the American boatman, environmental philosopher, nature writer, 'patron saint of swamps,' and pioneer conservation counter-theologian, Henry David Thoreau, the poetic bard and prose poet of the Concord River and Walden Pond. Thoreau guides the vessel of the present volume and its story of the Hopkins River and kindred wetlands from source to sea. He also leads its calls for the care and conservation of the lands and waters, the birds and fishes, of these places. Now that the captain of the vessel of this volume has been appointed and he has come aboard, it can be considered to be well and truly launched on its voyage down the Hopkins and into kindred wetlands to meet kindred spirits. May all who sail in the good ship *Middlemarsh* be blessed as it sails through Australia the blessed.

Chapter 2 begins the story of the journey of the river from source to sea in the upper Hopkins where the river rises in the hills near the town of Ararat with an account of the colonial exploration of the area and establishment of this town with its allusion to the biblical story of Noah, his ark of animals and his family coming to rest on Mt Ararat in present day Türkiye. This chapter also includes a side trip away from the river to Lake Bolac within the Hopkins basin. Fiery Creek flows into the lake and Salt Creek flows out of it, eventually joining the river. Both creeks are tributaries of the Hopkins. This area is rich in Aboriginal history and culture, poor in colonization and wealthy from pastoralism as this chapter relates.

Chapter 3 presents the Aboriginal and colonial history and culture of the wetlands of 'the Grampians' and of the area between this rugged mountain range and the Hopkins across the sweeping plains of 'Australia Felix' or 'Eden,' according to their colonial explorer and re-namer, Major Mitchell. This was also 'the promised land' and Mitchell was a kind of Moses leading the chosen people of colonists out of slavery on an exodus through the deserted land to it (as we have seen). This area was a happy hunting ground for the colonial artist, Eugene von Guérard, whose landscape paintings and sketches of the area are discussed in this chapter. This area was also home to the artist Carole Mules who was born and died here. Some of her artworks that portray its wetlands are discussed in this chapter too.

Chapter 4 goes on a peripatetic ramble upstream from the towns of Ellerslie to Wickliffe among these and other colonial places on the middle Hopkins. To begin with, the land-borne and not-so-conservation-minded guides are three ramblers, all naturalists, two from the late nineteenth century and one from the early twentieth century. To complete guiding the ramble in the present day are the ecologist and Landcare facilitator Ayesha Burdett and the artist and illustrator Howard Brandenburg. They live and work on the Burdett family farm on the Hopkins River in Wickliffe. They are 'riverkeepers' of the Upper Hopkins. The story of their lives, their lives on the river and their work conserving and promoting the conservation of the Hopkins basin concludes this chapter.

Chapter 5 relates the Aboriginal and colonial history of the wetlands along the middle Hopkins near the towns of Ellerslie and Mortlake focussing on the Aboriginal elder Kaawirn Kuunawarn, and the regenerative farmer and bird artist Richard Weatherly, both of whom were born in this area and made it their home for many years. Their lives in the area span over one and a half centuries. On their farm on the river Richard and his wife Jenny practiced a land ethic, soil conservation and a conservation aesthetic that produced healthy land, sound mental health, and valuable artwork. These are the principles of 'commandments for conservation' as first codified by Aldo Leopold, the Moses of managing lands and the patron saint of marshes who practiced what he preached on his family farm in the mid-west of the US. Similarly, the Weatherlys conserved and reengineered wetlands on their family farm and regenerated their farm in the mid-west of Victoria as this chapter goes on to discuss.

Chapter 6 considers the history and politics of the Aboriginal people and places of Framlingham and the Hopkins Falls on the lower Hopkins. Kaawirn Kuunawarn was removed from his traditional lands further upstream on the Hopkins to Framlingham where he died of a broken heart. It has also since been the home of some other remarkable Aboriginal people, such as Banjo Clarke and Robert Lowe (whose stories have been told extensively elsewhere; see Clarke with Chance, 2003; Lowe, 2002). Their stories and the story of this place are recounted in this chapter. This area is also threatened by the proposal for the development of a basalt stone quarry on the other side of the Hopkins to Framlingham. This chapter concludes by critiquing this proposal and calling for the conservation of the lower Hopkins.

Chapter 7 concludes the present volume and the journey of the Hopkins River from source to sea with a consideration of the ecology and the Aboriginal and colonial history of the Hopkins Estuary in the regional city of Warrnambool on the Bass Strait on the south coast of Victoria. The estuary is rich in fish species and is a favourite fishing spot for amateur anglers. The ecology of the estuary has been well-documented by John Sherwood and others. The Warrnambool Art Gallery hosted an exhibition in early 2021 devoted to artworks about the Aboriginal and environmental significance of this area. This chapter and the present volume concludes with a consideration of these rich artworks and with a call for the care and conservation of the Hopkins River and its kindred wetlands from source to sea, from where it rises to where it comes to rest.

1.

THE CAST OF CHARACTERS AND A COMPANION OF A CAPTAIN OF CONSERVATION

3 And God said, Let there be light: and there was light. 4 And God saw the light, that it was good: and God divided the light from the darkness. 5 And God called the light Day, and the darkness he called Night. And the evening and the morning were the first day. *Genesis* 1

The fertile, watery places of the Hopkins River and their kindred wetlands is in the present and was in the past the home and country of some remarkable people whose life-stories are retold to greater or lesser extent in the following chapters of the present volume and are introduced briefly in the present chapter. They are heroes of the Hopkins and of the stories of these places in the present volume. The relationships between these people and to these places are also introduced briefly. These characters are the major actors in the drama of these places that follows.

These watery places are not the mere stage and background for the life-stories of remarkable people. The more-than-human actors and agents of Middlemarsh, such as the basalt rock flows above and below ground in the past, the water flows above and below ground in the past and present, the charismatic and graceful brolga, the florescent and edible yam daisy, the shiny and slimy eel, the paradoxical duck-billed platypus, and the booming bittern emblematic of the creativity of womby wetlands, are introduced and play their role in the stories of the several chapters that follow. *Middlemarsh* tells the transnational life-stories of watery places in western Victoria.

The minor characters, supporting actors and bit players who did not live here, who crossed the stage fleetingly and made a cameo appearance, who are far more famous and whose stories are told extensively elsewhere and referenced later in the present volume, such as the explorer Major Thomas Mitchell (in chapters 2 and 3) and the colonial landscape artist Eugene von Guérard (in chapter 3), are not re-introduced here.

Coming on board the vessel of the present volume and captaining it is Henry David Thoreau, the patron saint of swamps[15] and 'the river boatman' whose voyage on the Concord and Merrimack Rivers is retold and related to *Middlemarsh* in the second half of the present chapter. He will make a cameo appearance in later chapters in keeping with his dictum (slightly modified) that the captain who captains the least, captains the best. The story of the rest of his life before, during and after his riverine voyage is extensively retold elsewhere.

Also coming on board and crewing the vessel of the present volume in chapter 5 on its voyage into the wetlands of the middle Hopkins is the first mate, Aldo Leopold, the patron saint of marshes,[16] the Moses of managing land, and the codifier of the commandments of conservation, such as a land ethic, soil conservation and a conservation aesthetic. Joining him on this leg of the voyage is the chief engineer of the vessel for chapter 5, Charles Massy, the patron saint of regenerative farming.[17] As their stories are told extensively elsewhere and referenced later, they are not re-introduced here either.

These are the main characters of Middlemarsh and *Middlemarsh*:

Kaawirn Kuunawarn ('Hissing Swan') was born in *c.*1820 at Lake Connewarren (or 'Hissing Swan Lake') that once flowed to the Hopkins River and that was later drained by colonizers (drainage is an instrument of colonization). This is not the nearby lake now known as Lake Connewarren (as discussed in chapter 5 of the present volume). He was an elder of the Girai wurrung people and died at Framlingham Aboriginal Mission Station (the 'Mish'), now Aboriginal Community Settlement, on the Hopkins in 1889.

His life-story and the story of his places are told by **Jan Critchett** in various locations and retold in chapter 5 of the present volume. Jan Critchett was a lecturer at Warrnambool Institute, later Warrnambool College of Advanced Education, now the campus of Deakin University in Warrnambool, and wrote about Framlingham, Kaawirn Kuunawarn and the Aboriginal peoples of mid-western Victoria in several places (Critchett 1990a, b; 1998; 2005).

Banjo Clarke, also an elder of the Girai wurrung (Kirrae Whuurong) people, was born at Framlingham Aboriginal Mission Station in *c.*1920 and died there in 2000. He told his life-story to Camilla Chance, much of it at Hopkins Falls on the river. It was transcribed and published in *Wisdom Man* (Clarke with Chance 2003). Banjo also retells briefly the story of some of his sons and daughters, including **Patricia Clarke** (Clarke with Chance 2003, 179-180). She in turn retells Banjo's story of the Rainbow Serpent of the Hopkins River in a book of that title and portrays the serpent in her painting of the 'Map of the Western District (Banjo Clarke's Country)' reproduced inside the front cover of *Wisdom Man* (and discussed in the previous chapter of the present volume). The story of Banjo Clarke and Framlingham are retold in chapter 6 of the present volume.

Robert Lowe was born in Melbourne in 1947 and grew up on

Framlingham Aboriginal Mission Station. He retells his life-story in *The Mish* (Lowe 2002). It won the David Unaipon Prize in 2001. Named in honour of David Unaipon (1872-1967), the first Indigenous author to be published and an inventor also honoured on the Australian $50 bill, this annual literary competition is open only to Aboriginal and Torres Strait Islander authors who have not previously been published. Robert is a prominent Aboriginal elder in Warrnambool active in many community activities, including giving Welcome to Country speeches at events, such as at the commencement of each semester at the Deakin University campus on the Hopkins River. The stories of Robert Lowe and Framlingham are also retold in chapter 6 of the present volume.

Richard Weatherly was also born in 1947 near Lake Woolongoon on *Woolongoon* station, grew up there and later spent 30 years farming on nearby *Connewarran* station on the Hopkins River where he and **Jenny Weatherly** engineered and rehabilitated wetlands, regenerated drylands and vegetation in both, became exemplary practitioners of regenerative farming, as well as him becoming an internationally noted bird artist who retells briefly his life-story in *A Brush with Birds* with his own illustrations (Weatherly 2020). The story of Richard and Jenny Weatherly as exemplary regenerative farmers and *Connewarran* station as an exemplary farm is also briefly retold by Charles Massy in *Call of the Reed Warbler* (Massy 2020, 217-229). This story and the stories of Kaawirn Kuunawarn and Richard Weatherly and their connection to the Hopkins River and the watery places of the wetlands west and south-west of the town of Mortlake are retold in chapter 5 of the present volume.

Jess Chatfield, from the Framlingham Aboriginal community, is a proud Gunditjmara woman, part of the Maar nation, who grew up at Framlingham and has since returned to live there with her two children and her extended family. She is helping the campaign to Save the Hopkins, Stop the Quarry. A basalt (bluestone) quarry is proposed for the banks of the Hopkins on the other side to Framlingham. She has made a powerful video with some stunning aerial footage of the Hopkins River in which she speaks passionately about her connection to country and voices her opposition to the proposed quarry. Her story is retold in chapter 6 of the present volume.

Carole Mules (née Anderson) was born at Willaura south-west of Ararat, grew up at Mount William Station east of Gariwerd where her father worked and when it was owned and run by the Chirnside family, went to Lake Bolac High School and Victoria College of the Arts, worked in state government departments in Queensland for many years and retired to Ararat before passing away in Ararat Hospital in September 2021. She created a number of artworks depicting the wetlands and other places of the region. These were exhibited at the Willaura Modern art gallery from December 2020 to March 2021. These and other works were included in a retrospective memorial exhibition of her artworks held at the Ararat Art Gallery Textile Art Museum Australia from October 2022 to February 2023. Her artworks depicting the wetlands of the region are reproduced and discussed in chapter 3 of the present volume. This chapter is dedicated to her memory. Before her illness, she was working on artworks for her project on the Hopkins River, one of which is reproduced in figure 1.1 and discussed in the first chapter of the present volume. Carole also provided advice and information for chapter 5 as acknowledged previously.

Bob McKenzie walked the length of the Hopkins River from source to sea in the spring of 2000 to showcase the life of the river and create educational opportunities about the river, its history, and its inhabitants for nearby schools on the way that were celebrated in the local media. The 300 km journey, from Skeleton Hills near Ararat to Warrnambool, took five weeks and began just after Bob's 74th birthday. He tells his story, illustrated with many of his own photographs, in his self-published account, *Down the Hopkins* (McKenzie 2001). He makes a cameo appearance in several chapters of the present volume. It is believed that he passed away some time in 2011.

Ayesha Burdett and **Howard Brandenburg** are two riverkeepers of the upper Hopkins. They live on a farm on a bend on the Hopkins River near Wickliffe where Ayesha grew up and where her parents, George and Barbara, did extensive replanting of native vegetation and are riverkeepers with them. **Ayesha Burdett** went to Primary School in Wickliffe, High School in Lake Bolac, and boarding school in Ballarat. She completed a double BA/BSc at the University of Melbourne and a PhD in Environmental Science at Charles Sturt University in Wagga Wagga in New South Wales. From there she gained a Post-Doctoral Fellowship and travelled to New Mexico where she worked on food webs in the Rio Grande at the University of New Mexico. She became the Curator of Bioscience at New Mexico Museum of Natural History and Science. She met and later married Howard. After living and working for 13 years in New Mexico, she returned to Wickliffe with Howard and their two daughters. Ayesha is a freshwater ecologist by training and profession. She continues to collaborate with colleagues in the USA. Howard and Ayesha work together on local ecology research projects and science outreach and communication. She is currently working as the Landcare Facilitator for the Upper Hopkins Land Management Group. Her role includes producing an informative and readily available quarterly newsletter. Ayesha is a leading ecologist and conservationist of the Upper Hopkins basin.

Howard Brandenburg is a native New Mexican and artist who, like Carole Mules, exhibited at the Willaura Modern art gallery from December 2020 to March 2021. He also had a solo exhibition of paintings there in 2019. He studied art and science at the University of New Mexico (UNM) and started working on endangered fish species during college when he was employed by the Museum of Southwestern Biology at UNM. He spent the next 20 years doing so. He is a scientific illustrator of fish and has illustrated all the native fish species in New Mexico rivers and some of the lesser known, non-game species that inhabit the Hopkins River and its tributaries. He takes the opportunity whenever possible to float a river as he puts it, which is a very Thoreauvian thing to do. He is a river floater and the artist of the fish of the Hopkins and its tributaries. Ayesha and Howard live transnational lives.

John Sherwood is an environmental chemist with expertise in the earth sciences who taught and researched for 30 years at the Warrnambool Institute, later the Warrnambool College of Advanced Education, now the Deakin University campus in Warrnambool. He headed its Research Priority Area and was Venture Manager for a $3million dollar State Government funded Sustainable Aquaculture project. He was instrumental in organising a public lecture series in 1984 in Warrnambool about the Aboriginal and colonial settlement of the Western District of Victoria from prehistoric times to the present and he was involved in co-editing the proceedings (see Coutts 1985). With colleagues and collaborators, he wrote about the estuary in *Tuuram: Hopkins Estuary and Coastal Environs* (Bantow, Rashleigh and Sherwood, eds, 1995). The story of the Hopkins estuary, intertwined with material drawn from this book and John's recent contributions, is retold in chapter 7.

The life-stories of these remarkable people, whose lives span two centuries, are linked by a common connection with, and concern for, the Hopkins River and its kindred wetlands. Their stories are interwoven with the stories of their places retold in the present volume. They were and are fertile places for the cultivation of this remarkable group of elders, artists, farmers, scientists, storytellers, walkers and writers. They are heroes of the Hopkins. *Middlemarsh* tells the transnational life-stories of these remarkable people. We (the writer and the reader, me and you) are blessed to sail with them in the vessel of the present volume, the good ship *Middlemarsh,* through Australia the blessed.

A Companion of a Captain of Conservation

The life-stories of heroes of the Hopkins are interwoven in *Middlemarsh* not only with each other, but also with the story of Henry David Thoreau travelling up and down the Concord and Merrimack Rivers in the north-eastern United States in 1839. He recounted his riverine travels in his first book, *A Week on the Concord and Merrimack Rivers.* He is a companion and his book is a guide on the journey of the vessel of the present volume as it makes its way down the Hopkins River from source to sea and takes side journeys along the creeks and into the wetlands that feed them and the grasslands along their courses. He and his writings are a guide to conserving the more-than-human creatures, such as birds and fish, that call these watery places home (or are their habitat), and to the human activities of bird-watching (and not bird-hunting) and fishing (or not). He is a captain of conservation of rivers and wetlands, and of the vessel of the present volume in its calls for the conservation of the Hopkins River, its tributaries and kindred wetlands. In addition, he is the conveyor of darkness and light as he said in *Walden* "the darkness bear[s] its fruit, and prove[s] itself to be good, no less than the light" (Thoreau 1982, 324). He did not subscribe to the biblical preference for light over darkness, nor to the biblical division between darkness and light, as proclaimed in *Genesis* 1: 4, but regarded both as equally valuable, such as the play of light and dark in the living black waters of swamps. He is a pioneering conservation counter-theologian as demonstrated in *A Week, Walden,* 'Walking,' his great essay, and his multi-volume, two-million-word journal.

In the introduction to the Penguin Classics edition of Thoreau's *A Week on the Concord and Merrimack Rivers* Daniel Peck writes that he regards it "as one of the most interesting, ambitious, and complex books written in mid-nineteenth-century America, and one of the major literary achievements of that era" (Peck 1998, vii). This is high praise indeed that is usually reserved for Thoreau's later and far more famous book *Walden*. After his journey on the two eponymous rivers, his sojourn at Walden Pond, and the writing of both of his books about them, Thoreau became what Robert Thorson (2017) calls "the boatman" in his original, exhaustive and exemplary study of Thoreau's later life and work on the Concord River and its tributaries. Thoreau's meticulous survey work mapping and documenting water flows supported local farmers in an early conservation and legal battle against the industrialisation of waterways (as Thorson shows in his great labour of love that is as meticulous as Thoreau's own work).[18] The present volume supports the local campaign in the current conservation battle against the proposal for a quarry on the Hopkins River in Panmure (as discussed later in chapter 6 of the present volume).

The title of *A Week on the Concord and Merrimack Rivers* for Thorson (2017, 8) suggests "a travel narrative," but for him the title is misleading as "the bulk of the book is a scattered anthology of transcendental musings, 'doggerel verse,' natural history description, events unrelated to the fictional chronology, which distils two weeks into one." One could say all the same things about *Walden* (except that it distils two years into one), or that it is about Thoreau building a house by a pond and hoeing beans in a nearby field he cleared of weeds. This is like saying Homer's *Odyssey* or Melville's *Moby Dick* are books about a man who goes on a sea journey. Similarly *A Week* is not just about the river journey of Thoreau and his brother took over two weeks in a boat he and his brother built in a week. Nor is it just, as Thorson

(2017, 93) puts it later, "a random collection of scholarly essays, poems, and digression." One could also say the same thing about *Walden,* which is for Thorson (2017, xiii) "arguably the most important work of American nonfiction." *A Week* is arguably the fourth most important work of American nonfiction after Rachel Carson's *Silent Spring* and Aldo Leopold's *A Sand County Almanac.*[19]

Like *Walden, A Week* weaves together nature writing, family and environmental history, mythology, philosophy, religion and science. The best bits of *A Week* are quotable and instructive as I go on show in this, the second part of the present chapter. I dub Thoreau the companion of a captain of conservation on the journey of the vessel of the present volume down the Hopkins River and into its kindred wetlands in advocating for their care and conservation.

Both *Walden* and *A Week* are exemplars for the present volume. Like both, *Middlemarsh* weaves together nature writing, family and environmental history, mythology, philosophy, religion and science in appreciation of some remarkable people who lived, walked or worked along the Hopkins River and among its watery places, including its accompanying wetlands. These people made these places their home for much of their lives. They were Thoreauvians without knowing it as they followed his injunction in *A Week* to "leave not your native land behind" (Thoreau 1998, 116). To be forcibly removed from their native land and dispossessed of it, as many Aboriginal people in mid-western Victoria and elsewhere in Australia were, meant dislocation leading to death (as we will see in chapter 4 of the present volume). Thoreau said in his journal:

> Here I am at home. In the bare and bleached crust of the earth I recognize my friend [...] the constant endeavour should be to get nearer and nearer *here* [...] A man dwells in his native valley like a corolla in its calyx, like an acorn in its cup. *Here*, of course, is all that you love, all that you expect, all that you are. Here is your bride elect, as close to you as she can be got. Here is all the best and all the worst you can imagine. (Thoreau, 1962, *XI*, 275)

Home is here; it is not there, someplace else. Home is also a sacred place and a multi-sensory, embodied space. Thoreau (1998, 139) said in *A Week* "I see, smell, taste, hear, feel, that everlasting Something to which we are allied, at once our maker, our abode, our destiny, our very Selves." This is religion for Thoreau.

Religion for Thoreau is what binds people to place. Religion is derived from ligature and ligament so re-ligion rebinds bodies internally and externally. In a letter Thoreau remarked that "religion is where our love is" (cited by Giblett 2021c, 181). A place we love is (our) religion, or where we find religion. He found it in the woods and swamps. Thoreau was a paludiphyte, a lover of swamps and marshes. As Carl Bode (1982, 686), the editor of the first *Portable Thoreau* observed, Thoreau loved swamps. Thoreau reminds his readers that the root of the word 'religion' is the same as the word ligature in the Latin '*ligare*,' 'to bind' and that religion should be the umbilical cord connecting people with divinity (Thoreau 1998, 63). Religion is the love that (re)binds people to place, feeds them nutrients and connects them to the sacred. Places along the Hopkins River and among its accompanying wetlands are religious in this sense and sacred for the people of these places.

For Thoreau myths are the stories that bind people to place. Religion and mythology are not separate categories for him. Institutionalized religion, such as Christianity, and its scriptures, such as those of the *Bible,* not only arose out of mythology, but are also (only) an addition to it. For Thoreau (1998, 54) in *A Week* "one memorable addition to the old mythology is due to this era,—the Christian fable. With what pains, and tears, and blood these centuries have woven this and added it to the mythology of mankind." Myths are stories that people live by, not falsities or untruths. For Thoreau (1998, 49) also in *A Week*:

> to some extent, mythology is only the most ancient history and biography. So far from being false or fabulous in the common sense, it contains only enduring and essential truth, the I and you, the here and there, the now and then, being omitted [...] In the mythus a superhuman intelligence uses the unconscious thoughts and dreams of men as its hieroglyphics to address men unborn.

This certainly applies to the myth of the Rainbow Serpent of the Hopkins River and of other water bodies in this area of mid-western Victoria and elsewhere in Australia.

Religion for Thoreau does not reside in churches, nor is confined to them. The bluestone churches in the four towns of Ellerslie, Hexham, Rossbridge and Wickcliffe along the Hopkins River are ugly, squat buildings. They bear out the contention of Thoreau (1998, 61) on his river journey that in a village "the church, not only really but from association, is the ugliest looking building in it, because it is the one in which human nature stoops the lowest and is most disgraced." Even out of sight, churches had negative associations for Thoreau (1998, 62) as "the sound of the Sabbath bell far away [...] does not awaken pleasing associations, but melancholy and sombre ones rather." Thoreau's travelling companion on his journey up and down the Concord and Merrimack Rivers in 1839 was his brother John, who died in 1842. Thoreau experienced this loss and writes about it later when he mourns the loss, not primarily of a loved one, or a separate object, or another, but the melancholic loss of himself, or a part of himself. The sound of a church bell conveys this sense of melancholia. It is a virtual, not a visual, presence.

The bluestone churches of Ellerslie, Hexham, Rossbridge and Wickcliffe are testament to the virtual presence and continued existence of God by virtue of the fact that most people nowadays are oblivious to Him. In *A Week* Thoreau (1998, 52) maintains that "no god ever dies." He said this about half a century before Friedrich Nietzsche proclaimed that "God is dead" in the sense that He is dead in the hearts and minds of his contemporaries with declining church attendance, adherence to the ten commandments, belief in creationism, etc. By referring to God, Nietzsche affirmed His existence, at least in name of whom death could be predicated. The existence of churches built to the glory of God affirms God's existence too. The fact that the majority of people are oblivious to God means that He is present by virtue of His very oblivion.

Thoreau was reputedly advised on his deathbed to settle his quarrel with God. He supposedly replied that he had never quarrelled with God. He certainly quarrelled with religious and other institutions. In his 20s and 30s Thoreau (1998, 78) in *A Week* called "good books" those which "make us dangerous to existing institutions." His own books are now numbered among these 'good books.' The institutions to which his books were dangerous were the dead ones, among which he numbered the church and the state. Thoreau (2001, 346) remarked in one of his political essays that "my thoughts are murder to the State." In *A Week* he reflected that "in my short experience of human life, the *outward* obstacles [...] have not been living men, but the institutions of the dead [...] I love man-kind, but I hate the institutions of the dead un-kind" (Thoreau 1998, 104-10; his emphasis). Thoreau was not a misanthrope he has often been made out to be. Rather than dead institutions, Thoreau preferred the living places of woods and swamps. In *A Week* Thoreau (1998, 83-84) also admired the swampy style of the neo-Platonist Iamblichus with his "long, stringy, slimy sentences." He praised "the wise Iamblichus [who] eddies and gleams like a watery slough" in his writings.

Rather than the Judeo-Christian God, the god at whose shrine Thoreau (1998, 52-53) was "constant" was the pagan god-monster Pan. For Thoreau, Pan was the god of the woods and the swamps. No god ever dies; Pan and God are no exception. Thoreau could entertain a belief in both, or acknowledge the existence and presence of both. Thoreau was an adherent of polytheism who made no hard and fast distinction between body and mind, matter and spirit. He states in *A Week* that he did not believe that "matter is independent of spirit" (Thoreau 1998, 207). He did not adhere to mind-body dualism in philosophy, nor body-spirit dualism in theology. He advised in *A Week* that "we must make shift to live, betwixt spirit and matter, such a human life as we can" (Thoreau 1998, 59). The swamp for him was the sacred site for being so where he could be fully immersed in body and present in spirit.

This is the case when Thoreau wrote in *A Week* that:

> I can fancy that it would be a luxury to stand up to one's chin in some retired swamp a whole summer day, scenting the wild honeysuckle and bilberry blows, and lulled by the minstrelsy of gnats and mosquitoes! [...] Surely one may as profitably be soaked in the juices of a swamp for one day as pick his way dry-shod over sand. (Thoreau 1998, 242-243)

One could even go one step further than Thoreau does by following in the footsteps of Aldo Leopold when he relates that "one day I buried myself, prone in the muck of a muskrat house. While my clothes absorbed local colour, my eyes absorbed the lore of the marsh" (Leopold 1949, 160). He was eye-deep in a wetland. Both men were swamp self- or auto-baptists, though Leopold did not practice total immersion to the point of blocking off the sense of sight. In Thoreau's case immersion in the swamp meant keeping all his senses still and being a good baptist. Thoreau wrote in his journal that "far from being poisoned in the strong water of the swamp, it is a sort of baptism for which I had waited" (Thoreau 1962, IX, 376–377).

The river is a figure for the stream of consciousness; the swamp is a figure for the unconscious. The unconscious of the swamp is the consciousness of the god Pan, or 'God,' or the divine. For Thoreau (1998, 265) in *A Week* "the unconsciousness of man is the consciousness of God." Or of the goddess. The swamp is the domain of the goddess. The fact that the majority of people are oblivious to the goddess of the swamps means that she is present by virtue of her very oblivion. The fact that the majority of people are oblivious to the swamp world that precedes cities and farms means that it is present by virtue of its very oblivion. No goddess ever dies. The fact that the majority of people are oblivious to the swamp world that supplies the fossil fuels that power the vehicles and generators of their cities and farms of carboniferous capitalism means that it is present by virtue of its very oblivion. The swamps accompanying the Hopkins River along its course should also be sacred sites, as many of them were for the Aboriginal peoples of these watery places (as we will see in the following chapters of the present volume).

Thoreau's river journey was mediterranean as for him "the smallest stream is *mediterranean* sea" (Thoreau 1998, 192) in the sense that all streams flows between two land masses in the middle of the earth. Some streams, such as the Hopkins, flow between wetlands so they are mesopalia, whereas the marshy area between the Tigris and Euphrates Rivers is Mesopotamia, between two rivers. Like the Hopkins River, the Potomac River (or Potomac Potamus) in Washington DC, from an Algonquian name meaning 'river of swans,' flowed between wetlands. The city was built in a swampy place and had reverted to a figurative swamp of lobbyists by the time that Donald Trump promised to drain it before and during the time he was President of the United States. He failed to do so thus breaking his promise.[20]

Following the course of Thoreau's riverine journey, on August 31, 2003 John McPhee and his companion began to re-trace by canoe Thoreau's and his brother's journey by boat along the same rivers beginning on August 31, 1839. McPhee (2004, xxviii) describes Thoreau's writing in *A Week* as "commentary, editorial, philosophical, homiletic," as "defying generic assignment" and as "between psychiatry and religion," all apt descriptors. Thoreau's and McPhee's journeys began in the town of Concord, Massachusetts, and then traversed the wetland of 'the Great Meadows' which "have levelled a fertile and juicy place in nature" as Thoreau puts it in *A Week* (Thoreau 1998, 7) and which are described by McPhee (2004, xiv) as "part floodplain, part swamp." Meadows for Thoreau are also quaking zones, such as when he refers to "the quaking meadow ground" (Thoreau 1998, 32). These are places where the earth trembles, and the body does too (for further discussion of Thoreau on meadows and quaking zones, see Giblett 2021c, 175-191). McPhee is a great writer of non-fictional or factual novels of true stories about American land, landscapes and their peoples. Following in McPhee's footsteps, or in his wake, *Middlemarsh* is a novel faction of true stories about Australian land, landscapes and their peoples in mid-western Victoria.

The journey of the Hopkins River from source to sea begins near the town of Ararat in mid-western Victoria and then traverses the wetlands of the floodplains and swamps that feed the fertile plains of 'Australia Felix.' Thoreau's and McPhee's journeys by boat and canoe were up and down the Concord and Merrimack Rivers. Thoreau (1998, 13) observed in *A Week* that rivers are "the natural highways of all nations." Two centuries before Thoreau, Blaise Pascal said "a river is a road that moves" (cited in Blackbourn 2008, 23). A river is an active road whose downstream flow can move vessels along its course providing some motive power for their propulsion unlike passive roads that don't move. Rivers, as Christof Mauch and Thomas Zeller (2008, 7) put it, are "themselves agents, providers of energy [not only of, for example, hydroelectric power generation, but also in their own movement *à la* Pascal], and resources, and a driving force in history". Rivers are not passive roads on which vehicles move, but active roads whose downstream flow also moves resources, such as water and nutrients, as Thoreau observed and noted later. The Hopkins is an active agent, energy provider, life source and driving force in the history of the past life of mid-western Victoria and in the story of its present life.

More than a decade after his weeklong riverine journey, Thoreau (1962, *V*, 404) wrote in his journal of the Concord River that "Nature made a highway [...] through this town [...] bordered by the most fertile soil in the town, a tract most abounding in vegetable and in animal life." Similarly the Hopkins River is a road for the transportation of life-giving waters and nutrients to the fertile plains of 'Australia Felix' and to its estuary highly productive of fish. Rivers, such as the Hopkins, convey river floaters "on their bosom [...] through the most interesting scenery," as Thoreau (1998, 13) puts it in *A Week*. They also convey nutrients in the milky, life-giving waters of their bosom. Along their banks and flanks and in their waters is "where the animal and vegetable kingdoms attain their greatest perfection," as Thoreau (1998, 13) also puts it *A Week*. Although the Hopkins is not deep or wide enough for large, waterborne vessels for most of its course to be a highway or road for the transportation of goods and commodities, it, its tributary creeks and wetlands nevertheless are blood vessels for the lifeblood of water.

Rivers are also roads that afford different points of view and scenery than their landbound counterparts. Thoreau observed in *A Week* that "the river steals into the scenery it traverses without intrusion, silently creating and adorning it" (Thoreau 1998, 190). The landbound road intrudes noisily, both in its construction and usage phases, into the scenery it traverses, often creating a place and point of view to take in the scenery and render the land into landscape. This certainly was the case with the construction of roads in national parks in the United States and Australia (as we will see in chapter 3 with the Grampians National Park in mid-western Victoria). The curving sweep of roads with stopping points to take in the spectacular view were created to entice the car-driving tourist to stop and experience the land as landscape, as dead, aesthetic surface for the eye and not as living, dynamic depths for all the senses and the whole body to move and live in and have their being.

Rivers, such as the Hopkins, provide a way for people to walk by and along its length as Bob McKenzie did in 2000 and as Aboriginal people have done for thousands of years before that. The Hopkins River is the lifeblood of people and culture. In a radio interview, Brett Clarke, a local custodian of the Gunditjmara nation and Kirrae Whurrong people in mid-western Victoria and a son of Patricia Clarke, reflected on his relationship with the Hopkins River and explained the importance of the local waterways to his ancestors. He tells how "the wetlands, river and ocean are very important to me and my ancestors. They were like highways back in the old days, with people travelling up one direction and others travelling the other direction, cooeeing to each other" (Hughson 2011).

Colonists sometimes remarked on the silence of the bush. Such was the case when 'F.R.' went on a ramble along the Middle Hopkins in 1917, despite hearing and noting bird calls (as we will see in chapter 4 of the present volume). Aboriginal people had been dispossessed, removed or massacred so there were no people cooeeing to him. When Bob McKenzie (2001) walked down the Hopkins in 2000, no one was travelling in the opposite direction on the other side of the river to cooee to him either. In addition, he had to get permission to cross the boundary fences demarcating private property and intersecting with the river.

Brett Clarke goes on to explain that "our relationship with water starts before birth. We come from the sacred watering hole of our mother's belly. Water is Aboriginal culture on the Hopkins River." In other words and in short, water is not nature for Aboriginal people on the Hopkins River. The road of a river runs through them. This flies in the face of the European binary opposition between nature and culture that assigns water to nature and people to culture. Arguably the European devaluation of water and valorisation of humans underpins and makes possible the mental and physical activities of abstracting water from specific water bodies and treating it as a resource to be bought, sold, consumed and wasted, as well as dredging, draining and reclaiming wetlands for dryland agriculture on farms and for dryland architecture in cities. Water is Aboriginal culture because it is the womb of life. How could it be nature, something outside and separate from human culture? Wetlands and other water bodies, such as swamps and meadows, are wombs for the creation of new life. Wombs are watery spaces for the creation of new life too.[21]

For Thoreau (1998, 12) at the beginning of his journey on the Concord and Merrimack Rivers "the sluggish artery of the Concord meadows steals [...] unobserved through the town, without a murmur or a pulse-beat." These meadows are about 50 miles long and convey "a huge volume of matter" along its natural highway. Meadows without a pulse are water in a meditative state. When Taoist Tai Chi Master Moy Lin-Shin meditated, his circulations became sluggish and his students could not find a pulse. By contrast with unobserved, sluggish meadows, rivers typically pulse with observable flowing matter. Thoreau does not distinguish greatly between the Concord meadows and Concord River. The river is a part of the meadows. In one case, Thoreau (1962, *XII*, 263) wrote in his journal late in his life:

> you can [...] feel the pulse of our river only in the shallowest places, where it preserves some slight passage between the weeds. It faints and gives up the ghost in deeper places on the least adverse wind, and you would presume it dead a thousand times if you did not apply the nicest tests, such as a feather to the nostril of a drowned man. It is a mere string of lakes which have not made up their minds to be rivers.

The meadows supply the string of lakes with lifegiving water and nutrients, just as the chain of lagoons of the Hopkins basin supply them to the river. They are all just one continuous body of water in contiguous watery bodies.

With or without a murmur or a pulse, all meadows and rivers, lagoons and lakes, are living waters, the lifeblood of the body of the earth. More than 20 years after his journey on the Concord and Merrimack Rivers, Thoreau (1962, XIII, 163) wrote in his journal that water is "the most living part of nature. This is the blood of the earth, and we see its blue arteries pulsing with new life now." Conversely, the blood of the body pulses through veins and arteries like "those waters, which are carried by brooks and rivers over all the earth," as Thoreau (2001, 78) and Ackroyd (2009, 8; see also 112) cite Sir Walter Raleigh. Blood is the lifegiving water of the body. The heart of the (body of the) earth is the equatorial region that pumps moisture-laden clouds to higher latitudes generating rain and bringing life-giving water to the surface and depths of the earth to be gathered and flow through aquifers, rivers and wetlands to the seas and oceans in the perpetual cycle of evaporation, transpiration, sublimation, precipitation and transportation.

The Hopkins River pulsing with fresh flows of water is exactly how Howard Brandenburg describes it (as we will see in chapter 4 of the present volume). The Hopkins River is a blue artery pulsing with the lifeblood of the earth (as depicted in one of Carole Mule's artworks; figure 1.1).

Typically rivers are depicted and coded in blue in the conventions of cartography, even though their water may be brown and muddy as in the famous case of the Yarra River in Melbourne that reputedly flows upside down (see Giblett 2021c, 168-169).

Even in winter, water is still an artery of lifeblood. Thoreau (1962, IX, 224) wrote three years earlier about how a brook in winter was "open in the meadow there, an artery of black water in the midst of the snow." Thoreau (1962, XIII, 138) wrote three years later that the "black artery" of the river in winter is:

> the wrists, temples of the earth, where I feel its pulse with my eye. The living waters, not the dead earth. It is as if the dormant earth opened its dark and liquid eye upon us.

Swamps for Thoreau (1982, 613) are also sacral spaces. In his final essay, 'Walking,' he called them "the holy of holies" of the temple, the innermost sanctum to which he, the self-appointed high priest, annually went on a pilgrimage. Here water and bodies (watery bodies) are in a meditative state, as in meadows. They are living waters, living black waters, not the dead black waters of a wet wasteland (or waste wetland) starved of oxygen that kill fish, such as occurs all too frequently in Australian rivers. Thoreau (1982, 613) found that in swamps "there is the strength, the marrow, of nature." They nurture and nourish the marrow the bones of the body of the earth and strengthen them.

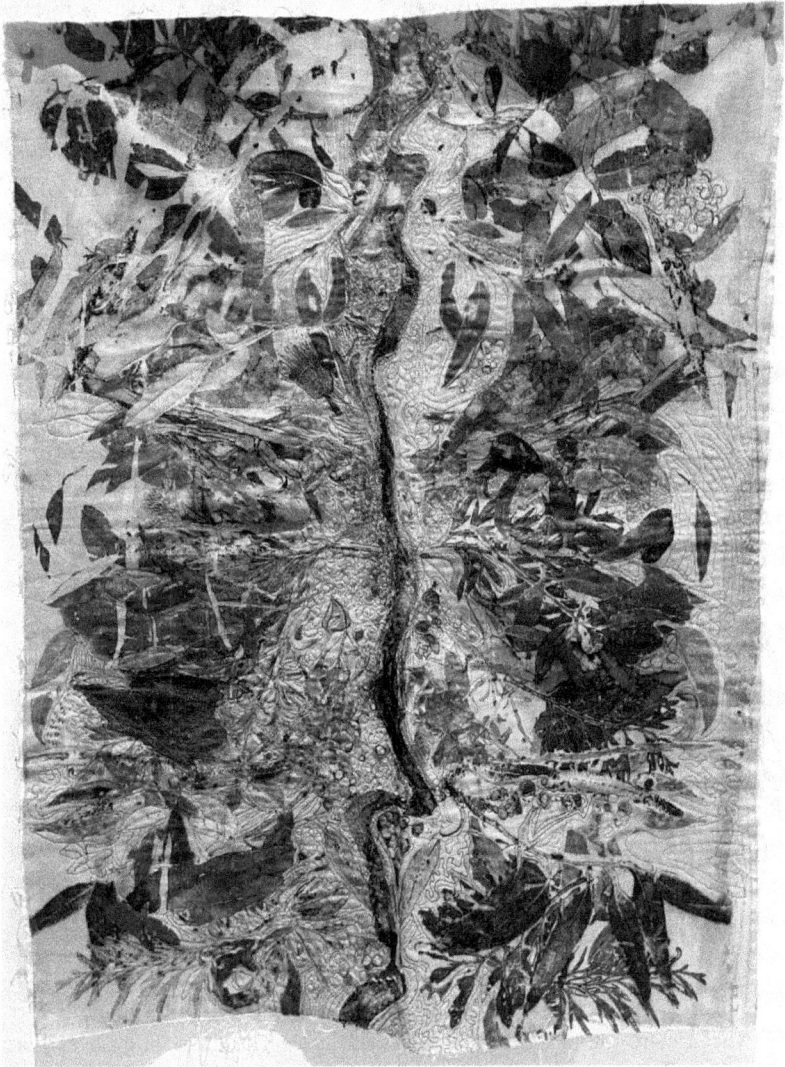

Figure 1.1 Carole Mules, 'The Hopkins River and Surrounds.' Free-motion machine embroidery of eco-dyed recycled textiles. © The artist's estate. Reproduced with the kind permission of Rachael Browning. Photo by Rod Giblett.

Home for Thoreau is variously the body and place in the present. Hope for the future for Thoreau lay in local, uncultivated places, in the country and not in the city. In 'Walking,' he announced that:

hope and the future for me are not in lawns and cultivated fields, not in towns and cities, but in the impervious and quaking swamps [...] I derive more of my subsistence from the swamps which surround my native town than from the cultivated gardens in the village [...] When I would recreate myself, I seek the darkest woods the thickest and most interminable and, to the citizen, most dismal, swamp. I enter a swamp as a sacred place, — a *sanctum sanctorum* [a holy of holies]. There is the strength, the marrow of Nature [...] A town is saved, not more by the righteous men in it than by the woods and swamps that surround it.[22] (Thoreau, 1982, 611-613)

Thoreau loved being immersed bodily in rivers and swamps with his senses all alive.

Unlike Ackroyd (2009) and Sciolino (2020) who are keen to locate *the* definitive, singular source of the Thames and the Seine on the ground, or in an underground spring, the source of all rivers is in the air, in the clouds, as Thoreau (1998, 153) reminds his readers of *A Week*:

Low-anchored cloud,

Newfoundland air,

Fountain-head and source of rivers,

Dew-cloth, dream drapery,

And napkin spread by fays;

Drifting meadow of the air,

Where bloom the daisied banks and violets,

And in whose fenny labyrinth

The bittern booms and heron wades;

Spirit of lakes and seas and rivers,

Bear only perfumes and the scent

Of healing herbs to just men's fields!

Clouds are the fens and meadows of fairies in the air. They are where the Hopkins River begins. The Australasian bittern and white-faced heron live on the Hopkins (as we will see in later chapters).

The bittern is a companion species for Thoreau on his river journey. For Thoreau in *A Week* the bittern is also emblematic of Thales, the pre-Socratic philosopher of water. In Thoreau's environmental philosophy of slimy swamps, water is not only "the melancholy element," as Ackroyd (2009, 18-19, 375) puts it, among the other elements of earth, fire and air, but also the element emblematic of the humour, or psychosomatic state, of melancholy. Melancholy is the watery humour. Water is also a creative element emblematic of the first day of creation in biblical theology, found also in Mesopotamian mythology. Water and melancholy come together in conservation counter-theology and contemplation of the primacy of watery wetlands.

Thoreau begins this reflection on his river journey by quoting Milton who described:

> the smaller bittern [as] the genius of the shore [...] It is a bird of the oldest Thalesian school, and no doubt believes in the priority of water to the other elements; the relic of a twilight antediluvian age which yet inhabits these bright American rivers with us Yankees. There is something venerable in this melancholy and contemplative race of birds, which may have trodden the earth while it was yet in a slimy and imperfect state [...] What could it tell of stagnant pools and reeds and dank night-fogs! (Thoreau 1998, 190-191)

Or should that be when the earth was yet in a slimy and perfect state?:

> In the beginning was the wetland. The earth and the water were without form and were chaotic, and darkness and light moved over the face and body of the earth and water. Earth and water were together one wet land. This was the first act of creation, the first coming into being, when the world was wetland, and the wetland was womb from which all later life sprung. Including human life. The wetland is not only the womb, but the womb is also a wet land, a slimy swamp of embryonic life. The wetland is not only the womb out of which all life came, but also the tomb into which all life dies and from which new life is (re)born. This was the world before the fall, when the world was good and without evil, before the swamp and the marsh became places of darkness, disease and death, home alone to grotesque monsters lurking in the uncanny depths of their murky waters evoking horror and fascination in any who should have been unfortunate enough to stumble upon them. [23] (Giblett 2018, 3)

Rather than subscribing to Robert Burton's 'anatomy' or psychology of melancholy that associated it with swamps, or to John Bunyan's theology of the slough of despond,[24] Thoreau (1962, X, 150) suggested in his journal that "if you are afflicted with melancholy [...], go to the swamp." Thoreau prescribed the swamp-cure for melancholy. In *Walden* Thoreau wrote that "there can be no very black melancholy to him who lives in the midst of Nature and has his senses still" (Thoreau 1982, 382). The place *par excellence* in which to live literally in the middle of Nature, even up to one's chin, is the swamp. Or at least on its edge. In 'Walking,' Thoreau (1982, 612) encourages us to "bring your sills up to the very edge of the swamp, then (though it may not be the best place for a dry cellar)." Which is exactly where Thoreau located his house at Walden Pond: on a rise next to the wetland of Wyman Meadow, but not so close or low that he did not build his house with a dry cellar too, nor so high that he could see the meadow from his house (see Giblett 2021c, chapter 8).

Following in Thoreau's footsteps in *Walden* (1982, 262) (a book which George Eliot reviewed sympathetically on its first publication in 1854) in which he figured debt as a slough, her *Middlemarch* (1994, 587) figures debt as "that swamp, which tempts men towards it with such a pretty covering of flowers and verdure" and suggests ironically that "it is wonderful how soon a man gets up to his chin there." Along similar, but different lines, Thoreau (1962, *IV*, 281) wrote in his *Journal* in 1852 that swamps are "the wildest and richest gardens that we have. Such a depth of verdure into which you sink." The surface of the swamp for Eliot is a garden figuratively hiding depths of debt into which the debtor sinks, whereas the depths of the swamp for Thoreau not only figures debt, but is also a garden for sinking into literally and getting out of melancholy. The ecological, financial and psychological economies are intimately intertwined as Thoreau knew and practiced. Both debt and melancholy involve loss and deficit. Debt involves loss of money and being beholden to others; both debt and melancholy also involve loss of oneself (Eliot's narrator is portraying the character - in two senses - of the indebted and melancholic doctor Tertius Lydgate who inevitably or predictably sinks further into Bunyan's 'slough of despond' invoked in the epigraph to chapter 79 of *Middlemarch*[25]). Sinking into the swamp in *Middlemarch* figures all three aspects of debt, whereas for Thoreau it also means getting out of the melancholy that he experienced with mourning the loss of his brother. He prescribes sinking into a swamp literally as the antidote or cure for the figurative cause of the disease of sinking into melancholy.

Despite his non-conformist love of swamps, Thoreau had a visceral horror of slimy creatures, such as eels. Writing about his river journey, Thoreau (1998, 28) describes in *A Week* "the Common Eel [...] *Muraena Bostoniensis* [American Eel (*Anguilla rostrata*)], the only species of eel known in the State [of Massachusetts as], a slimy, squirming creature, informed of mud." Eighteen years after his river journey Thoreau (1962, *X,* 114) came across a dead two-foot long eel hanging on a bough and exclaimed in his journal "what a repulsive and gluttonous-looking creature, with its vomer made to plow the mud and wallow in filth [...] It is more repulsive to me than a snake, and I think must be less edible." If Thoreau had eaten American eel (as I have done and as Australian Aboriginal people did and do with Australian eels), he might have felt differently.

Rivers also begin, not only in the past, nor only in clouds in terrestrial space, but also in the present, in the eternal now, as Thoreau (1998, 9) also reminds the readers of his river journey:

> as yesterday and the historical ages are past, as the work of to-day is present, so some flitting perspectives, and demi-experiences of the life that is in nature are in time veritably future, or rather outside to time, perennial, young, divine, in the wind and rain which never die.

Thoreau looked to a changeless and timeless nature in which wind and rain followed regular patterns. In the age of climate change, global warming and extreme weather, wind and rain have gone feral in many places and at many times. Strong winds and heavy rain wreak havoc at the time and later in flooding with devastating consequences.

History for Thoreau on his river journey is written not only in books, but on and in the earth. Of farmers he wrote:

> Look at their fields, and imagine what they might write, if ever they should put pen to paper. Or what have they not written on the face of the earth already, clearing, and burning, and scratching, and harrowing, and ploughing, and subsoiling, in and in, and out and out, and over and over, again and again, erasing what they had already written for want of parchment. (Thoreau 1998, 9)

The earth is a palimpsest that is written on in farms, roads and the grids of streets and lots in towns. The farms and towns of Middlemarsh are no exception. Their history is written on the earth. It erases by and large the history of the Aboriginal people of the place. Traces of that history remain and can be read in the names of places and the people of those places, such as Kaawirn Kuunawarn, Connewarran Station and Lake Connewarren. Subsequent generations of farmers rewrite their farms on the earth, such as in regenerative farming (as we will see in chapter 5 of the present volume).

Regenerative farming is akin to what was traditionally called in sexist terms 'husbandry.' Thoreau wrote in *Walden* how:

> Ancient poetry and mythology suggest, at least, that husbandry was once a sacred art; but it is pursued with irreverent haste and heedlessness by us, our object being to have large farms and large crops merely. By avarice and selfishness, and a grovelling habit, from which none of us is free, of regarding the soil as property, or the means of acquiring property chiefly, the landscape is deformed, husbandry is degraded with us, and the farmer leads the meanest of lives. He knows Nature but as a robber. (Thoreau 1982, 415)

The regenerative farming family, by contrast to Thoreau's lone stereotypical masculine farmer, regards the soil as a sacred trust and living material to build and nurture, leads the richest of lives practicing this sacred art and knows nature as both a giver and taker (as we will see in chapters 4 and 5 of the present volume with several farms on the Hopkins River).

The Hopkins River finishes its journey from source to sea in the nine-kilometre long Hopkins Estuary near the south coast regional city of Warrnambool on the Bass Strait (as discussed in the final chapter of the present volume). The precise extent of the estuary and reach of salt water is formed by solidified flows of basalt rock that also flow across the river at a couple of points further downstream. They indicate that there are not only flows of water above and below ground, but they were also flows of ore above and below ground too. For Thoreau in *A Week* there are rivers of water and rivers of ore:

> The hardest material seemed to obey the same law with the most fluid, and so indeed in the long run it does. Trees were but rivers of sap and woody fibre, flowing from the atmosphere, and emptying into the earth by their trunks, as their roots flowed upward to the surface. And in the heavens there were rivers of stars, and milky-ways, already beginning to gleam and ripple over our heads. There were rivers of rock on the surface of the earth, and rivers of ore in its bowels. (Thoreau 1998, 266)

Rivers of ore once crossed the river of water in the bowels of the Hopkins estuary. These rivers in the earth below share a common morphology with the branching sap of trees and the rivers of the stars in the heavens above. Later Thoreau found the same branching morphology in the flow of "sand foliage" "like lava" down a railway cutting beside Walden Pond. He noted and elaborated on it for several pages in *Walden,* as well as referring to the same branching of internal organs in the animal body (Thoreau 1982, 544-549). These branching flows are all life-giving. The earth is not composed of dead strata; "there is nothing inorganic" for Thoreau (1982, 548); everything is organ-ized, everything flows.

Being on the surface of the water and "floating a river," as Howard Brandenburg puts it, and as he does, is a unique way to experience a river on its own level and along its length, rather than crossing it on bridges or intersecting it on roads that terminate at it, and viewing it from above or from the shore. Highways and roads running east-west cross the Hopkins River at many points on the majority of its southerly journey from north of Ararat to the sea. Many of these crossing points, which were fords, such as at Hexham, Wickcliffe, Ellerslie and Allansford, now have bridges. The Hopkins Bridge crosses the widest point of the river's estuary in Warrnambool. Where the estuary of the Hopkins flows westward, local roads run southerly from Princes Highway to terminate at the river. A journey on the river recounts the flow of the river's story, whereas dipping into it at various points on land only tells parts of the story. I hope that those who can and do experience the river by boat, kayak or canoe, or view the Hopkins River from the land, or who walk by it, or fish in it, or live by it or near it, will appreciate and look after the Hopkins in all its length and variety, including its kindred wetlands.

The journey of the Hopkins from source to sea is guided by the American environmental thinker and river boatman Henry David Thoreau who undertook and recounted a weeklong riverine sojourn. It is interwoven in *Middlemarsh* with the life-stories of the remarkable people who have called (and still call) and made (and still make) these watery places their home over the past two centuries. These people include Aboriginal elders, English explorers, Australian ecologists and regenerative farmers, as well as German, American and Australian artists. Weaving the lives of these people together in the places of Middlemarsh makes *Middlemarsh* transnational in width and depth.

2.

WHERE THE RIVER RISES: THE UPPER HOPKINS, ITS CREEKS AND LAKE BOLAC

> 6 And God said, Let there be a firmament in the midst of the waters, and let it divide the waters from the waters. 7 [26] And God made the firmament, and divided the waters which were under the firmament from the waters which were above the firmament: and it was so. 8 And God called the firmament Heaven. And the evening and the morning were the second day. *Genesis* 1

The 'head' of the catchment for the Hopkins River lies in the hills near the town of Ararat in mid-western Victoria. The upper Hopkins then flows roughly due south through the rich volcanic plains of 'Australia Felix' as Major Mitchell called the area in 1836. The 'head' of the catchments and the upper reaches of other rivers, such as the Wannon that flows south to join the Glenelg River and the Wimmera that flows north, also lie in this watery region. A watery place indeed. By alluding to the biblical stories of creation and of Noah, his ark and the 'Great Flood,' the name of Ararat memorializes an elevated, dry place in a low, watery landscape and the fulfillment of the divine covenant not to flood the earth again (*Genesis* 6-9). When God created a firmament in the midst of the waters, and so divided the waters above from the waters below as related in *Genesis* 1: 6-7, and so proved to be the first civil and hydraulic engineer rolled into one, it did not mean that He could not reverse the process by flooding the earth in a time of wickedness and as punishment for it, such as when Noah, his family and the contents of his ark were chosen by God to survive. After the 'Great Flood' Noah's ark came to rest on Mt Ararat.

An early colonial settler named Mt Ararat in mid-western Victoria. The Victorian Places website relates that:

> The city of Ararat is on the Western Highway, 85 km west of Ballarat and 198 km north-west of Melbourne. Its name arose from a pastoralist/explorer, Horatio Wills, who arrived in the district in 1841 and named a rise 'Mount Ararat,' for 'like the arc, we rested there.' Mount Ararat (618 m) is about 7 km south-west of Ararat. (Victorian Places, nda)

By taking a name from a mountain in present day Türkiye and the setting for a story in the book of *Genesis* in the Bible, Wills made sense of the unfamiliar watery landscape by telling a familiar and re-assuring story about a mountain on the other side of the world. Naming it 'Mt Ararat' also expunged the Aboriginal name of the place.[27] Wills also anoints himself as God's chosen one elected to survive in a wicked world and tells his own story with himself as heroic Noah with his animals ready to repopulate an ostensibly empty earth (*terra nullius*) prepared for him by God, and not by the traditional owners, users and inhabitants, the Aboriginal people of the area.

Unlike Noah's ark full of a variety of paired animals ready to repopulate the earth, Wills "and other adventuring squatters" mounted on an equine species of animal drove flocks of woolly animals into the area to colonize a place on earth already populated by other humans and more-than-humans. Mounted on horseback they drove their flocks of sheep to "the headwaters of the Hopkins and Wimmera Rivers" where they "settled a vast stretch of country in the shadow of the Grampians," as the history of Ararat puts it (Banfield 1986, unp., 1), as if the country were unsettled when they arrived. Flocks of sheep were the infantry and squatters the cavalry in the colonial army of invasion who fought against the Aboriginal settlers, dispossessed them, resettled their country and largely destroyed the structures (built, social, spiritual, etc.) of their civilizations. Sheep and horses were pressganged into service in the colonists' war against Aboriginal settlers and their lands that had been regarded, in the words of Ararat's historian, as "a nomad people's hunting-ground but destined to become the rich Western District of Victoria, the home of the fine wool merino" (Banfield 1986, 4). And of the wealthy western district pastoralist whose wealth was founded on stealing land and who quickly rose up the social scale as a result of doing so.

Aboriginal people of this "district" are now regarded as semi-nomadic, semi-sedentary settlers who hunted, fished, damned, fired, foraged, cultivated and cared for their "grounds and waters" and who held and practiced spiritual beliefs, such as in the Rainbow Serpent, "the longest continuing religious belief documented in the world" dating from 7,000 to 9,000 years ago (Giblett 2018, 149; 2020e, 35). They were not the "tribes of savage heathens" constructed by "civilized settlers", as Horace Wheelwright (1861, viii, 259) called both parties in his book about 'Australia Felix.' He was referring in this case, at that time, to the whole of "the Port Phillip district" of the colony of New South Wales that became the colony of Victoria in 1851, rather than specifically to Mitchell's "green and pleasant land" of mid-western Victoria. Aboriginal people were civilized settlers too as they made improvements, lived in settlements, mixed their labour with 'nature' and owned the land. They were sophisticated builders of stone houses, oven mounds and eel traps, as well as basket-weavers, tool-makers, plant-cultivators and -foragers, and graziers and hunters of native animals, all performed in time with the rhythm of the seasons. "Local Aboriginal bands" in "resource-rich zones, such as at Lake Condah in mid-western Victoria" built "eel traps and more substantial shelters constructed from stone that enabled them to have a quasi-sedentary lifestyle" (Clarke 2018b, 58-59; see also Clarke 2018a, 83-84, 93) with "semi-sedentary seasonal shifting of camp sites" (cited by Clarke 2018d, 279).

The cluster of these camps amounted to a village, as George Robinson called one in May 1841 when he encountered several camps at the Great Swamp at "Konnung-i-yoke," probably near Hamilton in western Victoria (Cahir 2018, 161-162). Typically and unsurprisingly these villages were located close to, or around, water sources, such as wetlands and rivers. Wetlands are the birthplace of civilizations and the cradle of settlements, villages, towns and cities (as we saw in the introduction to the present volume). Aboriginal villages are akin to the ancient Greek *polis* defined as *synoecism*, "the bringing together of households," or *oikoi* (households)*,* as Wilson (2020, 75) defines it. Wilson (2020, 76) goes on to argue that "the *polis* was not primarily a physical place; it was a community. Greeks referred to 'the Athenians' when they talked of the city rather than saying 'Athens.' It is a telling distinction." The *polis* is the synthesis of the *oikoi* within the *oikos* of the earth (see Giblett 2011, chapter 2). Australian Aboriginal villagers believed in and practiced the vital links between the private sphere of the household, the public sphere of the community and the biosphere of the earthly household (ecosphere) and the greater cosmos (see Giblett 2011, chapter 11).

Aboriginal villages are testament not only to Aboriginal civilizations in John Stuart Mill's definition of a civilization as making improvements (as we also saw in the introduction to the present volume), but also to their inhabitants as citizens in the etymological sense deriving from the Latin '*civis*' for "citizen" (*The New Shorter Oxford English Dictionary*, I, 407), not just for "town" as Wilson (2020, 111-112) suggests. '*Civis*' gave rise to '*civitas*' for city and citizen, "an inhabitant of a city or town" (*The New Shorter Oxford English Dictionary*, I, 407). Before the city, is the citizen; no city without citizens. Aboriginal villagers were citizens of their civilizations. *The New Shorter* cannot muster a definition of 'civilization,' except to contrast it with barbarism. Barbarians are defined earlier as foreign, pagan, non-Christian, uncivilized or savage (*The New Shorter Oxford English Dictionary*, I, 181). Colonial settlers applied most of these terms to Australian Aboriginal peoples at one time or another and were used to justify dispossession and genocide.

Australian Aboriginal civilizations are a case in point of civilizations that did not have cities in the sense of a collection of large physical structures constructed over an extensive area by their inhabitants. They are a case in point of civilizations that had cities in the sense of communities with well-developed cultural and social structures living in small physical structures constructed over a small area by their inhabitants. Aboriginal peoples were not only inhabitants of their villages of households, but also citizens of their civilizations and of their country in the earthly household. A citizen is, or should be, a participating member of a co-located community of other beings, including human beings and more-than-human beings (plants, animals, rivers, wetlands, woodlands, grasslands, etc.) in a bioregion within the earthly household and the greater cosmos.

The 'head' of the Hopkins catchment and the upper Hopkins River is the country in the earthly household of the Djab Wurrung people. Ian D. Clark relates that:

> The Djab Wurrung are the people of the plains, hills, woodlands and grasslands that lie east and south of the Grampian Ranges [Gariwerd] as far east as the [upper] Hopkins River and Fiery Creek. They are notable for their determined resistance to the invasion of their land by [colonial] settlers between 1838 and 1844 through guerrilla warfare. (Clark 1990, online)

Fiery Creek flows into Lake Bolac (see figure 2.1). The area demarcated by Clark is the topic and topos of the present chapter. Clark later elaborated that:

> The Djab wurrung (literally meaning 'soft language') people were the traditional owners of the Ararat, Stawell and Hamilton districts of western Victoria. This country is mostly volcanic plain punctuated with large numbers of perennial and intermittent lakes and swamps. The only elevated portions are the Mount William Range [eastern part of Gariwed or 'the Grampians] and the western end of the Pyrenees Range. Their territory is drained by the northward-flowing Wimmera River and the headwaters of the southern-flowing Hopkins River. Vegetation was predominantly savanna woodland and grassland. (Clark 1995, 57; 2007, 1)

Their territory is also watered and drained by the roughly southern-flowing Wannon River east of the Mount William Range that flows into the Glenelg River and hence to the sea at Bass Strait. The Glenelg and Hopkins Rivers are lumped together for catchment management purposes into a single authority. The wetlands of Gariwerd and of the area demarcated by Clark here and previously are the topic and topos of the following chapter.

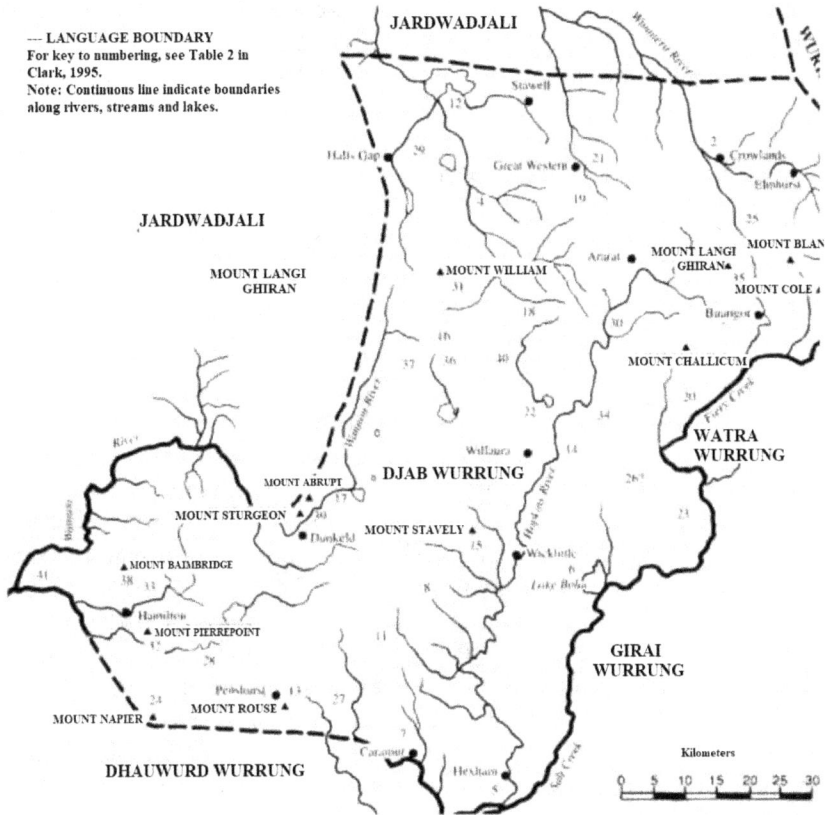

Figure 2.1: Djab wurrung language area and clans. Clark, 1995, figure 8, 58. Reproduced with the kind permission of Ian Clark.

A recent cultural heritage management plan identified 'Some Aboriginal Places in the Geographic Region' of Ararat:

• Along the Hopkins River near its confluence with Denicull Creek a number of scarred trees are present;

• Along the course of Jacksons Creek, particularly near its confluence with Captains Creek, a dense cluster of mound sites was found; and

• Along the Hopkins River where the western highway crosses it a number of artefact scatters and low density artefact distributions are located. There is also another small cluster of mounds approximately one kilometre east of that. (Chamberlain, 2015)

Several of the scarred trees along a notoriously dangerous section of the western highway slated for development into a dual carriageway were recently saved from being cut down with the negotiated realignment of the duplication of the highway (Eastern Marr Corporation 2020). Other culturally significant trees in the same area were cut down in October 2020 after a controversial confrontation when police removed protesters who had been camped there for over three years (Perkins 2020). The Premier of Victoria stated in a news conference at the time that "a balance must be struck" between the demands for road safety and "respect for Aboriginal cultural heritage." He was implicitly acknowledging that it had not been respected in this instance. Culturally significant trees were removed to make way for a safer road for culturally significant humans. Such is the impossibility of striking a balance between Aboriginal cultural heritage, Australian natural heritage and culturally significant drivers. Such is the lot of politicians in power to make such a decision.

The Victorian Volcanic Plains (VVP) is a widespread area of natural temperate grasslands which stretch from Melbourne to the South Australian border and cover an area of 22,000 square kilometres. The bioregion of the Victorian Volcanic Plains dates back five million years and embraces "wetland formations [that] include inland salt marshes, permanent and intermittent freshwater and saline/brackish lakes, permanent freshwater ponds and marshes and inland, subterranean karst" (Victorian State Government Department of Environment, Land, Water and Planning ND). Middlemarsh is wetlands central indeed. The VVP Biosphere Committee (2017) is "working towards establishing a UNESCO Biosphere Reserve over the VVP bioregion in Victoria." The basis and rationale for this proposal is that "the two major ecosystems in the VVP are Native Grasslands and Grassy Woodlands. Both are critically endangered" (VVP Biosphere Project Inc. 2020).

In 2015 the Commonwealth Scientific and Industrial Research Organization (CSIRO) published a definitive collection of multi-disciplinary chapters and case studies devoted to the native grasslands of south-eastern Australia covering every imaginable aspect of their ecology, conservation, restoration and management and totalling over 400 pages (William, Marshall and Morgan, eds 2015). One chapter on 'The Wildlife of our Grassy Landscapes' describes how "wetlands and wetland margins are […] home to one of the grassland's most charismatic birds, the Brolga. These graceful cranes require shallow wetlands for nesting, but are quite content to forage in otherwise dry grasslands" (Antos and Williams 2015, 96). Brolgas are one of the most charismatic birds and graceful cranes of the wetlands and grasslands of Middlemarsh. They are beautifully illustrated in both of these habitats in many of Richard Weatherly's paintings in *A Brush with Birds* (Weatherly 2020, 24, 96-99, 248-249). They make a cameo appearance in chapter 3 of *Middlemarsh* as a noted inhabitant of the wetlands of 'Australia Felix' and in chapter 5 as an indicator species of the health of the land for Richard and Jenny Weatherly on their farm with kindred wetlands on the Hopkins in mid-western Victoria.

Remnants of the Native Grasslands can be found in the Mortlake Common Flora Reserve west of the town. This Reserve:

> contains one of the largest remnants of the nationally listed critically endangered Natural Temperate Grassland of the VVP. The reserve consists almost entirely of grassland, merging into a large (32 ha) seasonal wetland in the centre of the reserve. A shallow drain has been dug from the wetland, connecting it to Blind Creek [...] The Mortlake Common Flora Reserve represents one of the largest and most herb-rich grasslands within the Western Volcanic Plains region. The large grassy wetland helps to support a high diversity of grassland species, including a number of rare and threatened species. (Grasslands Biodiversity of South-East Australia ND)

Hence the work towards establishing a UNESCO Biosphere Reserve for the VVP bioregion which should acknowledge the importance of wetlands for maintaining native grassland and other biodiversity in the bioregion. Blind Creek flows into the Hopkins River.

The VVP bioregion with its fertile wetlands was an abundant food source for the Djab wurrung. Clark continues that:

> The Djab wurrung camped along ecotones (areas of overlap between major vegetation regimes) and along streams, where timber and fuel were more abundant [...] In season, eels were a staple food, and Djab wurrung and nearby clans moved to the fishing grounds at Mount William Swamp and Lake Bolac, where in early autumn up to 1000 people gathered to take advantage of the annual migration of eels. During mid-summer, clans gathered for ceremony and hunting at Mirraewuae, a large marsh rich in emu and other game, near Hexham. Djab wurrung cultural heritage includes rock paintings in the Black Range, Mount William Range, and Mount Langi Ghiran, and a stone arrangement at Lake Bolac. Ground drawings were known to have existed at Challicum and the Hopkins River. (Clark 1995, 57; 2007, 1)

The heritage-listed Kuyang stone arrangement in the shape of an eel on private property at Lake Bolac was recently damaged by a grader, despite being an Aboriginal registered site since 1975 (Wahlquist 2021). Naturally this vandalism caused a great outcry of concern and criticism. Mount William, Mount William Swamp and other nearby wetlands are discussed in chapter 5 of the present volume.

Clark notes that "the last known massacre in western Victoria is reported to have occurred in 1859 at Lake Bolac station, near Lake Bolac in Djab wurrung country, however it is unsubstantiated" (Clark 1995, 9; for previous massacres of the Djab wurrung see Clark 1995, 57-83). Civilized colonial settlers became, or were, heathen savages if and when they massacred civilized Aboriginal settlers who resisted and fought back against the colonizing invaders and dispossessors with sheep-hunting and guerrilla warfare (and so reinforced the colonial perception of them as savage heathens). The fundamentalist imagination of the colonizing invaders constructed civilized Aboriginal settlers as "tribes of savage heathens" to constitute themselves as "civilized settlers" and justify their own heathen savagery.

Lake Bolac is a significant Aboriginal site. It was especially important for catching eels and as a gathering place for people. Both aspects were observed by George Robinson in the mid-nineteenth century, noted by James Dawson in the late nineteenth century and remembered by Banjo Clarke in the early twentieth century. In April 1841 Robinson described how the "masses" of "a collection of representative tribes" hold "great social and political meetings" at such places as Lake Bolac, a place that he found "the most interesting" as:

> this spot, celebrated for its eels and its central situation, appears to have been fixed upon by general consent for the great annual general meeting of the tribes of the interior [...] (cited by Clark 2018a, 234).

Lake Bolac is Middlemarsh indeed, partly because it also provided water during drought. Following the wet year of 1836 when Major Mitchell was in the area and drew mistaken conclusions about the ongoing abundance of water in the area (as we will see in the following chapter), south-eastern Australia was in the grip of a severe drought from the late 1830s to the early 1840s (Clark 2018b, 105). George Robinson observed Aboriginal people digging for water in the dry bed of Lake Bolac during a drought in March 1841 where water was still readily obtainable (cited by Clark 2018b, 100). In August 1841 at Lake Bolac the clan head of the Djab wurrung, the clan to whom the lake belonged, presented Robinson with a reed straw symbolising the granting of temporary access to water for strangers (Clark 2018b, 107).

Twenty years after Robinson, the rambling naturalist Horace Wheelwright (1861, 244) observed that "eels abound in all the swamps" of 'Australia Felix' and noted that "the Blacks are very expert at spearing eels on the swamps with a long-pointed spear." When Aboriginal people demonstrate dexterity by spearing eels in the swamps of Victoria they are 'Blacks;' when they are "wandering about among Christians in the close vicinity of a large city" (such as Melbourne) they are "savage heathens" (Wheelwright 1861, 259). Blacks belong in the swamps with the eels; whites belong in the city with the other Christians; the bush is the contested middle space between the two.

Twenty years after Wheelwright, Dawson described how:

eels are prized by the aborigines as an article of food above all other fish. They are captured in great numbers by building stone barriers across rapid streams, and diverting the current through an opening into a funnel-mouthed basket pipe, three or four feet long, two inches in diameter, and closed at the lower end. When the streams extend over the marshes in time of flood, clay embankments, two to three feet high, and sometimes three to four hundred yards in length, are built across them, and the current is confined to narrow openings in which the pipe baskets are placed. The eels, proceeding down the stream in the beginning of the winter floods, go headforemost into the pipes, and do not attempt to turn back. Lake Boloke [Bolac] is the most celebrated place in the Western District for the fine quality and abundance of its eels ; and, when the autumn rains induce these fish to leave the lake and to go down the river to the sea, the aborigines gather there from great distances. Each tribe has allotted to it a portion of the stream, now known as the Salt Creek; and the usual stone barrier is built by each family, with the eel basket in the opening. Large numbers are caught during the fishing season. For a month or two the banks of the Salt Creek presented the appearance of a village all the way from Tuureen Tuureen, the outlet of the lake, to its junction with the Hopkins. The Boloke [Bolac] tribe claims the country round the lake, and both sides of the river, as far down as Hexham, and consequently has the exclusive right to the fish. No other tribe can catch them without permission, which is generally granted, except to unfriendly tribes from a distance, whose attempts to take the eels by force have often led to quarrels and bloodshed. Spearing eels in marshes and muddy ponds is a favourite amusement. Armed with two eel-spears, the fisher wades about, sometimes in water up to his waist, probing the weeds and mud, at the same time gently feeling with his toes. On discovering an eel under his feet, he transfixes it with one spear pushed between his toes, and then with another, and by twisting both together he prevents its escape, and raises it to the surface. He then crushes its head with his teeth, and strings it on a kangaroo sinew tied to his waist. In instances where old men have very few or bad teeth, it is amusing to see them worrying the heads, while the tails of the eels are wriggling and twisting round their necks. If the marsh is shallow, the eel can be seen swimming in the water. It is followed to its hole in the ground. The fisher probes the spot with an eel-spear, and, feeling that he has transfixed the eel, he treads in with his heel a round portion of the mud and weeds, lifts the sod to the surface of the water, and removes the eel. Sometimes two spears are needed to secure the fish. In summer, when the swamps are quite dry on the surface, but moist underneath, eels are discovered by their air-holes, and are dug up.

(Dawson 1881, 94-95)

Lake Bolac was a significant site of Aboriginal settlement and for social and political meetings in mid-western Victoria. The present day bi-annual eel festival at Lake Bolac celebrates and commemorates its significance for eels and as a gathering place (Anonymous NDB). In this respect, Lake Bolac is like its more famous counterpart of the Budj Bim site in the wetlands of Lake Condah (Gunditjmara People with Wettenhall 2010), gazetted as a National Historic Landscape in 2004 (Cahir, Clark and Clarke 2018, 283) and now a World Heritage Site (AAP 2019).

Banjo Clarke relates that when he was a child in the 1920s at Framlingham further south on the Hopkins River:

> the Old People would talk about wonderful times long ago at Lake Bolac, on the western border of my tribal country. Eels would travel in huge numbers downriver from the lake there to the sea during the autumn rains. The Buluk Bara tribe owned all the country around the lake, also land on both sides of the river for a very long way down. No other tribe was allowed in without permission, or there would be fighting. But every autumn they would welcome us to a huge gathering on the banks of the Salt Creek, which would become like a big village. Each tribe would be lent its own bit of the creek, which it returned to year after year. The families would camp for about two months beside their own stone rivermarks, where they would lay their eel traps. It was a time of celebration – wise talking, corroboree, making marriage arrangements and meeting old friends. Sometimes there'd be important talks and decisions to be made, like about a problem with food or a neighbouring tribe or whatever, and the Old People would get together and hold a council to seek spiritual guidance. They would always try to have everyone agree on whatever it was, helped by the spirits. (Clarke with Chance 2003, 25)

Lake Bolac was a place of physical and spiritual sustenance and communal celebration. Banjo Clarke's story of growing up and living for much of his life at Framlingham is told in *Wisdom Man* (Clarke with Chance 2003) and is retold in chapter 6 of the present volume.

Native black swans were also an abundant food source in the wetlands of mid-western Victoria. Dawson related that:

> swans are killed in marshes, by the hunter wading among the tall reeds and sedges, and knocking the birds on the head with a waddy. When the nullore blossoms, the swans commence laying. The eggs are generally eaten raw, especially by the men while wading in the cold swamps, as they believe an uncooked egg keeps them warm. The penalty for robbing a swan's nest in a marsh belonging to a

neighbouring tribe is a severe beating. Ducks and the smaller waterfowl are captured among the reeds and sedges with a noose on the point of a long wand. The hunter approaches them under the concealment of a bunch of leaves, and slips the noose over their heads, and draws them towards him quietly, so as not to disturb the others. In summer, when the long grass in the marshes is dry enough to burn, it is set on fire in order to attract birds in search of food, which is exposed by the destruction of the cover; and, as the smoke makes them stupid, even the wary crow is captured when hungry. Sometimes a waterhole is surrounded with a brush fence, in which an opening is left. Near this opening a small bower is made, in which the hunter sits; and, when the birds come to drink, he nooses them while passing. (Dawson 1881, 93)

Aboriginal people practiced seasonal fire management in sync with the lives and life cycles of plants and animals for the health of the land and their own health, a practice (or "praction") now increasingly recognized, repracticed and valued (Steffensen 2020). Aboriginal '*ignis procuratio*' (Latin for 'fire management') needs to be included among Aboriginal agriculture, paludiculture, pasturalism, aquaculture and aquaorniculture as one of their means of cultural caring for country and deriving sustenance for their people and sustainability for their societies and as one of their triumphs of improvement in their civilizations.

Black swans figure later in chapter 5 of the present volume in the name of one of the prominent elders of the Girai Wurrung, Kaawirn Kuunawarn, which means 'hissing swan' as he stole eggs from the nest of a swan when he was young and the swan hissed at him. He was most likely named after Lake Connewarren where he was born (as we will also see in chapter 5 of the present volume). Ian Clark (email to the author January 30, 2021) wrote that "the word for swan, *kunawurr*, is ubiquitous throughout western and central Victoria, and found in quite a few placenames," such as Lake Connewarre, Lake Connewarren and Connewarran station. The black swan is a common bird in southern Australia and an iconic bird of Perth, Western Australia with its Swan River.[28] It is not a rare bird, nor an ugly bird, nor an improbable event, nor an impossible woman, as it has been in the European imaginary for centuries, including the last one.[29]

A century after Dawson the Victorian government archaeologist concurred of western Victoria that:

from the viewpoint of *Aboriginal settlement*, the most significant features of the area are the large numbers of perennial and intermittent lakes, swamps, streams and rivers which attract abundant wildlife and provide favourable environments for aquatic plants. (Coutts 1985, 23; my emphasis).

Western Victoria was already settled by Aboriginal peoples when colonizers came to (re)settle it. For the colonizers to settle the already settled land, and so in fact to *re*settle it, they had to dispossess the original settlers by one means or another.

Coutts goes on to state that of the wildlife and aquatic plants "special mention needs to be made of eels and the daisy yam," or yam daisy (*murnong*, Native Dandelion, *Microseris lanceolata*).[30] The yam daisy was one of a number of what Philip Clarke calls "calendar plants" which "to Aboriginal people indicate the change of the season" (Clarke 2018d, 274). Drawing on Clarke's work, John Charles Ryan elaborates that calendar plants "provide—often simultaneously—a time-keeping measure and a source of physical sustenance" (Ryan 2021, 118). The yam daisy is seasonal eating.

Traditionally botanists might classify the yam daisy as a helophyte, literally "sun lover," a category of plants that "rests in water or in soaking soil" with its petals turned towards the sunlight and soaking up solar energy to photosynthesise, though recent botanists would regard it is an example of a plant that can adopt "an aquatic habitus" (and so perhaps as a hydrophyte, literally "water lover" with its roots in water) in response to ecological constraints, such as excessive saturation in a rainy season (Ryan 2020, 101-102). Wetland plants, like wetlands themselves, defy and upset taxonomies based on a hard and fast distinction between wet and dry lands. Like wetlands, wetland plants transition between the two.[31] The yam daisy can be classified as a helophyte and a hydrophyte depending on the dryness or wetness of the land and the season. Either way, the yam daisy is a lover (whether of sun and water) which attests to what Ryan (2020, 101) calls "the affective affinities" between it and its "paludal habitats." Affective affinity was also exercised between Aboriginal people and their paludal habitats in mid-western Victoria with their love of country and their seasonal 'habitations,' or *wurrns*, of built houses (as we will see in chapter 5 of the present volume). Aboriginal people of mid-western Victoria are paludiphytes, lovers of wetlands.

An early European encounter with the yam daisy illustrates and affirms its seasonality and relation to water, but not its vital importance as a food source. In the very wet spring of September 1836 Major Mitchell captioned an illustration of a "yellow flower abundant on the plains of Australia Felix" and saw it is as a sign of reaching "the good country." No doubt for him this meant fertile and well-watered country good for pastoralism. Mitchell did not equate the sight of the visible yellow flower of the yam-daisy above ground in spring with the presence of an invisible food source for Aboriginal people below ground, "one of the major food sources for Victorian Aboriginal people" (Clarke 2018b, 55-56; Cahir and McMaster 2018, 120).

A European encounter five years later with the yam daisy illustrates and affirms its seasonality, relation to water, importance as a food source and use of fire to harvest it. Aboriginal people's use of fire in summer flushed out black swans and in winter made the presence of the yam daisy and their invisible roots visible. In the winter of July 1841 George Robinson observed and described "Aboriginal (presumably Djab wurrung) women" using fire to harvest the yam daisy by burning "the grass, the better to see these roots but this burning is a fault charged against them by the squatters" (cited by Cahir and McMaster 2018, 120). For Cahir and McMaster (2018, 120) this wet season cool burning "supports the argument that Aboriginal people in Victoria deliberately used fire as an agent of greater yield change for tuberous food plant ecosystems," such as the yam daisy.

This is no longer the case. Philip Clarke relates that, "although once common, the Yam Daisy has disappeared from many regions through being trampled out by European grazing stock" (Clarke 2918b, 66), and their roots eaten by sheep (Wettenhall 1999, 16). Sheep, horses and cattle were indeed the foot soldiers of the European invasion of colonization led on horseback by explorers and followed up by squatters with the result that, as Clarke (2018d, 274) later puts it, "the yam daisy […] has become locally scarce since the country was transformed into a rural landscape." More precisely, Aboriginal country was transformed from their agricultural, aquacultural, pastoral and paludicultural drylands and wetlands with cultivated native plants and animals and managed fire into a European-style pastoral and rural landscape with introduced plants and animals. The irony and now cliché of history is that Aboriginal people co-created lands looked like European park lands. Colonists thought they were a gift of God or nature (and not a co-creation of Aboriginal cultures) and so that they were ready and available for transformation into a rural landscape. In a further irony, Aboriginal people were graziers of mobs of kangaroos on the grasslands they managed through the use of fire in what has come to be called "fire-stick farming" (Wettenhall 1999, 35-36) and what could be called pasturalism to distinguish it from the European aesthetics of the pastoral and practices of pastoralism of sheep and cattle that were transported to Australia where sheep and cattle stations grew to industrial scale.

Some squatters charged Aboriginal people with the fault of lighting fires because the squatters saw Aboriginal people's use of fire as a dangerous and destructive threat, quite rightly when Aboriginal people used it as an offensive weapon against the squatters (Cahir and McMaster 2018, 124-128). In symmetrical reciprocity, tit for tat payback, some squatters used fire as an offensive weapon against Aboriginal people such as when they "deliberately burnt a village of large Aboriginal huts […] in a bid to spatially dislocate Aboriginal people from districts which the squatters coveted" (Cahir 2018, 170). Squatters stole land, water and fire and wrested rights to them from Aboriginal people. Squatters arrogated to themselves the position and role of the titan Prometheus in Greek mythology who stole fire from the gods and brought it down to earth.

Similarly fire in Aboriginal mythology originated in the Skyworld, was stolen and brought down to earth. One legend from Lake Condah in western Victoria tells how an Aboriginal man "threw a spear towards the clouds; to the spear a string was attached. The man climbed up with the aid of the string and brought fire to the earth from the sun" (cited by Clarke 2018c, 12-13; Clarke 2018c, 258). This sounds like an ancient antipodean version of Benjamin Franklin's experiment in the early eighteenth century of attaching a long piece of wire to a kite and confirming that storm clouds carried electricity and that lightning was a heavily charged spark of electricity. The legend from Lake Condah is also an antipodean, or upside down, version of Franklin's experiment as the Aboriginal man went up his string and brought fire down to earth whereas Franklin's string brought fire down to earth where he had stayed.

Whereas fire was only a destructive agent for titanic squatters to be used or feared, fire for Aboriginal people was a sacred trust to be used wisely and productively. It was a delicate and productive instrument that they adroitly and seasonally applied in caring for country that not only maximised the yield of food sources, but also minimised the build-up of fuel loads. The devastating consequences of *not* using Aboriginal fire techniques to do the latter has been seen in Australia recently with disastrous conflagrations and devastating consequences with the loss of human and more-than-human lives, and the destruction of the habitats of both with burnt bush and houses. The cross-cultural struggle between Aboriginal people and colonists over fire, land and water continues to this day, with some hopeful recent signs of dialogue and willingness on the part of non-Aboriginal people to learn from Aboriginal people about their traditional use of fire in caring for country (Steffensen 2020).

The land these squatters stole from Aboriginal people was the product of Aboriginal people's use of fire to create the park-like landscape of the pleasing pastoral prospect the squatters coveted, found and re-settled. One squatter in the 1840s in Victoria (then the Port Phillip District of the colony of New South Wales) observed that "the fire stick" is "an [Aboriginal] instrument [...] which must be credited with results it would be difficult to over-estimate" (Curr 1883, 188). By and large squatters did not estimate it at all, except as a threat, nor recognize, nor acknowledge Aboriginal people's work in co-creating the land with creator beings, nor their ownership of the land, nor their settlement of it, nor their improvements, nor their civilizations. All these aspects of Aboriginal people and their place were beneath estimation and not worthy of esteem, let alone respect and acknowledgement – legal, cultural, or any other way.

Recent debates about Aboriginal peoples' cultivation of native plants and their use of fire and whether they constitute farming in the narrow sense of dryland agriculture apply the European value-laden yardstick of stages of human development with agriculture as the pinnacle of land use and constitute "hunting and gathering" as lower in a hierarchy of value (Clarke 2018b, 71). They fail to appreciate not only the sophistication of the latter, but also Aboriginal peoples' differing uses of fire in their cultivation of native plants on the drylands and in the wetlands of Australia according to season, vegetation and type of country (as recently brought together brilliantly by Victor Steffensen 2020). Aboriginal peoples' attitudes to wetlands contrasts with colonizing Anglophone farmers who typically denigrated and abhorred wetlands, an attitude they brought with them from England as part of their cultural baggage (Gearey et al, 2020[32]). They typically drained or filled wetlands to create dry land for agriculture, or converted them into dams or 'irrigation lakes' to store water, as acerbically illustrated in 1950 by Arthur Boyd (Giblett 2020a, figure 3.3, 58-59). Anglophone farmers in Australia did not cultivate wetland plants in them. They were unlike their Francophone counterparts in Canada who used the clapper valve technology of the *aboiteaux* they brought with them from France to regulate the flows of water in marshes in order to water their crops and pastures and mitigate flooding (Giblett 2014). Australia might look a lot different today if it had been colonized by the French whose explorers visited Australia in the late eighteenth/early nineteenth centuries at about the same time as British explorers did, periodically encountering each other on the odd occasion.

Coutts (1985, 23, 63 n2), the Victorian government archaeologist, concludes that in mid-western Victoria its:

> wetlands were potentially [*sic*] rich and reliable sources of food for the Aborigines and were the focus of much economic activity during […] the period immediately prior to the European invasion, *circa* 1830 CE.

This period dates back about two thousand years and is usually described by archaeologists as the period of "intensification" of nomadic hunting and gathering (see Coutts 1985, 62-63; Lourandos 1987), rather than as a shift to the construction of settlements and the cultivation of wetlands in paludiculture (as discussed in the introduction the present volume). No greater evidence for the abundance of wetlands as food sources for Aboriginal people is the number of oven mounds, or *myrnongs*, constructed around them dating back five thousand years (Coutts 1985, 31-38 and as discussed in chapter 5 of the present volume).

The wetlands of mid-western Victoria, such as Lake Bolac, were at the pointy end of the contact and conflict between colonial squatters and Aboriginal settlers. Lake Bolac was a place of physical and spiritual sustenance and communal celebration that changed with the invasion of the colonists, as Banjo Clarke goes on to relate:

> I was told that at the beginning of the 1860s a group of white men from Ararat took to arriving at the lake every year as soon as it began overflowing – the only time when eels can be caught there. They would place their nets across the whole of its only outlet and not allow any Aboriginal people near. That was the end of the great gathering for the five south-western Victorian tribes which made up the Gunditjmara or Mara Nation. (Clarke with Chance 2003, 25)

Lake Bolac is a thus a significant site of colonial dispossession of Aboriginal people from their country and colonial repossession of it. The group of white men from Ararat were not only stealing land and food from Aboriginal people and destroying their lifeways and livelihoods, but also enclosing the common wetland owned by one tribe and shared with other tribes into their own private property and clearing Aboriginal people off their estates in an act of conquest and dispossession. These were two "tragedies of improvement" as Simon Winchester (2021, 171-193) calls them that destroyed Aboriginal triumphs of improvement in a third tragedy (and as we saw in the introduction to the present volume).

Just as the Thames River in eastern England was a 'heart of darkness' of Roman colonization for Joseph Conrad in his novella of this title, so the Hopkins River in mid-western Victoria was a heart of darkness of English colonization as this episode about the white men displacing and dispossessing Aboriginal people at Lake Bolac demonstrates, as it does as a possible massacre site. Conrad's narrator Marlow intones conspiratorially to his listeners moored on the Thames, "this, also, has been one of the dark places of the earth" invoking variously its swampy beginnings or the Roman colonization of England or both. Just as it was, at that time, at "the very end of the world" as Marlow puts it in Conrad's novella, so English colonization of Australia was at the very end of the world in its time. Just as the African river of Conrad's *Heart of Darkness* goes into the heart of the 'dark continent' of Africa and Kurtz's monomaniacal psychopathology, so does the Hopkins River go into the heart of darkness of European colonization of Australia and its psychogeopathology of the squattocracy, violence and industrial pastoralism. Just as Marlow's journey up the African river in Conrad's novella goes into both hearts of darkness of murder and mayhem, so does the journey of the Hopkins to the sea go into the heart of darkness of the colonial psychopathology of greed with the dispossession and massacre of Aboriginal peoples. Just as the Thames has not only been "one of the dark places of the earth," but also "one of the blessed places of the earth" as Ackroyd (2009, 78) puts it, so the Hopkins was deemed by Mitchell to be one of the blessed places of the earth.

Just as the Hopkins River is a Rainbow Serpent (and vice versa) for Aboriginal peoples, so Marlow's African river was a serpent on a map he saw in a shop window that he saw when he was a boy on which Africa:

> had ceased to be a blank space of delightful mystery—a white patch for a boy to dream gloriously over. It had become a place of darkness. But there was in it one river especially, a mighty big river, that you could see on the map, resembling an immense snake uncoiled, with its head in the sea, its body at rest curving afar over a vast country, and its tail lost in the depths of the land.

Rather than a white screen on to which to project his boyhood phantasies of glory, Africa had become a place of the darkness of colonialism into whose dark heart a fascinating and horrifying serpentine river coiled. Marlow's serpentine river inverts the anatomy of the Rainbow Serpent of Patricia Clarke's painting of Banjo Clarke's country. His river has its head (and so its mouth) in the sea and its tail (and so its cloaca) in "the depths of the land." He could safely enter its open mouth, travel warily up its inner passage into the heart of darkness and never reach or experience its lost depths and horrors (encountering the horror of Kurtz on the way was enough), whereas the Hopkins has its head in the top of the catchment, its tail and cloaca in the estuary, its wetlands in the depths of the land above and below the surface and its body at rest curving gracefully through home country (as portrayed in Clarke's painting), or squiggling and wriggling through mid-western Victoria (as in figure 1.1).

Just as the lagoon in Conrad's first published story of this title is a womb for the creation of new life (Giblett 1996, 96-97), so the lagoons of the Hopkins basin are wombs for the nurturing of embryonic life. Mitchell described the Cockajemmy Lakes connected to the Hopkins by the aquifer as "a chain of lagoons" (as we will see in the following chapter of the present volume). These lagoons are uncanny places, places of fascination and horror, of life-giving and death-dealing water, where monstrous maternal creatures, such as the Rainbow Serpent, and sacral serpents, such as the Rainbow Spirit, live in wetlands, creeks and the river.[33]

The upper Hopkins is the home of some remarkable people who have been caring for the wet and dry land, the creeks and the river for many years. The Ararat Landcare Group (ALG) has been active protecting Cemetery Creek and the Hopkins River from gorse infestation since the early 2000s. Cemetery Creek is a tributary of the Hopkins that joins the river near the Western Highway just outside of Ararat. Ayesha Burdett (2021a), the Facilitator of the Upper Hopkins Land Management Group (UHLMG), writes that:

> Gorse is an upright, woody shrub with bright yellow flowers that can

produce huge numbers of seeds. The seeds spread rapidly and can remain dormant in the soil for up to 30 years. Gorse is one of the worst weeds in Victoria. It degrades pasture and creates habitat for rabbits, foxes, and feral cats. It is a tough weed to tackle and requires ongoing vigilance. [...] The existing native vegetation has been supplemented by tree planting projects by Landcarers, high school students and other community members. [...] Part of the success of the weed control program in Ararat is due to the dedicated volunteers and the partnership between ALG and UHLMG with support and coordination from Peter Forster and Una Allender [the Facilitator of UHLMG for 20 years]. This partnership has resulted in control of the gorse infestation around Ararat, on public land, and along key waterways and roadsides. The groups continue to share equipment and knowledge. [...] Other leaders in the war on weeds in the region include John Graham, Keith Little, Aileen Banfield and Stephen Hughan. [...] John was an incredibly active member of the ALG, committing two mornings every week to spraying gorse and other weeds, while carefully avoiding native vegetation. John spent 14 years controlling gorse and training others to identify and control weeds. His efforts have made a remarkable difference.

The war on weeds and the struggle to revegetate the wetlands, drylands, creeks and river with native plants is also taking place in many other places in the Hopkins basin with many other local heroes whose work sometimes gets the recognition it deserves.

Two such land-carers are Don and Goldie Rowe. Ayesha Burdett (2021c) writes that they:

> have hosted numerous paddock walks, field days and social gatherings for the Upper Hopkins Land Management Group (UHLMG) on their property [just west of Maroona with a magnificent view of the Grampians]. Don is an important mentor and role model for other farmers who share his commitment to soil health and sustainable farming, as well as enhancing indigenous vegetation, protecting wetlands and waterways, and controlling pest plants and animals. As a teacher at Ararat Secondary College, Don promoted sustainable farming practices and organised students to work on many tree planting projects from Elmhurst to Tatyoon. Well before UHLMG was formed in 1991, Don and Goldie were erecting land class fencing and planting biodiversity corridors on their property, transforming the agricultural landscape. Many of the new trees and shrubs were grown from seed Don had collected. He also pioneered the use of direct seeding in the region as a way of sowing large areas with indigenous trees with excellent results. Don

has also worked tirelessly at the Maroona Reserve, adjacent to the Hopkins River, planting trees and controlling weeds with the local primary school. In November 2021 Don won the prestigious Australian Government Individual Landcare Award. This award acknowledges the significant contribution made by an individual who has demonstrated outstanding leadership and commitment to Landcare.

The Upper Hopkins has also been the home of some remarkable people whose artwork decolonizes nature and the wetlands of the area. Prominent among these is the work of Carole Mules, whose work is also discussed in the following chapter of the present volume. A recent artwork of hers depicts the Hopkins River from above in an aerial view like a map. It shows the river as a strong blue line that snakes its serpentine course from source to sea (see figure 1.1). It portrays (it is a portrait, it is not a landscape) the river as a living being, like the Rainbow Serpent in Patricia Clarke's painting of Banjo Clarke's country (frontispiece to Clarke with Chance 2003). It does not betray the river as dead matter, as a resource to be transported, bought and sold, a view of water that persists in colonial settler history up to the recent past (as we will see in the following chapter). The work of other environmental artists of the Hopkins River, such as Richard Weatherly and Howard Brandenburg, are also discussed in later chapters of the present volume. They all contribute to portraying the life of the Hopkins River and its kindred wetlands in all its richness and vitality.

WETLANDS OF 'AUSTRALIA FELIX': BETWEEN 'THE GRAMPIANS' AND THE UPPER HOPKINS

9 And God said, Let the waters under the heaven be gathered together unto one place, and let the dry land appear: and it was so. 10 And God called the dry land Earth; and the gathering together of the waters called the Seas: and God saw that it was good. 11 And God said, Let the earth bring forth grass, the herb yielding seed, and the fruit tree yielding fruit after his kind, whose seed is in itself, upon the earth: and it was so. 12 And the earth brought forth grass, and herb yielding seed after his kind, and the tree yielding fruit, whose seed was in itself, after his kind: and God saw that it was good. 13 And the evening and the morning were the third day. *Genesis* 1

6 There went up a mist from the earth, and watered the whole face of the ground. […] 8 And the LORD God planted a garden eastward in Eden. […] 9 And out of the ground made the LORD God to grow every tree that is pleasant to the sight, and good for food. […] 10 And a river went out of Eden to water the garden. *Genesis* 2

Gariwerd, or 'the Grampians,' in Australia are largely known collectively as the mountainous region in western Victoria centered around the town of Halls Gap nestled in the valley between spectacular ranges and accessible from the east through a gap (hence the name of the town) in the ranges.[34] Hardly surprisingly, these ranges "running in a north-south direction" and lying in "the path of rain-bearing westerly winds" (Wilkie 2020, 6) created and recreate magnificent wetlands with the water cascading off the ranges, collecting in basins in the ranges and flowing out around their base in the surrounding country. The Grampian mountain ranges are a watershed with water catchments flowing down to the east and west, feeding rivers flowing to the north and south, and creating surrounding wetlands and well-watered plains in some of God's best work. The Grampian mountain ranges are 'the head,' or top, of these catchments with former wetlands there too.

The first Englishman to record the existence of Gariwerd and its wetlands was the explorer/surveyor Major Thomas Mitchell in 1836.

Mitchell described the rugged mountain ranges and sweeping blessed plains in terms of the European aesthetic conventions of the sublime, the beautiful and the pleasing pastoral picturesque. He dubbed western Victoria 'Australia Felix,' meaning 'Australia the blessed,' or 'blessèd', because of its well-watered grasslands. He did not recognize and acknowledge that these grasslands were the product of Aboriginal fire practices. In his 'Description of Australia Felix' he noted how "small rivers radiate from the Grampians" (Mitchell 1839). Not surprisingly, this area was the happy hunting ground for colonial squatters as the well-watered and blessed plains lent themselves readily to establishing sheep stations where Aboriginal people grazed mobs of kangaroos on their hunting grounds. It was also the happy hunting ground for the colonial-settler landscape painter Eugene von Guérard who depicted the rugged mountains and blessed plains in terms of the European aesthetic conventions of the sublime, the beautiful and the pleasing pastoral picturesque too. Pastoralism and landscape painting went hand-in-hand and were mutually reinforcing colonizing enterprises. The picture told the story; the story enacted the picture.

The Grampian mountain ranges are important geologically and biologically. The Heritage Council of Victoria (2005) states of their significance that:

> The Grampians comprise a complex of sandstone ranges rising abruptly from the Western Plain. From a distance they are most spectacular with their serried ranks of precipitous peaks rising to 1,164m at Mt. William. The area provides some of the most beautiful and diverse habitats for native flora in Victoria with over 1,000 species of ferns and flowering plants, many endemic to the area. A wide range of habitats resulting from the diverse topography, micro-climates and vegetation have provided secure refuges for many wildlife species including a number of rare species.

To what extent this "statement of significance" includes the wetlands surrounding the Grampians National Park is not clear (for further discussion of the geology and biology of the Grampians, see Wilkie 2020, 1-11).

Looking down from a plane flying from Melbourne to Perth, the Grampians mountain ranges are certainly spectacular and their "serried ranks" are clearly visible, as are many of the magnificent Grampians wetlands, even when they are dry, such as Mt William (or Big) Swamp. Mountain ranges in traditional Chinese cultural geography are dragons. They are the backbones of the land. Without the spine of the land, the land would fall apart. The Grampians have four distinct ranges lying back to back or face to face with each other like four intertwined dragons. Water bodies in traditional Chinese cultural geography are places where the Tao, or the Way, begins, where new life springs. They are the internal organs of the land that hang off the spine. Without these organs, the land would die. They give and nourish life by supplying and purifying water. Traditional Australian Aboriginal cultures have a similar view of water bodies (Giblett 2020d).

The Grampians are generally not known for, or associated with, the wetlands that encircle the mountain ranges like a sapphire necklace. Sapphire for Pastoreau (2001, 7) is "a truly celestial color. Its blue, often compared to that of the sky, is said to have healing powers." Blue waters depicted in paintings, such as von Guérard's of swampy Fyans Creek near the Grampians (see figure 3.1 and the cover of the present volume), reflect the sky:

Figure 3.1: Eugene von Guérard, 'Mount William From Mount Dryden,' 1857 Oil on canvas, 61.5 x 91.5 cm.
Collection: Art Gallery of Western Australia
Reproduced with kind permission.

All living waters reflecting the celestial blue sky are truly terrestrial and have life-giving and restorative powers. On maps of the Grampians National Park and the surrounding area, they are shown in blue in accordance with mapping conventions that show water bodies, or not at all.[35] Sapphires can also be black which is fitting for the mainstream denigratory, western cultural colour-coding of swamps as black waters, as blots on the landscape and in the ledgers of colonial farmers and pastoralists.[36]

Benjamin Wilkie in *Gariwerd*, his otherwise largely exemplary and useful recent environmental history of the Grampians, is so fixated on the mountains, the ranges and the national park that he ignores, with a couple of exceptions, the larger bioregion and its wetlands. He might have discussed them, but does not, in relation to water, waterways, reservoirs, rivers and drainage systems (see, for example, Wilkie 2020, x, 7 and 85). Water is abstracted from the specific, living bodies of wetlands, and turned into a dead commodity to be transported, bought and sold. This is a sad and sorry story which seems to be the wont of environmental historians, cultural geographers and urban designers who neglect the life-giving properties of wetlands (as we will also see later in the present chapter and in later chapters of the present volume).

The exceptions are when Wilkie acknowledges wetlands coincidentally, either in mapping Aboriginal country (though there is no key to this map; Wilkie 2020 fig.2.1, 25), or in discussing George Augustus Robinson, the Protector of Aborigines, and his account of 1841 of Aboriginal peoples' uses of marshes (Wilkie 2020, 31-32). Wilkie (2020, 31) describes this usage as "aquaculture," but it is more precisely paludiculture. When Wilkie (2020, fig.3.1, 48) maps pastoral stations, he also shows the prominent mountains, major rivers, bigger towns (not Halls Gap), main roads, Lake Lonsdale, but no wetlands. It is as if pastoral stations wiped pre-contact wetlands off the face of the earth and wrote them out of the history and geography of the Grampians, which they did try to do, and Wilkie largely follows suit. It is as if wetlands are relics of a bygone Aboriginal era. Neo-colonialism is alive and well in 2020. Wetlands are still there!

Despite being a blot, or black spot, on the landscape and in the ledgers of colonial farmers and pastoralists, these wetlands played an important role in the lives of Aboriginal and European peoples. Weaving together the strands of local and environmental history with Aboriginal story of Gariwerd, and illustrated with landscape paintings by von Guérard and with environmental artwork by the local artist Carole Mules in mixed eco-dyed fabric free-motion machine embroideries creating textured renderings of the wetlands of western Victoria, the present chapter celebrates the life of the wetlands in and around the mountain ranges of the Grampians in western Victoria and their role in the lives of the people who have called this place home for many generations. The Grampians wetlands are found in the region bounded by the roads between the towns of Horsham to the north, Ararat and Stawell to the east and north-east, Willaura to the south-east, Dunkeld to the south and Mooralla to the west. Based on archival and contemporary research into Grampians wetlands, this chapter conserves and conveys the natural and cultural heritage of the wetlands of the area for present and future generations.

Aboriginal Significance

Aboriginal peoples have had a long association with Gariwerd, the

Grampian mountain ranges and its surrounding wetlands. Gib Wettenhall (1999, 6) in *The People of Gariwerd: The Grampians' Aboriginal Heritage* states that the Grampians have "immense importance as home and spiritual sanctuary to the two Aboriginal language groups and their predecessors who had shared the ranges [and wetlands, I would suggest] for thousands of years." Their home was the Grampians catchment. Wettenhall (1999, 6) goes on to describe how "Aboriginal people's territories were often catchment-based with rivers and mountain ranges acting as natural boundaries" and encompassing resourceful wetlands (as he goes on to discuss and as I will discuss below).

The *Grampians National Park Management Plan* begins by stating that:

> The Indigenous Nations have a long association with the Grampians–Gariwerd. The use of one site in the Victoria Range (Billawin Range) has been dated from 22 000 years ago. Recent archaeological investigations have demonstrated that there was intensive Aboriginal occupation of Grampians–Gariwerd. The draining of Lake Wartook in 1997 for maintenance works exposed 32 sites around the margin of what was once a swampy basin. (Parks Victoria 2003)

The *Management Plan* is plagiarising Wettenhall (1999, 6 and 25), but neglects to go on to mention that "the 32 sites" around "the swampy basin" of 'Lake' Wartook are now submerged beneath Wartook Reservoir. In other words, Wartook was once a wetland, or more precisely, a tarn, a perched, mountain wetland, though for Wilkie (2020, 85) it was merely "a natural basin." By contrast with Wilkie, Wettenhall (1999, 25) does not neglect to go on to mention that "similar in distribution and content in other western Victoria wetlands […] the Werdug ['Wartook' is a corruption of this Aboriginal name] complex bears all the hallmarks of village life, often established for months at a time." The established hallmarks and built structures of Aboriginal occupation and inhabitation were ignored by the early explorer Major Mitchell who remarked that the territory was "in the state of nature," when in fact it was in the state of culture.

According to the regional water utility, "Lake Wartook is located on the MacKenzie River in the central Grampians. It is an important water resource in the region […] The lake also provides important environmental flows" (GWM Water ND, online). For what or for whom these environmental flows are provided is not specified. It certainly provides continual environmental flows to MacKenzie Falls, the scene of spectacular thrills for tourists (discussed in greater detail below). GWM Water neglects to mention that MacKenzie River is seasonal, and so would the Falls be if it were not for the artificial 'Lake' of Wartook Reservoir.

Despite the loss of these sites and this wetland, the Management Plan goes on to argue that "the park's Indigenous culture is rich, diverse, and living, but will need support and protection to be sustained" (Parks Victoria 2003, 22). Part of that support can come through providing knowledge and interpretation of the rich, diverse, and living culture and nature of Grampians wetlands (for further discussion of the Aboriginal significance of the Grampians, see Wettenhall 1999 and Wilkie 2020, 13-36).

European Exploration

The first Europeans to visit the area noted its wetlands. Rod Bird (2014, 3) in his self-published history of wetlands in south-west Victoria writes that "at settlement [sic] by Europeans the land was full of swamps and lakes," yet it was hardly full of wetlands as it also had mountain ranges, such as the Grampians, that Europeans could easily see and note, and did so. Paul Carter (1987, 111) describes how the explorer/surveyor Major Thomas Mitchell "traversed the Grampians regions during a very wet season; during a very dry season the same country wears a quite different appearance." Quite so, as much of it was made up of wetlands. In fact, the very wet season of 1836 made the region into what Wettenhall (1999, 6) calls "the maze of swamps." Wilkie (2020, 6) remarks that "the region was relatively wet just before the arrival of the Europeans in the late 1830s [...] It was fateful that the Europeans would first encounter the region in a period of relatively high precipitation and moisture, and therefore lush, alluring vegetation."

On 30th June 1836 Mitchell (1839) climbed Pyramid Hill and later waxed lyrical in his journal that "I stood, the first European intruder on the sublime solitude of these verdant plains as yet untouched by flocks or herds." More specifically, the country "appeared to be undulated, open, and grassy" with forested land that "opened into grassy and level plains" and "open grassy plains, beautifully variegated with serpentine lines of wood" (Mitchell 1839). This country was, as Mitchell first indicated and as Wilkie (2020, 70) recently reiterates, "precisely the kind of landscape sought after by nineteenth-century pastoralists." Mitchell was an ex-army man and an explorer/surveyor by profession or trade and appointment to and for colonial pastoralists. One followed the other in lockstep with devastating impacts on indigenous peoples and places. In 1938 James Cowell (cited by Wilkie 2020, 69) wrote in *The Horsham Times* that "with man's sheep came destruction of this verdant growth," precisely the very object of desire that attracted them in the first place, and that they then destroyed. Some white men kill the things they supposedly love, like grasslands, and those they hate, like wetlands.

The Grampians wetlands were seasonal, as are many Australian wetlands, a situation often held against them by colonial explorers and setters (see, for instance, George Webb's denigration of Lake Monger in Perth for not being "like a lake at home" and "drying up" seasonally and inconsiderately according to Eurocentric criteria; Giblett 1996, 57-58). Yet the seasonal wetting and drying of Australian wetlands as noted by one of the earliest European observers of western Victoria in George Augustus Robinson, the 'Protector' of Aborigines from 1839 to 1849, makes them highly productive and important as a food source for Aboriginal people (both discussed below).

In what Powell (1970, xxv) calls "an unusually wet winter – almost uncannily avoiding some of the least promising areas," Bird (2014, 3) describes how Mitchell "struggled across these landscapes," or more precisely wetlandscapes, in south-west Victoria and named the area initially as 'Eden' and later famously as 'Australia Felix' (Wettenhall 1999, 34). Mitchell wrote that:

> We had at length discovered a country ready for the immediate reception of civilised man; and destined perhaps to become eventually a portion of a great empire. Unencumbered by too much wood, it yet possessed enough for all purposes; its soil was exuberant and its climate temperate; it was bounded on three sides by the ocean; and it was traversed by mighty rivers, and watered by streams innumerable. Of this Eden I was the first European to explore its mountains and streams, to behold its scenery, to investigate its geological character and, by my survey, to develop those natural advantages certain to become, at no distant date, of vast importance to a new people. (Mitchell 1839; cited by Carter 1987, 111 and 254-255)

Rather than the biblical Eden, Mitchell may have had more in mind Milton's pastoral and pastoralist Eden in *Paradise Lost* (4, 247) described as "a happy rural seat of various view" complete with an aquifer ("the nether flood"), a lake "with fringed banks", "lawns, or level downs" and "flocks grazing."[37] Perhaps Mitchell was evoking nostalgically Milton's Eden in retrospect and projecting it imaginatively as a pleasing prospect into the future. To imagine flocks of sheep grazing, however, he would have needed to block out the sight of mobs of kangaroos grazing peacefully in a happy pastoral estate of Aboriginal ownership. What he didn't see was that the land was ideal for pasturing sheep because Aboriginal people grazed and pastured kangaroos and wallabies on the grasslands that they cultivated and regenerated with fire.

Carter (1987, 255) concludes of Mitchell's account that, "in short, Australia Felix was a picturesque country," or more precisely, some aspects of it were. Carter overlooks the fact that 'Australia Felix' for Mitchell was also, in short and in part, a sublime country, or more precisely, some aspects were, as Mitchell goes on to write (but Carter does not cite) how:

from the summit of Mount Abrupt I beheld a truly sublime scene; the whole of the mountains, quite clear of clouds, the grand outline of the more distant masses blended with the sky, and forming a blue and purple background for the numerous peaks of the range on which I stood, which consisted of sharp cones and perpendicular cliffs foreshortened so as to form one grand feature only of the extensive landscape, though composing a crescent nearly 30 miles in extent: this range being but a branch from the still more lofty masses of Mount William which crowned the whole. (Mitchell 1839; cited by Wilkie 2020, 44 and in part by Wettenhall 1999, 6)

The sublime in European landscape aesthetics has generally been concerned with vertiginous mountainous landscapes and Mitchell follows this convention. It is as if Mitchell were singing here from the song-sheet of the sublime penned by Edmund Burke and elaborated by Immanuel Kant in the eighteenth century (see Giblett 1996, chapter 2). The sublime is one of the major European aesthetic and cultural modalities that goes back to Longinus in the first century of the common era and comes forward to Lyotard in the twentieth century. For Lyotard (cited by Giblett 1996, 25), "around the name of the sublime, modernity triumphed," not least over wetlands in the short term with draining and dredging, but not in the long term with floods and storm surges. The sublime is what could be called "a secular theology," a theology for a world without the Judeo-Christian God, or for a world in which "God is dead" (see also Giblett 1996, chapter 2).

The sublime was part of Mitchell's cultural baggage that he carried with him on his expeditions in the nineteenth century and used in his descriptions of the "the sublime peaks" and "the sublime solitude of these verdant plains." Mitchell quite rightly associates the sublime with immensity in the vertical and horizontal planes (plains) and evokes the affect (bodily or visceral emotion) of solitude conjoining subject and object. The sublime is not a quality of the subject (the 'I') alone, nor of the object (the 'scene') solely, but of their conjunction. The sublime is also a product of the position and stance of the subject ('I stood') in relation to geometrical objects (e.g., "sharp cones and perpendicular cliffs," etc.) as famously depicted and evoked in Caspar David Friedrich's painting of a solitary 'Wanderer above the Mist,' or 'Mountaineer in a Misty Landscape,' of *circa* 1818. In Mitchell's terms, this painting could be called 'in sublime solitude in, or of, the mountains.' It is as if Mitchell were transporting and translating the horizontal mid-ground in Friedrich's painting from grey mist to green plains, from image to word, from Germany to Australia only 18 years later.

Carter (1987, 255) goes on to note that "in Mitchell's published narrative" the description quoted earlier about Eden "occurs in the entry for 13 July, *before,* that is, Mitchell had entered Australia Felix." Mitchell, in fact, had called this area at the time 'Eden,' not 'Australia Felix' at all; he had called it 'Eden' when he had seen it and before he had entered it. 'Eden' was the view of the country from afar as picturesque scenery in a pleasing pastoral prospect, whereas 'Australia Felix' was his name for the region as productive pastoralist country close-up after he had entered it and when he later described it (as we will see shortly, and which Carter does not quote for some strange reason). The biblical gates of Eden are closed and guarded by an angel with a flaming sword for anyone wishing to re-enter it (*Genesis* 3: 24), while the portals of 'Australia Felix' are open for any white male settler wanting to enter it (or her) guided by Mitchell with a flagrant pen – an exceptional case in which the pen *is* mightier than the sword.

Mitchell serves as a pander or pimp for white men entering 'Australia Felix' when in his later description of, and introduction to, it he waxes lyrical that:

> The land is [...] open and available in its present state for all purposes of civilised man. We traversed it in two directions with heavy carts, meeting no other obstruction than the softness of the rich soil; and, in returning over flowery plains and green hills fanned by the breeze of early spring, I named this region Australia Felix, the better to distinguish it from the parched deserts of the interior country [...] flocks might be put out upon its hills or the plough at once set to work in the plains. (Mitchell 1839; cited in part by Bird 2014, 3)

In other words, 'Australia Felix' is soft, flowery and virgin land that is open and available for 'civilized' white men to penetrate and deflower it (or her). 'Australia Felix' is also moist, green and fertile land, unlike the dry and barren desert of the interior of Australia. 'Australia Felix' is ready and ripe for insemination and procreation by white men in industrial agriculture and pastoralism in which they are active and the land is a passive receptacle or incubator. Mitchell colour-codes, genders and sexualizes the land. Strangely Carter does not cite this particular description of 'Australia Felix' in his extensive use and discussion of Mitchell's work in *The Road to Botany Bay,* nor does Michael Cathcart (2010) in *The Water Dreamers,* his environmental history of water in Australia (Giblett 2021c, chapter 7). Are they embarrassed by, or squeamish about, Mitchell's old-fashioned patriarchal sexual politics? They are fairly typical for his day, age, masculine gender, heterosexuality and politics.

George Augustus Robinson, the Protector of Aborigines from 1839 to 1849, was an early dissenter from Major Mitchell's bucolic view of 'Australia Felix' and 'the Major's Eden,' as Robinson put it. As Carter (1987, 110) points out, "according to Robinson, most of what Mitchell called 'lakes' were never more than 'lagoons covered with thick reeds and grass'," an apt description of an Australian wetland. Carter goes on to point out that

Robinson wrote that "two 'lakes' south of Mount Abrupt at the southern end of the Grampians:

> called by Mitchell lakes, had no doubt water in them [at the time]. But even then it must have been so shallow that had he examined them he would have seen the grass. They are now dry. (cited by Carter 1987, 110)

In other words, lakes aren't shallow, don't have grass, and they don't dry up in Robinson's landscape lexicon. Robinson, like Webb, applies European criteria for lakes to Australia. Mitchell for Robinson should have known better and not called these water bodies 'lakes' when they didn't deserve the name, or fit the criteria. Yet Robinson writes here another apt description of an Australian wetland that can be, and usually is, shallow, can have grass, and can and does dry up.

In July 1841 Robinson (1998, 306) was among the Grampians wetlands where he "passed several dikes dug by the natives for draining small lagoons into the large ones for the purpose of catching eels." The following day Robinson (1998, 308) was at "the confluence" of a creek and marsh where he:

> observed an immense piece of ground [of at least 15 acres] trenched and banked, resembling the work of civilized man[,] but which on inspection I found to be the work of the Aboriginal natives, purposely constructed for catching eels.

"Resembling" belies the fact that, indeed, this "piece of ground" *was* the work of civilized people as Aboriginal people, in John Stuart Mill's definition of civilization, undertook "human improvement" and were "rich in the fruits of agriculture" (cited by Mayes 2018, 36), or more precisely aquaculture and paludiculture in this case. So much for the country being ready for the reception of civilization, as Mitchell stated previously as it was already civilized and had been for tens of thousands of years. So much for civilization beginning in Australia in the late eighteenth century, as famously claimed as the opening gambit of Manning Clark's monumental, multi-volume history (cited by Mayes 2018, 26). Clark implied that barbarism existed in Australia until the late eighteenth century when it was superseded by civilization. Clark later regretted whitewashing Aboriginal civilizations out of the history of Australia and acknowledged that civilization in Australia began forty or fifty thousand years ago.

Aboriginal people also demonstrated ownership of their property as they, in John Locke's terms, "mixed their labour with nature" (cited by Mayes 2018, 34). Yet contra Locke and his theory of property, rather than transforming the commons or waste land into private property, their labour maintained the commons in common. Robinson (1998, 308) commented repeatedly that "these works must have been executed at great cost of labour" and "they evinced great perseverance and industry of the part of these Aborigines." "The plan or design of these ramifications" for Robinson (1998, 308) were "extremely perplexing" and he found "it difficult to commit to paper." He still tried to do so though (Robinson 1898, figure 7.10). Robinson (1998 307) had previously commented that "these people must labour to get precious food."

Not only does Mitchell boost 'Australia Felix' as available for colonization by industrial agriculture and pastoralism, but also by roads, towns and "county divisions" along English lines:

> this territory, still for the most part in a state of nature, presents a fair blank sheet for any geographical arrangement whether of county divisions, lines of communication, or sites of towns etc. etc. (Mitchell 1839)

This territory was, in fact, in a state of culture with villages (as we have seen), fish weirs and eel traps (as we will see later). In accordance with the prevailing doctrines of *terra nullius* and *tabula rasa*, Mitchell equates Aboriginal people and their territory with nature, and thereby writes Aboriginal people, wetlands and other specificities of their place out of history and geography and denies their culture. The traces of their lives and their cultures are wiped clean from the slate of the land (including wetland) in Mitchell's rendition of the landscape, the surface of the land presented to the eye. Aboriginal people were genocided by word, as they were soon in fact as many were massacred in this region, beginning with Mitchell's expedition, even though they were dependent on Aboriginal guidance and knowledge of the country (Koori Heritage Trust 1991; Wilkie 2020, 42, 62-63). The depths of the earth (including wetlands) are smoothed into the surface of a blank sheet for the inscribing of roads, towns and counties.[38]

The surface of the earth is also available for Mitchell as the basis for erecting monuments on it to the greater glory, power and wealth of the British empire. Mitchell (1839) concludes that such an enterprise "would be establishing a lasting monument of the beneficial influence of British power and colonization." Such boosterism of the beneficent colonial master is the stock-in-trade of colonialism, when in fact it brought pain, disease, death, dispossession and destruction (as Mbembe 2019, remarks on many occasions). Erecting monuments on monstrous marshes, the grotesque lower earthly stratum, thus inscribing a place in space and a moment in time as a lasting memorial to itself, is also the stock-in-trade of patriarchal capitalist colonialism (see Giblett 2011, chapter 1; for further discussion of European exploration of the Grampians, see Wilkie 2020, 41-50).

Landscape Painting

Mitchell (1839; cited by Wilkie 2020, 70) wrote of his expedition that "we had been for some time travelling through forest land which now opened into grassy and level plains, variegated with belts and clumps of lofty trees giving to the whole the appearance of a park." Following literally and metaphorically in Mitchell's footsteps, Wettenhall (1999, 34) points out that "early settlers described the plains of western Victoria as looking 'just like a gentleman's park'." One such early settler was John G. Robertson (Bride 1898, 34) who wrote in 1853 that "all the landscape looked like a park." Such a simile was the stock-in-trade of early explorers and colonial settlers throughout Australia (Giblett 2011, 91-92). It belied the fact that, indeed, the landscape *was* a park, the product of Aboriginal firing and hunting practices in "the biggest estate on earth" (Gammage 2011; see also Giblett 2011, 93-94). The pastoralist's desideratum is the gentleman's park estate — on Aboriginal peoples' estates. The arriviste squatter could rise quickly up the social scale and class ladder by dispossessing Aboriginal people, acquiring their landed property and exploiting its resources cultivated by Aboriginal people. Scottish settlers, who made up at least two-thirds of the pioneer settlers of western Victoria (Kiddle 1961, 14, 517 n1) and who had been cleared off estates in Scotland, cleared off Aboriginal people, in turn, from their estates in Victoria (as we saw in the previous chapter; see also Wilkie 2020, 46).

To illustrate the simile of the country being like a gentleman's park estate, Wettenhall (1999, 34) reproduces von Guérard's painting, 'Mount William from Mount Dryden' of 1857 and captions it as "depicting the park-like beauty of western Victoria" (see figure 3.1 and the cover of the present volume). Indeed, this landscape painting based on a sketch of 1856 (Pullin 2018, figure 6.12, 180) does depict a park-like pastoral scene in the foreground with kangaroos grazing peacefully on grassland bathed in beneficent sunlight and ripe to be dispossessed by grazing sheep and cattle, but the mid-ground between the two mountains is unmistakeably swampy, with Mt William in the background. This swampy area is probably around Fyans Creek with Lake Fyans in the left background, another of the Grampians wetlands turned into a lake and a reservoir, the home of the Stawell Yacht Club and the source of drinking water for the town of Stawell and others. The depiction in this painting of grazing kangaroos implies Aboriginal graziers who used fire to manage grassland to provide feed for kangaroos, to then hunt. Grazing segues into hunting. Grazing kangaroos in the painting is evidence for Aboriginal graziers.

Von Guérard's 'Mount William From Mount Dryden' was bled-off (or cropped) and used as the cover illustration for the catalogue of the 1998 touring exhibition, *New Worlds from Old: 19th Century American and Australian*

Landscapes, held at, among other places, the National Galleries of Australia and Victoria. Keaney (1998, 155) notes in her catalogue entry for this painting in the 1998 touring exhibition catalogue that contemporary newspapers "commented favourably on the beauty of the natural landscape [...,] commending von Guérard for his composition and the chosen vantage point. The artist was praised for his empathy with the Australian landscape." He was not praised for his empathy with the Australian wetlandscape that makes a cameo appearance in this painting in the mid-ground and that appears centre stage in his painting of Mt William (figure 3.2 discussed below in the present chapter).

Contemporary newspaper reports also described von Guérard's painting "in terms of his national significance" (Keaney 1998, 155). More to the point, von Guérard was an Australian artist of national*ist* significance for his paintings of the colonial-settler landscape that made the unhomely land homely by depicting it in terms of the conventions of the European landscape aesthetic of the sublime, the beautiful and the picturesque, often in a single painting, as in 'Mount William From Mount Dryden.' Nothing much has changed to his status in over a century as he is still regarded as "arguably Australia's, and certainly [the state of] Victoria's most important colonial landscape painter," as McDowall (2014) puts it.

Keaney (1998, 155) relates how von Guérard's 'Mount William From Mount Dryden' was acquired by the Art Gallery of Western Australia in 1972. She concludes that this painting "remains one of that gallery's most significant colonial Australian paintings." She does not give any reasons for this conclusion, but I hazard a guess that it has this status because it contains many well-worn clichés of landscape painting in mainstream western cultural aesthetics executed dexterously, such as the pleasing and picturesque pastoral foreground with a mob of kangaroos grazing peacefully ready to be supplanted by introduced farm animals, a wetland subsumed fleetingly in the mid-ground (as all wetlands should be fleeting according to mainstream western thinking about the landscape) providing a source of water for the settler, a sublime mountainous background topped by beneficent, rain-bearing clouds and overseen by a raptor flying magisterially in the sky above the immensity and expansiveness of the land below as an emblem of God's providence over all (but also a trace of the all-creating Bunjil eagle). The Aboriginal graziers who tended the mob of kangaroos and cared for the country with cool burning to make it suitable for grazing are absent from the painting.

Unlike von Guérard, who saw the land in terms of the sublime, the picturesque and the beautiful, and Mitchell, who also saw the land in sexual, sublime and picturesque terms, Mitchell's second-in-command, Assistant Surveyor Grenville Chetwynd Stapylton, saw the flat or undulating land in similar picturesque and pastoral terms to both men when he saw the Grampians as "a beautiful and romantic appearance" (Andrews 1986, 185; cited by Wilkie 2020, 44), unlike Mitchell (1839) who saw them as "the sublime peaks" (as we have seen). Stapylton did not differentiate the two landscapes of the flat or undulating plains and the rocky or steep mountains from each other in terms of two different modes of aesthetics of the sublime and the picturesque as both Mitchell and von Guérard did.

Bird describes how south-west Victoria was "a soft land" and quotes from Dennis Conley's contribution to *The Western Plains: A Natural and Social History* published by the Australian Institute of Agricultural Science in Victoria in 1986:

> the untroddden sward [...] was literally comparable to a bed of sponge; our horses sank to their fetlocks with every step [...] A two years' occupation in most instances rendered a station so 'firm' that horse racing, kangaroo, emu and dingo hunting [...] formed one of the principal sources of amusement to the light-hearted settlers. (cited by Bird 2014, 3).

The sward, the upper layer of soil covered by short grass and so desirable pastoralist land, was trodden by Aboriginal people for tens of thousands of years before the arrival of Europeans. The transformation of soft and spongy wet land into firm dry land marks the sad and sorry story of occupation, dispossession and colonization by the armies of settlers with their cavalry of mounted hunters, stockmen and drovers and their infantry of cattle and sheep. It marks the transformation of the native quaking zone of wetlands where the earth trembles and where Aboriginal people tread lightly into the feral quaking zone of drylands where introduced animals tread heavily and native animals are hunted and tremble in fear.[39]

Mount William Swamp

'The Wartook Reservoir,' as Wettenhall (1999 25) prefers to call it, was not alone in submerging an Aboriginal village and a Grampians wetland. He also goes on to state that "archaeologists now consider that other wetlands, such as the Moora Moora Reservoir [also in Grampians National Park ...], could well exhibit similar signs of intensive occupation by Djab wurrung or the Jardwadjali" peoples (Wettenhall 1999 25). So much for *terra nullius*. These signs were also evident much farther away in what Wettenhall (1999 24) calls "the Mt William wetlands" with the construction of fish weirs and the use of eel traps (as noted and illustrated by George Augustus Robinson in his journal of 1841; see Presland 1977; Wettenhall 1999, 24; Wilkie 2020, 31-32). They practiced both aquaculture and paludiculture, the cultivation of wetlands, also observed by Robinson (cited by Bird 2014, 4) when he noted that "the great swamp abounds in rushes, the roots of which are edible and afford the natives an ample supply." Wettenhall (1999, 34) describes how, "on the plains [of western Victoria], large numbers of lakes and swamps offered a wide range of reliable food resources, both plant and animal." The fact that Aboriginal people regulated the flows of water in wetlands and rivers with weirs and channels, not only for catching fish and eels, but also for cultivating edible roots and rushes and attracting waterbirds shows that they were practitioners of paludiculture. Aboriginal people also netted waterbirds as noted by Major Mitchell (1839) in his journal when he observed them constructing wetland structures and practicing what could be called traditional 'aquaorniculture.'

Looking at the land from the point of view of food resources (as Aboriginal people did) is different from that of the landscape painter (as Eugene von Guérard did). Swamps and marshes may be viewed in the midground of the picturesque pleasing prospects as in von Guérard's 'Tower Hill' of 1855. This painting housed in the Warrnambool Art Gallery depicts in the mid-ground what Andrew Sayers (1998 154) describes in *The New Worlds from Old* exhibition catalogue as "the shallow marsh […,] part of a connected series of wetlands and a fertile breeding ground for birds and other wetland animals." The wetland is a water-filled, dormant volcanic crater now in the Tower Hill Wildlife Reserve in the Warrnambool area of south-western Victoria. The painting also depicts an Aboriginal person in the foreground tending a small cooking fire and another outside a 'humpy' or 'mia-mia.' A dog that looks more like a greyhound than a dingo is in attendance. Aboriginal people are shown performing domestic pursuits at a campsite complete with a domesticated dog as if they are on holiday, rather than grazing or hunting kangaroos on their pastures, or cultivating and hunting waterbirds and other animals in the wetland.

Ten years later von Guérard painted a painting of another wetland in western Victoria in the mid-ground of a picturesque pleasing prospect. It is based on a sketch he had done about ten years before while he was travelling and staying in the region (figure 3.2; see Pullin 2011, 126-127; see also Pullin 2018, 179 and map unp.).

According to one writer on this painting, "although this scene was on Mount William Station, von Guérard chose to paint it as a primeval landscape." In other words, although the scene was part and parcel of pastoral land use, von Guérard chose to paint it as a primeval hydrological wetlandscape of marsh and slime in the fore- and mid-ground, and as a primeval geological drylandscape of rock and the sublime in the background. The horizontal, supine wetlandscape is countered by the vertical, erect drylandscape in the background in a classic, masculinist gendering of the land. Mountainous clouds surmount the scene and shroud the top of Mt. William as an emblem of God's overarching omnipotence, if not beneficence.

Figure 3.2: Eugene von Guérard, 'Mount William and part of the Grampians in West Victoria,' 1865
Oil on cardboard, 30.3 x 40.6 cm
National Gallery of Victoria, Melbourne
Collier Bequest 1955 (1562–5)
Reproduced with kind permission.

It is as if von Guérard set out in this painting to illustrate Mitchell's description of "the sublime scene" from the summit of Mt Abrupt cited earlier in which he was singing from the song sheet of the sublime. Von Guérard's painting with its strong horizon in the mid-ground and with placid water and marshy vegetation in the foreground could also be called a depiction and evocation of the slime in the horizontal of wetlandscapes, as distinct from the sublime in the horizontal of the verdant plains (as Mitchell did as we have seen), or of desert landscapes (as identified and discussed by Rudolf Otto 1950, 69). Sheep and cattle are *not* grazing safely in this pastoral landscape and no damage by their hard hooves is evident in the exposed foreground. Rather, native waterbirds wade and browse placidly in the water or fly smoothly above the water, emus congregate convivially in the marshy vegetation and a lone pelican floats magisterially in the air above. In the sense of being a benign, prelapsarian landscape of God's good earthly creation, the scene depicted is pastoral; in the sense of being a scene of chaos, it is also a primeval wetlandscape before the fall into evil, into wetland drainage and into agricultural and pastoral damage.[40]

This painting was not included in the *New Worlds from Old* exhibition (and so not reproduced or discussed in the catalogue either) for some strange reason, especially as this touring exhibition was held for several months in the National Gallery of Victoria where this painting is housed. Perhaps it was not included because von Guérard expressed too much empathy in this painting for the slimy swamps of the Australian wetlandscape, and/or for playing around with the conventions of the European landscape aesthetic in the s(ub)lime (slime is the secret of the sublime, as Zoë Sofoulis construes it in her parenthetical portmanteau; see Giblett 1996, chapter 2) and/or for not singing from the same song sheet about the grandeur of nature, etc., as most of the paintings in this exhibition do from which there were some other noteworthy absences (for further discussion of these absences and of the s(ub)lime in Australian wetlandscape painting and photography, see Giblett 2020a).

The wetland on Mount William Station in von Guérard's painting was called (unoriginally) 'Mount William Swamp.' The scene depicted in this painting is also a primeval wetlandscape before the fall into evil and land abuse.[41] The "untrodden sward" and primeval slime in von Guérard's painting of swampy Fyans Creek in flood in his painting of 'Mount William from Mount Dryden' (figure 3.1 and the cover of present volume) becomes the devastated and desolate pre-industrial agricultural landscape of a blighted and drought-stricken farm in Arthur Boyd's painting 'Irrigation Lake, Wimmera' painted in 1950 depicting the other side of the Grampians, the dark side of the pastoral wet day dream, a drought-stricken nightmare, or day-mare. This painting depicts a desolated wetlandscape and tree graveyard on a farm in the Mallee/Wimmera region of western Victoria west of the Grampians with trees in a dam dying from salination or inundation or both. The lake looks like it is well on its way to becoming irredeemably saline caused by the clearing of native trees and stripping of the topsoil (Giblett 2020a, figure 3.3, 58). Perhaps this painting is the visual expression of the dark side of Mitchell's verbal explorer-settler water dreaming, 'Australia Execratus,' 'Australia the Cursed,' to Mitchell's 'Australia Felix.'

The living wetland is transformed into a dying wetlandscape, a landscape painting of it, and a stark portrait of a once living being. This wetland that was once living is now a ghost swamp. Land is transformed into landscape and the face of the land ('land-face') into portrait. As land is to landscape, so face is to portrait, as naked is to nude (see Giblett 2009, 177-178). In Boyd's painting the ruined wetland and dry desert is desublimated into dried paint on the dry surface of the painting. The life of the land and the depths of the wet-land are surfaced into painterly surface. Soft, wet paint is applied to a hard, dry surface. Soft, liquid paint dries hard into solid painting. In von Guérard's painting of Mount William (or Big) Swamp, solid mountain is sublimated into the ethereal sublime while liquid swamp is surfaced into aquaterrestrial slime. The two paintings are a diptych presenting in the now, a dialectical image of a moment in the past and in the present of absent wetlands, 'Australia Felix' and 'Australia Execratus.'

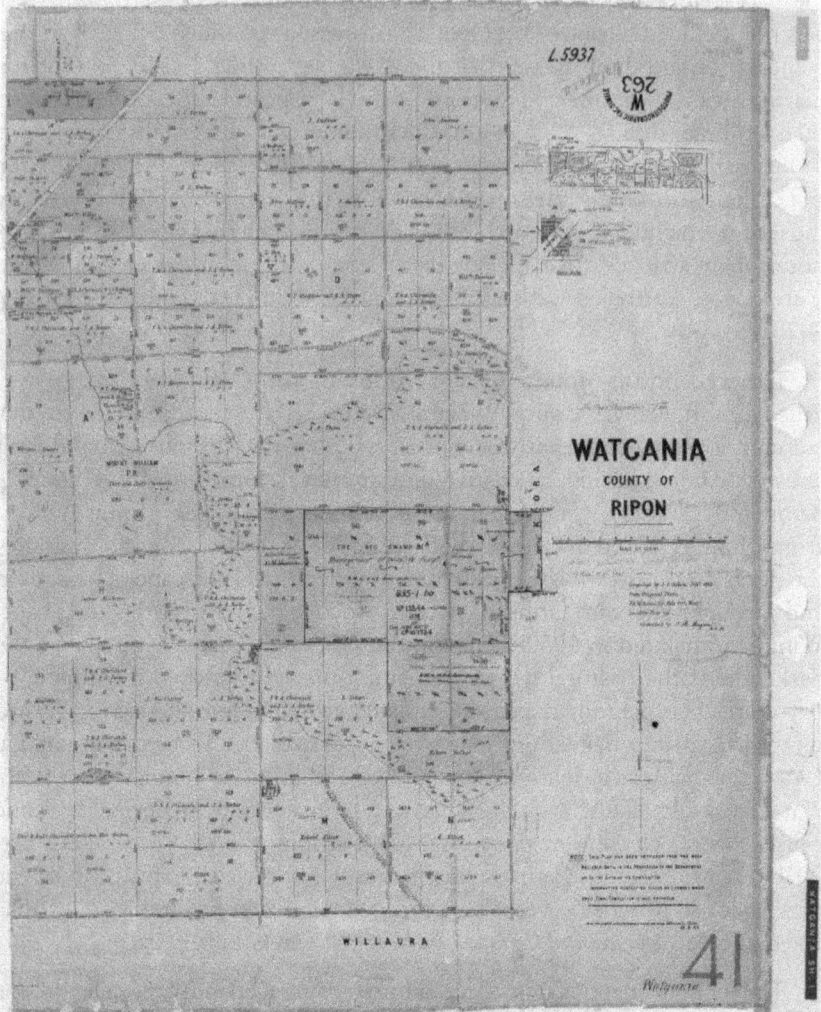

Figure 3.3: 'Watgania Parish, County of Ripon, 1880.' Public domain. I am grateful to Carole Mules for passing on a copy of this map.

Eugene von Guérard's swamp still survives, or at least the middle of it is protected, perhaps because it is too boggy for farming and "only good" for water-birds. Bird (2014, 18) describes how "some 635 ha of unfenced Crown Land remains in the centre of the 1900 ha Mt William Swamp, but is not accessible to the public." This area is named as "The Big Swamp WR" on the accompanying map (Bird 2014, 18). 'WR' is short for 'Wildlife Reserve' (not 'Refuge'), or previously 'Management of Wildlife Purp[s],' in other words, a hunting preserve, as in a survey map of 1880 figure 3.3).

Mitchell's lines of communication and counties are writ large here in a rectilinear grid of lots on the surface of the earth. The fluid outlines of the swamp are subsumed beneath the grid, the life of the Great Goddess/Mother (or Mater) of swamps buried beneath a mathematised matrix ruled by set square and tee square. From mater to matrix marks the sad and sorry fate of many wetlands. The commons of Aboriginal land are enclosed and 'alienated' into private property. Bird (2014, 18) captions a photo of "Mt William Swamp as it was in August 2011 – nearly full for the first time in 65 years. Most of the area has been alienated and sown to pasture (note the fence across the lake)." The fence is another line, another inscription on the surface of the (wet)land (for further discussion of colonization of the Grampians and pastoralist dispossession of Aboriginal people, see Wilkie 2020, 59-76).

Other Grampian Wetlands

Other Grampian wetlands experienced a similar fate to Mt William Swamp. Bird (2014, 14) relates how "Bradys Swamp was once a magnificent wetland, filled by fresh water from the Wannon River, flowing out of the park from its alluvial fan. It was host to hundreds of Magpie Geese, Ibis, Brolga and other waterbirds." The Grampian wetlands are noted as Brolga habitat. The water flow was reversed with devastating consequences. Bird (2014, 2) describes how:

> Heifer Swamp to the east was drained in about 1900 and the water was directed via a deep channel through a lunette into Bradys Swamp. In the late 1940s a shallow drain was dug across the swamp to create a new outlet into the upper Wannon River. As a consequence of the drain, Bradys Swamp is usually dry by January or February. Works to restore this picturesque wetland are required.

Even if it were not picturesque, it should still be restored. Being picturesque is not the only reason for restoration. Being water-bird habitat is a reason for protecting it.

As it is for another Grampian wetland in Lake Muirhead, close to Mt William Swamp. Rod Bird (2014 20) describes how:

> This wetland, comprising both shallow and deep freshwater marsh, is a prime flocking site for Brolga in Victoria, with several hundred birds sometimes seen there. At least parts of the lake dry out annually and the birds seek crickets and other insects on the flats. In summer and autumn Brolga spend much of their time in flocks on stubble areas in the Willaura area [...] Lake Muirhead is also prime habitat for rare species such as the Freckled Duck. The south-west

section has an area of flats that are subject to inundation. Parts are generally covered with reed and rushes while the rest is mud flats when not under water.

This temporal and spatial variation is fairly typical of Australian wetlands.

A much more positive story of a Grampians wetland is told recently with Walker Swamp. In June 2019:

> The landmark purchase of the 192-hectare Walker Swamp Reserve has been celebrated by partners and the community as a major step towards protecting the critically endangered wetlands in the Grampians. The reserve will permanently protect this important link in the large wetland system on the Wannon River Floodplain [...] Work to date to protect the Grampians wetlands includes: [...] 430 hectares of wetlands protected by landholders through the Wetland Defence Program and six one-day Farmplan21 workshops have been held, with 12 landholders attending. The workshops gave farmers the knowledge and skills needed to make sustainable land management decisions [...] The Eastern Maar Aboriginal Corporation and Martang Pty Ltd are involved in the ongoing cultural management of the wetlands of the Greater Grampians. A series of 'Water and Country' events involving Traditional Owners included tours of the Budj Bim landscape, a children's school holiday program and an Aboriginal art competition and exhibition. The events promoted the unique wetlands and their biodiversity and cultural values to the community. (DELWP 2019, online; for Budj Bim see, Gunditjmara with Wettenhall 2010, 7, 13-16, 67)

The wetland cultures of the Grampians wetlands are finally being celebrated.

National Park

Grampians National Park was 'set aside' in 1984 as an area of outstanding natural beauty and sublimity with mountain ranges and waterfalls, such as Kalymna and MacKenzie Falls, in accordance with the European landscape aesthetic transported and reproduced in the American template for National Parks. Using the presence of a waterfall as an essential criterion for a national park is part of the modern tradition of aestheticising nature in terms of what Dean MacCannell (cited by Giblett 2011, 159) calls "outstanding features of the landscape" (including not just a waterfall, but "a large waterfall"). It is also part of what he goes on to call "the modern touristic version of nature" which treats it as "a common source of thrills." Waterfalls, as Paul Shepard (cited by Giblett 2011, 159) points out, "have been primary tourist attractions for a thousand years;" national parks, usually with waterfalls, have been primary tourist attractions for a hundred years. Yet national parks are usually more than just tourist attractions. Or more precisely, the touristic functions of national parks are tied up with other colonialist, capitalist and nationalist agendas and only comparatively recently with conservationist ones (for further discussion of national parks along these lines, see Giblett 2011, chapter 8).

The Grampians were, in the words of the *National Park Management Plan* (Parks Victoria 2003, 25), "generally unsuitable for farming," while Mitchell eulogized the surrounding fertile and well-watered plains as highly suitable. The unsuitability of the rugged mountain ranges of the Grampians for farming conforms to the American template of 'worthless lands' that was one of the impetuses for the setting aside of national parks in the United States. In the United States, as Alfred Runte (cited by Giblett 2011, 166) argues:

> national parks, however spectacular from the standpoint of their topography, actually encompassed only those features considered valueless for lumbering, mining, grazing or agriculture [what has come to be called the 'worthless lands' thesis]. Indeed, throughout the history of the national park idea, the concept of useless scenery has virtually determined which landmarks the nation would protect as well as how it would protect them [. . .] not until the 1930s would wilderness preservation be recognized as a primary justification for establishing national parks, at least in the eyes of [the US] Congress.

The inclusion of wildlife preservation in the US came as late as 1934 with the creation of the Everglades National Park in Florida. Perhaps it is hardly surprising that the preservation of wildlife should be brought about in relation to that most useless and worthless of areas for industrial lumbering, mining, grazing and agriculture, and to that least aesthetically pleasing of landforms, a wetland (see Giblett 1996, chapter 1). The wetlands surrounding the mountain ranges and later National Park, are largely in private hands, with the exception of the middle of 'Big Swamp' (as we have seen). These wetlands had some worth and usefulness as hunting preserves, sources of food and water for stock and summer refugia for them too.

The Grampians National Park also followed the American template as the site for what the Management Plan (Parks Victoria 2003, 36) calls "scenic driving." The railway and the car did more than conservationists to create national parks in the United States and in Australia: "Stephen T. Mather, the first director of the US National Park Service [established in 1916] recognized that park development was linked intimately to the growth of tourism, so he energetically built a second 'pragmatic alliance' . . . between the NPS and automobile interests throughout the country" (cited by Giblett 2011, 160). The touristic functions of national parks tied up with other colonialist, capitalist and nationalist agendas were worked out in the use of modern transportation technologies, such as the car. The car created a more dynamic set of picturesque or pleasing prospects with various stops for taking in the view. The car driver and passenger looked out front and side windows at sweeping panoramic vistas surrounding the car. Wetlands do not generally lend themselves to this point of view (for further discussion of the development of Grampians National Park, see Wilkie 2020, 102-112).

Environmental Artwork

Wetlands do not generally lend themselves to a sweeping panorama in landscape painting, or to any sort of representation in landscape painting for that matter that use the conventions of the European landscape aesthetic of the sublime, beautiful and picturesque. Eugene von Guérard's paintings of the Grampians with a swamp in the foreground or the midground are the exception that largely proves the rule (as we saw previously in the present chapter). Wetlands are much more suited to the close-up point of view in the mixed media of environmental artworks, such as that by Carole Mules, of Grampians wetlands. Mules depicts (they are not landscapes) these wetlands in fabric and stitching with flowing lines of waters and clumps of vegetation (see figure 3.4).

Located near the Willaura Golf Course and south-east of the Grampians National Park, the Cockajemmy Lakes are what Mitchell (1839) called a "chain of lagoons" that leads from Gariwerd to the Hopkins River, feeds the river and expresses above ground level the subsurface groundwater flows underground. "A chain of ponds" or "a chain of lagoons" were noted by many early European explorers of northern and southern Australia, including Mitchell in both areas (Massy 2020, 130; Mitchell 1839).

Mitchell (1839) named the Cockajemmy Lakes on 20th September 1836 and noted their hydrogeology:

> I observed that the lakes occurred at intervals in a valley apparently falling from the westward in which no stream appeared, although it was shut in by well escarped rocky banks. [...] No connection existed by means of any channel between them although they formed together a chain of lagoons in the bed of a deep and well defined valley. On the contrary, the soil was particularly solid and firm between them, and the margin of the most eastern of these lakes was separated by a high bank from the bed of another valley where a running stream of pure water flowed over a broad and swampy bed fifteen feet higher than the adjacent valley containing the stagnant salt lakes.

Figure 3.4: Carole Mules, 'Cockajemmy Lakes.' Free-motion machine embroidery of eco-dyed recycled textiles. © The artist's estate. Reproduced with the permission of Greg Mules.

Wetlands aren't just what is visible on the surface, but are also manifestations and surface expressions of underground flows. Water isn't just a resource that can be seen, transported and commodified, but the life-blood of the body of the earth that flows through its internal, unseen veins and arteries.

Wetlands on the surface can dry up and disappear underground only to re-appear later in a wet year, as depicted in this artwork by Mules (see figure 3.5).

Mules reprises and reconstructs Eugene von Guérard's two paintings of Mount William (figures 3.1 and 3.2) with their abundance of water in the foreground or midground. In Mules's depiction the land is dry and parched with the Cockajemmy Lakes in the foreground and with abundant vegetation in the midground and background as a sign of underground water. The (wet) land has become textural, rather than primarily visual. It has ceased to have the smooth surface of water as in von Guérard's paintings, and has become the rough surface of cracked dry land. The wet land has disappeared in a dry season or year. The wet land may re-appear in a wet season. The wetland portrayed (it is not a landscape) in Mules' artwork is reminiscent of Arthur

Boyd's paintings of drought-stricken waterholes (Giblett 2020a, figures 3.3, 58; 3.4, 59) and Sydney Nolan's 'Carcase in Swamp,' yet with the hope and possibility that the wetland will re-appear as seen in von Guérard's paintings.

Figure 3.5: Carole Mules, 'Mt William from beyond a Cockajemmy Lake.' Free-motion machine embroidery of eco-dyed recycled textiles. © The artist's estate. Reproduced with the kind permission of Greg Mules and Glenys and Geoff Allum.

Carole Mules depicts other Gariwerd wetlands, such as Lake Buninjon shaped as an embryo, in mixed fabric (see figure 3.6).

Two figures gather at, or in, the water, perhaps to share it and its bounty. Or two guardian angels of the wetland stand guard on either side to protect its waters, its plants and animals. Or two ghostly virtual figures from the past. This artwork alludes to and plays intertextually with the biblical story of the Samaritan woman at the well. In the new Testament gospel of Saint John the story begins by relating how Jesus stops by Jacob's well, sacred to both Jews and Samaritans. Jacob was a Hebrew patriarch of the pastoralist type so he is a fitting figure to invoke in relation to the 'Australia Felix' of Middlemarsh and Mules' artwork (*John* 4: 6-26). A conservation counter-theological rewriting of the biblical story in dialogue with Mules' artwork could go something like this.

Not so long ago an Aboriginal woman and a white pastoralist accidentally arrive at this embryonic-shaped wetland at the same time. She was dressed in a long white flowing robe and he was wearing a full-length brown moleskin coat, the standard uniform of the Middlemarsh pastoralist. Both had come to this place for water, the woman to draw water for herself and others, the pastoralist to get a drink of water for himself and to water his horse. The disciples had gone looking for food. The pastoralist was too lazy or arrogant to get down off his horse. Besides, he did not want to get mud and slime on his shiny boots, so he said to her, 'Will you give me a drink?' The woman replied to him, 'You are a white man and I am an Aboriginal woman. How can you ask me for a drink?' (for white people do not associate with Aboriginal people as a rule). The man answered her, 'If you knew that I own this land and water, you would give me a drink.' The woman replied, 'My people own this land in common and this body of water. Everyone who drinks this water will be thirsty again, but whoever drinks the living water that our ancestors give them will never be thirsty. Indeed, the water they give them will become in them a spring of water welling up to eternal life.' The man got off his high horse, came down to the wetland (as depicted in Mules' artwork) and said, 'where is this water? Where can I get some?'

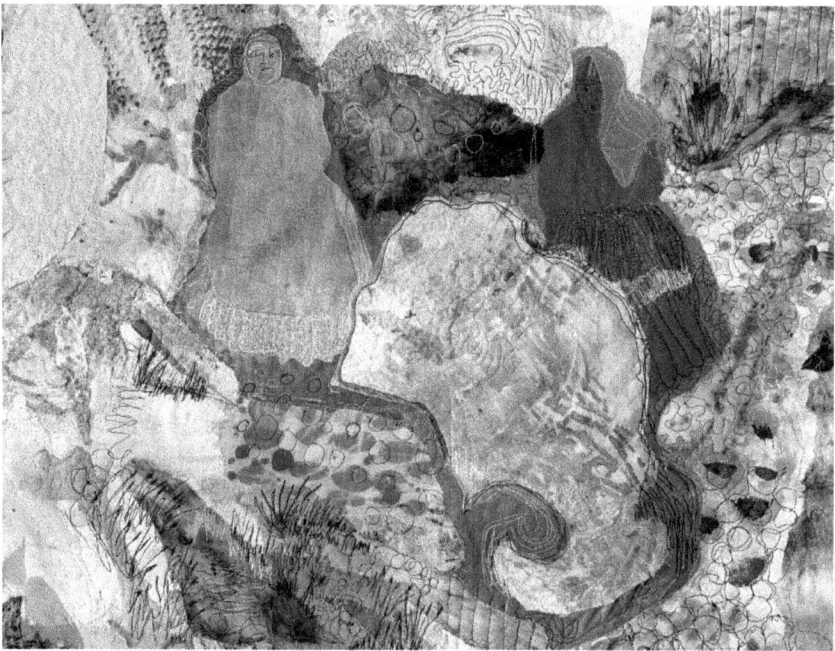

Figure 3.6: Carole Mules, 'Women at Lake Buninjon.' Free-motion machine embroidery of eco-dyed recycled textiles. Reproduced with the kind permission of Ararat Gallery Textile Art Museum of Australia. © The artist's estate, Ararat Gallery TAMA, and Ararat Rural City Council. Gift of Helen Miller and Warwick Mules.

The woman went on, 'The time has come, the time is now, when all human beings should be worshipping neither God the father (the patriarch), nor (on) the mountain, nor (in) the city (eternal or temporal, celestial or terrestrial, Jerusalem or Rome), but worshipping the god who is breath, or air, or oxygen, the spirit that is over all and in all life, and most matter for that matter. All living creatures need the breath of life to live, and need living waters to live too. The waters of wetlands are living waters welling up in the eternal now giving birth to life. Both air and water are sacred gifts that should not be polluted, but kept clean, owned in common and shared by all. The messiah and her disciples, the twelve apostles of conservation, explain this to us.' The pastoralist had never heard of them so he asked, 'who is this 'messiah'?' Then the woman declared, 'I, the one speaking to you—I am she.' Just then the twelve environmental apostles showed up right on cue with food that they had gathered. The pastoralist could now see who they were as they introduced themselves to him. What a motley bunch of men and women they were. He declined their invitation to join them for lunch of bush tucker and rode back to his station mansion for his lunch of roast mutton and potatoes washed down with a glass or two or three of western districts' shiraz.

In the Eastern Orthodox and Eastern Catholic traditions, the Samaritan woman at the well is venerated as a saint, Saint Photine (literally, 'light'), also transliterated as Fotini. She is the bearer of light, even the patron saint of light. She is a goddess of light as wisdom. She is also the goddess of living water in the well and elsewhere, such as wetlands as portrayed in Mules' artwork. She brings light to the white pastoralist's heart of darkness and his benighted ideology of colonialism and private property. She explains this to him and to us. She is a prophet who proclaims prophecy in poetic language. She is the leader of the twelve environmental apostles who explain her message to us too (Giblett 2020c, 35). She is the messiah of conservation who has come and is coming again and again. She is depicted with Jesus in many paintings engaged in what is called 'The Water of Life Discourse' in which he delivers his institutionalised theological sermon to her as his sole recipient in a one-person congregation. Yet rather than a monologue, the biblical story is a dialogue. She is a prophet who proclaims prophecy in impassioned speech in dialogue with her listeners. Mules' environmental artwork depicts two equal figures engaged in the material and spiritual 'water of life' dialogue around a wetland. Black waters live!

A RAMBLE ALONG THE RIVER: THROUGH COLONIAL
PLACES ON THE MIDDLE HOPKINS

14 And God said, Let there be lights in the firmament of the
heaven to divide the day from the night; and let them be for signs,
and for seasons, and for days, and years: 15 And let them be for
lights in the firmament of the heaven to give light upon the earth:
and it was so. 16 And God made two great lights; the greater light
to rule the day, and the lesser light to rule the night: he made the
stars also.17 And God set them in the firmament of the heaven to
give light upon the earth, 18 And to rule over the day and over the
night, and to divide the light from the darkness: and God saw that
it was good. 19 And the evening and the morning were the fourth
day. *Genesis* 1

Ellerslie, Hexham, Chatsworth, Wickliffe and Rossbridge are small towns
located on the middle Hopkins. The first four towns had fords across the
river created by basalt rock flows across the land and the course of the river.
These four towns are where they are because the river was fordable at this
point. They are at the intersection of two flows – rock and water. The town
of Allansford further south on the Hopkins, as the name suggests or implies,
is also a ford town. The five ford towns now have bridges over the Hopkins.
Rossbridge, as the name also suggests or implies, is not a ford town. The
river at this point is more a wetland with extensive floodplains than a stream
between banks. As a result, the town was liable to flooding. Some houses
built on the floodplain became uninhabitable and were demolished recently.
A new, all-weather bridge was constructed recently too. The main structures
to survive on higher ground in Rossbridge are a bluestone church and a
bluestone school, as well as the nearby former teacher's residence. Ellerslie,
Hexham and Wickliffe also have at least one bluestone church, beacons of
God's light in the darkness of the heathen savagery of colonialism. The
Hopkins, like "the Thames[,] is a river of churches" (Ackroyd 2009, 87).

In 1917 a naturalist travelled in a horse-drawn buggy through Hexham,
Chatsworth and Wickliffe along the Hopkins River. He continued on to
Willaura, Moyston, Stawell and Halls Gap. Under the by-line of his own
initials, 'F.R.' published an article in June of 1917 in the now defunct weekly
newspaper *The Australasian* whose headquarters on the corner of Elizabeth

and La Trobe Streets in Melbourne survive to this day as a heritage-listed building. As he was mainly interested in ornithology, and in natural history more generally, he is a useful guide to these aspects of the area (as we will see). He completely ignored the Aboriginal and colonial history of the area. This chapter weaves together ornithology, natural history and colonial history of five towns on the middle Hopkins and goes on to the other places he visited, including the wetlands of Fyans Creek depicted on the cover of the present volume (and figure 3.1).

'F.R.' was on what he called, and he entitled his article, "a ramble to Stawell." Rambling was a popular past-time for amateur naturalists in Europe and Australia dating back to the nineteenth century. The more famous Horace Wheelwright indicates and demonstrates as much on both continents in his *Bush Wanderings of a Naturalist: Notes on the Field Sports and Fauna of Australia Felix* first published in 1861. After "rambling in the forests and fells of Northern Europe" for six years, he came to Australia and decided to "face the bush on my account" (Wheelwright 1861, ix-x). The resulting account of his rambling and facing the bush on his own account is an early field guide to the fauna of Victoria that was primarily aimed at guiding fishers and shooters in filling a bag of "game" (edible animals). It would have also guided some later naturalists on their rambles in identifying and appreciating the sight and sounds of some species of fauna in their wetland and grassland habitats. He is also a guide on the ramble of the present chapter.

Samuel Hannaford's *Sea and River-Side Rambles in Victoria: Being a Handbook for those Seeking Recreation during the Summer Months* first published in 1860 is in the same tradition as Wheelwright's book. It concludes with a chapter devoted to the Hopkins River, or at least to its lower stretches from Allansford to the sea (Hannaford 1860, 100-119). His river-side ramble is in fact a river-side ramble of the Hopkins estuary. He is also a guide on the ramble of the present and final chapters.

'F.R.' was not among those who followed Hannaford's or Wheelwright's guides on his ramble over half a century after theirs. For instance, he regards pelicans as clumsy, whereas Hannaford calls them noble. 'F.R.'s naming of species also varies from Wheelwright's and he was not a shooter or a fisher. 'F.R.' also does not follow Wheelwright's denigratory descriptions of "dreary swamps," "dreary impenetrable marshes," "wild and dismal swamps" and "the wild marshy nature of the country" (Wheelwright 1861, 66, 87, 128, 171, 207, 217). Wetlands were generally only good in Wheelwright's view as habitat for "game," such as ducks, to shoot and sell in Melbourne. Wetlands were not good when they were habitat for the black swan that "is hardly worth shooting" as they fetch a low price and are "a heavy bird to carry about." Or they were good when the young black swan can be shot, cooked and eaten for the traditional Sunday roast (Wheelwright 1861, 69). Yet wetlands could be good when he also waxed lyrical about the musical call note of the black swan and call it a graceful, elegant bird, presumably in flight. He appreciated the visual, auditory and culinary features of black swans appealing to the senses of sights, hearing, taste and smell, but not the tactile experience of carrying dead ones to market.

A far more reliable guide for the ramble of the present chapter to the birds of the grasslands and wetlands of Middlemarsh, including ducks and black swans, is the erstwhile local artist and regenerative farmer Richard Weatherly (2020) in his book of illustrations and reflections, *A Brush with Birds*. Richard's life-story painting birds, as well as living and working on the Hopkins River and with some kindred wetlands west of Mortlake for 30 years is retold in the following chapter of the present volume.

Rambling was not only a leisurely walk in the countryside popular in the nineteenth century, but is also a pejorative term for peripatetic writing or a roundabout way of speaking. Wheelwright"'s *Bush Wanderings* are a case in point of rambling in both senses, including in the second sense as indicated by his going out of his way to make repeated detours to denigrate wetlands. 'F.R.'s ramble does so in both senses too, though it is his horse who does the bulk of the walking. The present chapter is also a ramble in the same area with an interest in natural history, especially birds, and colonial cultural history, as well as in contemporary regenerative farming by focussing on family farms on Salt Creek at Woorndoo and on the river at Chatsworth and Wickliffe. The chapter concludes with a discussion of the life and work of an ecologist and artist who live on the farm at Wickliffe.

'F.R.' commenced his ramble by travelling via Mortlake to the Hopkins River at Hexham. He bypassed **Ellerslie**, also on the Hopkins. It is worthwhile taking a short detour via Ellerslie on the ramble of the present chapter as it has a bizarre colonial history, especially as it is named after the birthplace of Sir Walter Scott, the nineteenth-century Scottish historical novelist. The Scottish connection was also secured with the construction of a Presbyterian church. Ellerslie re-appears in the following chapter of the present volume.

Ellerslie rates a mention in the online compendium of 'Victorian Places:'

> Ellerslie is a rural village in western Victoria, 32 km north-east of Warrnambool on the road to Mortlake. In 1841 John Eddington took up the Ballangeich pastoral run (named after his birthplace) west of the Hopkins River. At the place where the track from Mortlake crossed the river a ford was laid down, and the locality was known as Lettsford. During the early 1860s a bridge was constructed, and the Bridge Inn was opened. In 1865, at the

suggestion of Eddington, the place was renamed Ellerslie, probably after the birthplace of the author and poet, Sir Walter Scott. During the late 1860s and the 1870s farm selections were taken up. A school and a Presbyterian church were opened in 1871. Many of the farms were used for dairying and in 1891 the Ellerslie and Framlingham Butter Factory was opened. (Victorian Places. NDB)

Both Ellerslie and Wickliffe also had Anglican churches. English and Scottish colonists of western Victoria could exercise and display simultaneously their denominational preference, national allegiance and cultural background in attending either a Church of England or a Church of Scotland. John Eddington inscribed the names of birthplaces over the Aboriginal names for these places in an attempt to erase them from the land and from history, to create a *tabula rasa* of a *terra nullius,* and to give birth to a new land out of the brainbox of his head by linking the old land of Australia back to 'the old country' of Scotland.

'F.R.' commenced his bird-watching ramble by relating how:

At **Hexham** I crossed the Hopkins. The Hopkins is a fair stream yet. The heavy rains of the beginning of December have kept up the supply of water. By the side of the bridge there is a large pool of water, and on its edge is a blue crane. The blue crane (or the white-fronted heron, to give it its proper name) is, I fancy, our commonest waterbird in these parts. It is everywhere. Very few people molest it; so that it is holding its own very well. Occasionally I come across one of its cousins, the Pacific heron, but they are not nearly so common.

The blue crane (or the white-fronted heron) is now called the white-faced heron. Wheelwright (1861, 87) on his ramble refers to "the heron" (presumably the white-faced heron) and notes that it is "very common on the low marshy ground." Richard Weatherly (2020, 84-85) has completed illustrations of the white-faced heron.

Hexham also rates a mention in the online compendium of 'Victorian Places':

Hexham is a rural village in western Victoria, situated on the Hamilton Highway, 47 km north-east of Warrnambool and 15 km north-west of Mortlake. Hexham was surveyed as a settlement [in 1841] only two years after Mortlake. It was situated on an important regional route which had a ford where the Hopkins River was crossed. Pastoral occupation in the Mortlake-Hexham area began in 1839 with the Mount Shadwell pastoral run.

The Mt Shadwell "pastoral run" also appears in the following chapter of the present volume as it is both a significant Aboriginal and colonial site.

The online compendium continues:

> In 1848 the western part of the run was severed to form Hexham Park. By then there was the Woolshed Inn at the ford, possibly as early as 1842. Its successor, the former Hexham Hotel, was built in 1854 […] [I]n 1855 Hexham was surveyed for township lots. A post office and a school were opened in 1857 and 1858. In common with much of the Western District, the dominant religious group was Presbyterian, and a bluestone church was constructed in 1862. It was replaced with another [bluestone] building with a crenelated tower in 1864. (Victorian Places NDD)

It survives to this day. The dominant religious group was Presbyterian because the colonists of the district were predominantly Scottish.

'F.R.' continues his ramble by describing how:

> From Hexham to **Chatsworth** 10 miles—the country is very quiet. Not a sound is heard beyond the bleating of the neighbouring sheep. All is still. It is a deadly and oppressive stillness. I stop my buggy sometimes and just listen.

The country is very quiet and the stillness is "deadly and oppressive" because Aboriginal people who lived in the area have been removed, including to Framlingham where the sound of laughing children playing by the Hopkins River was a feature of Banjo Clarke's childhood in the 1920s and 1930s and he enjoyed hearing later (as we will see in chapter 6 of the present volume). Their cooeeing to each other as they walked up and down on either side along the natural highway of the Hopkins River no longer enlivens the soundscape, a feature of the Hopkins in the past as noted recently by Brett Clarke (as we saw in the first chapter of the present volume).

Despite the quiet, 'F.R.' continues by describing the soundscape:

> Far away on my left I hear the wild clang of a plover. He is wheeling in the air, but he does not come near. Away down on my right runs the river. As I gaze at it I see the long, startled necks of a couple of wood-duck stretched out. They have their eyes on me, and are trying to make sure that I am an ordinary traveller along the lane, and not a sportsman with an eye to themselves […] At Chatsworth I cross the Hopkins again. It is here also a broad, swift, stream.

Unlike Wheelwright, 'F.R.' is not a sportsman, a euphemism for a shooter. Many nineteenth-century naturalists, like Wheelwright, were also shooters; some, like Thoreau, gave up shooting.

In *Walden* Thoreau (1982, 458) wrote that:

I sold my gun before I went to the woods. Not that I am less humane than others, but I did not perceive that my feelings were much affected. [...D]uring the last years that I carried a gun my excuse was that I was studying ornithology, and sought only new or rare birds. But I confess that I am now inclined to think that there is a finer way of studying ornithology than this. It requires so much closer attention to the habits of the birds, that, if for that reason only, I have been willing to omit the gun.

Thoreau came to a similar conclusion regarding fishing and "attending to the nature of fishes" (as we will see in the final chapter of the present volume).

Chatsworth does not rate a mention in the online compendium of 'Victorian Places,' though nearby Chatsworth House and its pastoral estate cannot escape notice as it was a village unto itself. Joel Robinson (2018) describes how:

Chatsworth House [is] one of Victoria's grandest Western District's properties [...] It is named after the grand home of the Duke and Duchess of Devonshire, in Derbyshire. The historic property dates back to the late 1850s when it was erected for pioneer pastoralist John Moffat [...] His rise in fortune, on the back of a Merino stud, is well demonstrated by the expenditure of £20,000 on the house, outbuildings and landscaping. He entertained Prince Alfred at Chatsworth in 1867. Prominent Hamilton architect James Henry Fox, who also created the iconic Werribee Park mansion for the Chirnside family, designed the conservative classic style house with Doric portico and encircling verandah.

The Chirnside family makes a cameo appearance in the following chapter of the present volume as they were a prominent pastoralist family in western Victoria in nineteenth-century colonial Australia. Their palatial mansion of Werribee survives to this day on the outskirts of Melbourne as a heritage-listed building within a public park.

Robinson continues to describe Chatsworth House:

The 1,200 sqm, single-storey Victorian bluestone mansion features a grand entrance hall with Roman Corinthian style columns, gilded ornate cornices, over door entablatures and original multi-paned skylights. The six bedroom home also has a drawing room, billiards room, ornate formal dining room, office, and private library. All feature marble open fire places. On the 2,400 hectare property sits a bluestone Baronial hall with commercial kitchen and refurbished accommodation, as well as fully renovated bluestone stables and coach houses. There are two manager's residences and four country style cottages. One of the substantial bluestone building now known as the Longroom was once the men's quarters on the original Cobb & Co route and the stables that run parallel to them have been well maintained and were completed in 1867. The complex also originally included a school and church. The kindergarten that rests opposite the Longroom today was relocated to Chatsworth House farm by the Jones family in 2008 to save the building from demolition. The Longroom was renovated by the current owners in 2002 and then completed in 2006, when the remaining quarters at the western end of the building were converted to accommodation. Chatsworth has been described as one of the most versatile property holdings in the district. The gently rolling fertile grey and red sand loam soils has seen canola, red and white wheat, barley and oats all grow with success. It's fattened livestock, held ewes and produced lambs. It currently holds 12,000 composite ewes which annually produce around 15,000 lambs. There's an 11 stand woolshed, experts room, and full shearers facilities with stagg kitchen. Up to 300 steers are grazed twice annually on the property, and pasture set aside for hay and silage. The property has two dams and paddocks with access to the permanent Hopkins River and Churrup Creek [...] The gardens surrounding the substantial home were laid out by noted garden designer Edward La Trobe Bateman in the late 1860s. They then comprised of more than 5,000 plants and shrubs. Bateman, a cousin of Charles Joseph La Trobe, the superintendent [later Governor] of the colony, was one of Victoria's first garden designers. He earned praise from botanists von Mueller and Harvey, who were famous for developing Melbourne's Royal Botanical Gardens [see Giblett 2020b, chapter 7]. Bateman who excelled as an illustrator and artist, however turned to garden design as a more likely way of earning a living. He was commissioned on a three year contract to create the extensive gardens at Chatsworth, but paralysed his right arm in a buggy accident while doing so. The gardens with cascading symmetrical hedge lined rose gardens now includes a solar heated swimming pool. The garden is entered through a planting of Monterey Pines and is laid out within a perimeter planting of mainly conifers. A feature of the garden is a curved cypress hedge which encloses the garden on the east side. Another curved planting of pines, cypress cedars and carobs, once surrounding a church, occurs west of the drive, to the farm buildings. An unusual landscape feature is the raised banks used for tree planting. The planting makes extensive use of conifers – pines, cypress and cedars – oaks and figs, blue gums and remnant river red gums as specimen trees and in stands to create a 'picturesque' arrangement of trees in a parkland setting. A feature of the garden around three sides of the house is the impressive bluestone steps and sloping retaining wall capped by a cast iron rail. The planting features old camellias and several large dramatic English box (*Buxus sempervirens*) 'balls' and hedges. The new parterre garden is planted on the site of a former tennis court.

The landscaped gardens of Chatsworth House are very much a little piece of England set in a gentleman's park estate with its pleasing, picturesque parkland transported holus-bolus from England's 'green and pleasant land' and plonked down in Australia. Chatsworth House itself is a western district pastoralist's mansion built of local Victorian bluestone with an Australian vernacular verandah wrapping around it to provide shade from the blazing summer sun and shelter from the blasting winter storms.

Bluestone (basalt) is a local building material commonly sourced from the Victorian Volcanic Plains that stretch from Melbourne to the South Australian border. It was widely used in Victoria in the gold rush era of the second half of the nineteenth century when Melbourne was the richest city in the world (Giblett 2020b). It can readily be seen today in the buildings, kerbing and laneways of inner Melbourne, including the infamous Pentridge Prison where the last man to be hanged in Australia was hung in 1967, and whose bluestone quarry is now Coburg Lake and the prison now the gentrified residential, restaurant and entertainment precinct of 'Coburg Quarter.' A new basalt quarry is proposed for the eastern banks of the lower Hopkins River to Framlingham on the other side (as discussed in chapter 6 of the present volume).

The current owners of Chatsworth House and its estate acknowledge the history of the house and gardens, and move on with a focus on the future. On their website they state that:

> At Chatsworth House, we do a lot of things. It's a family farming property. A historic one at that. But while we love the beautiful, historic surrounds of the property, we're definitely not stuck in the past. Our focus is firmly on the future, and how we can help make it better for everyone. As a sheep and cattle farming property, we're always searching for better ways to do things. For us, that means a more environmentally friendly, healthier way. What we're building at Chatsworth House is an ever-evolving ecosystem that grows in diversity and resilience every day. So, while we continue to embrace our history, we also look for ways to improve our ever-changing biodiversity for better farming. There's a certain circle of life aspect to farming that many people often forget. For us, we feel it all starts with healthy soil. Healthy soil leads to healthy plants from which our animals feed. These healthy animals lead to healthier humans and a

healthier planet. This interconnectedness is something we focus on here at Chatsworth House, and we always hope to educate others on our progress. Harnessing the power of biodiversity and healthy soil doesn't mean sacrificing profits in farming, and we love the opportunity to share what we do with others. Just like our ecosystem, we're constantly evolving and growing, and we love bringing others along for the journey. (Chatsworth House Pastoral, ND)

Healthy soil is also the mantra of regenerative farming espoused and practiced by the Gubbins family at Coolana, also on the Hopkins River at Chatsworth. Richard Weatherly (2020, 83) describes how the farm and the family have "an excellent conservation history over three generations and a series of exemplary wetlands." The farm has been in the family since 1930. Arthur was the first of the Gubbins family to own and run the farm. His son John was born at Coolana in 1934. He married Jennifer Young in 1959 and they had four children, including two sons, one of whom is Mark who currently owns and operates Coolana with his wife Anna.

The Hopkins at Coolana is fed by saline springs. Arthur told Mark not to worry about the salty water flowing into the property and only to worry about what happened to it next. To mitigate and reduce salinity, wetlands were constructed to retain water and dilute salinity. Some of the wetlands on Coolana don't dry up and provide habitat for waterbirds all the year round. The Gubbins have not only rehabilitated or constructed wetlands, but also planted trees suited to the salinity, such as the Western Australian Swamp Yate. The flood of 2011 produced a flush of red gum seeds that germinated and created a fine forest. On top of their work with wetlands, they have also planted 13 km of riparian frontage along the Hopkins River. They have fenced it off and planted it on the bank tops with native trees. The lower margins and river bed reclaimed itself in an amazing short period of time (Mark Gubbins email to author October 4, 2021).

Dave and Nick Allen have also done a lot of regenerative work on their property 'Boorook' near Woorndoo on Salt Creek that flows out of Lake Bolac and is a tributary of the Hopkins River:

> David and Nick have planted thousands of trees on the farm, replacing Cyprus and some of the Old English varieties with natives, such as Eucalyptus, Wattle and Casuarina species. In total, there are currently 224 acres of trees planted on the farm, providing shade for cattle, as well as habitats for birds and wildlife. (Flagship Farmers ND)

One of their core values and goals is to "implement practices that protect native grasslands, wetlands, riparian areas and water resources" (Flagship Farmers, nd). The Allens also practice rotational grazing of their cattle that allows grasslands to recover and regrow.

Their farm has also been included in the Lake Bolac Eel Festival. Dave relates that:

> In 2005 we were privileged to have a group of people walking up the creek. They started in Warrnambool, came up the Hopkins River and up the Salt Creek, right up to Lake Bolac, over a period of about a week.

Following in the footsteps of 'F.R.', they continued the fine tradition of rambling along the Hopkins River and of Thoreau of spending a week on the Hopkins River and one of its tributaries.

'F.R.' continues his ramble by describing how:

> On the road to **Wickliffe** the same unearthly silence prevails. Not the breaking of a twig disturbs the silence. The whole of the countryside is wrapped in slumber. From some of the few tea-tree along the road several noisy rosellas fly out presently and their screams seem to tear the air [...]

The unearthly silence is broken violently by squawking rosellas illustrated by Richard Weatherly (2020, 76-77).

Despite the quiet and the prevailing unearthly silence, 'F.R.' continues his ramble by describing how he hears:

> At Wickliffe away down the river—it is still the Hopkins—comes the wild shrill call of the curlew. It is some years since I have heard this weird, wild, and plaintive call. It is not the real curlew, of course, but the stone-plover [...]

For Wheelwright (1861, 113) "the long melancholy whistle of the stone curlew in the Australian forest at night often strikes a chill in the heart of the benighted traveller; for an imitation of this bird is a signal-whistle from the bushranger here to his mates at night." The "wild shrill call" of the stone curlew acquires melancholy overtones because it has been appropriated by the dangerous bushranger. Wheelwright associates the call of the stone curlew with what Marcus Clarke a decade later called the "weird melancholy" of the Australian bush (Giblett 2011, 132-134). Perhaps Clarke was singing from Wheelwright's song sheet.

Wheelwright (1861, 87) also associated the boom of the bittern with the dreariness of Australian swamps. He expressed the sentiment that "it is no wonder that a country like this should abound in swamp birds of every birds of every description, and the Bittern, which more than perhaps any other shuns the haunts of man, is one of the commonest of the wild tenants of the Australian waste." The Australasian bittern is a famously discreet bird and a rare sighting. 'F.R.' did not see one on his ramble to Stawell. Wheelwright finds with the Australasian bittern that the "after evening has closed in over the dreary swamp, the dull measure boom of this solitary bird appears to add to the desolation which reigns over all" (Wheelwright 1861, 87).

Wheelwright's view of the Australasian bittern and the stone curlew can be contrasted with Thoreau's view of the American bittern. Like Wheelwright and the stone curlew, Thoreau associated the boom of the bittern with melancholy, a watery, creative humour that he found and embraced in swamps (as we saw in the first chapter of the present volume). Thoreau also saw it (as we also saw) as an emblem for the pre-Socratic philosophy of water as the primary element. The bittern could also be used as an emblem for the contemplation of the watery first day of creation in biblical theology and of creation out of water in Mesopotamian mythology. It could also be used as an emblem in the post-Socratic and Thoreauvian philosophy of slimy swamps. All four come together in conservation counter-theology and contemplating the primacy of watery wetlands.

Wickliffe rates a mention in the online compendium of 'Victorian Places':

> In 1840 John Dixon Wyselaskie, born of Polish parents in Scotland, took up the Narrapumelap pastoral run in the Wickliffe district. The track which preceded the Glenelg Highway crossed the Hopkins River at a convenient ford. An inn was opened by an Irishman, Farrell, at the crossing in 1843 and the place was known as Ford's Crossing, Hopkins Crossing and Farrell's Inn. By 1850 it was known as Wickliffe Government Township, possibly at the behest of Wyselaskie. A school was opened in 1858 [that closed in 1986] and a substantial bluestone Presbyterian church was built in 1861. By 1860 Wyselaskie had acquired a property of 105 sq km, and in 1878 built the Narrapumelap homestead. He also built Wickliffe House in the Melbourne suburb of St Kilda. Balliere's Victorian gazetteer (1865) recorded Wickliffe as having a post office and a court, and being set in good pastoral country which was well timbered and with numerous lakes. There was also the Hopkins Hotel. (Victorian Places NDF)

Wickliffe also has a Common on the Hopkins where it loops around the town. The Common was probably too low and wet to be useful for European agriculture and architecture. It is now the 'Hopkins River Wickliffe Streamside Reserve.' It has old River Red Gums and a good patch of *Themeda* (kangaroo grass) (Ayesha Burdett email to author, September 16, 2021).

'F.R.' continues his ramble by describing how:

> From Wickliffe, I travel north to **Willaura**. The road is still lonely

and very quiet [...] I pass a lake, set like a jewel in the hills. On its placid bosom are a group of black duck and [grey] teal is, of course, the close[d] season, and no one interferes with them.

Richard Weatherly (2020, 244-245) completed an evocative painting that "portrays Black Ducks flying in to the flats of the Hopkins River during a flood, something I had grown used to seeing since I was child" (as he retells in chapter 5 of the present volume). His portrait of these ducks places them against the backdrop of a wetlandscape and in situ in their habitat, one of the distinctive features of some of Weatherly's paintings that are not of birds as species abstracted from their home.

'F.R.' continues his ramble by describing how "nearer Willaura I see a few black swans on another lake. They swim about with great confidence. Very few people trouble the swan." Presumably the people he refers to are colonial settlers as Aboriginal settlers hunted and ate them and collected and ate their eggs (as we saw in the previous chapter). Very few colonial settlers trouble the black swan because it is not considered good eating, except in Wheelwright's (1861, 69) view for "the flesh of the young swan [which] is excellent" when roasted in the duck-shooter's camp oven for the traditional Sunday dinner of roast meat. Before extolling its culinary virtues, its lack of economic value for the market and the expenditure of labour to carry such a heavy bird, Wheelwright (1861, 68) calls the black swan "a graceful, elegant bird."

He describes in detail the red markings on its beak, its white flight feathers easily visible when it is flying and its "very musical call-note" and "soft musical hoop" (Wheelwright 1861, 68, 76). One evening he "listened with pleasure to the soft low notes of a pair of swans answering each other, while floating on the lagoon, by the side of which I lay at flight-time. At night they always fly low" (Wheelwright 1861, 69). They do so to navigate by the light of the moon reflecting off the water. Despite its lack of economic value, the visible and audible features of the black swan have aesthetic value for his senses of sight and hearing. The black swan also has culinary value when young for his senses of smell and taste. He also appreciated the soundscape of the bush in general, such as the dawn chorus of birds in "this land of wonders" (Wheelwright 1861, 128). Richard Weatherly (2020, 101) has completed an illustration of floating black swans.

Like Wheelwright, Hannaford (1860, 116) on his river-side ramble by the Hopkins appreciated the sight of the black swan, but unlike Wheelwright he did not appreciate its call when he observed "a fine Black Swan (*Cygnus atratus*) floating majestically along. Certainly no 'Rara avis' is this bird in Victoria, inhabiting all the Western lagoons in flocks [... T]hey generally move from one place to another at night, uttering most discordant cries as they fly." 'Rara avis' comes from Juvenal's sixth satire of the second century

CE in which he likens an impossible woman to "a rare bird, as strange to the earth as a black swan" postulating such a creature before a European had even seen one (see Giblett 2013, chapter 13).

Lagoons for Hannaford and Wheelwright are the habitat of the more charismatic species of waterbirds, such as black swans. Wheelwright compares lagoons to dreary swamps and marshes, "these morasses and fens," that "swarmed with wild fowl" (Wheelwright 1861, 66). Wild water fowl are not included in the interdiction enunciated in *Leviticus* 11: 13-19 against killing and eating swarming birds, including possibly pelicans, because they are an abomination. Wheelwright could justifiably shoot and sell them for people to eat. As the subtitle to his book indicates, Wheelwright gained his livelihood by shooting "game" in "field sports." Shooting is not much "sport" for "the game" though. The bird does not get much opportunity to test its skill against the shooter as the continuing campaign against duck-shooting in Victoria shows. His three-page list of birds includes a one-page list of "game birds" (Wheelwright 1861, 181-183).

Unlike Wheelwright, 'F.R.' does not describe in any detail the untroubled black swans on the lake near Willaura. Instead, he goes on to observe and note in greater detail that:

> On the far side of the lake there are a pair of pelicans, preening their feathers. One sees a good number of pelican on the western lakes nowadays. It is always a puzzle to me when I see them soaring away up in the air. I have seen a pelican, apparently a mile high, floating with motionless wings, like an eagle. For such an apparently clumsy bird it is, or appears to be, an acrobatic feat.

'F.R.' was observing eagles and pelicans riding the thermal air currents, as they do in Eugene von Guérard's paintings (figures 3.1 and 3.2). Pelicans also perform an aerobatic feat of flying low over water. Rather than a clumsy bird, Richard Weatherly (2020, 69) has always been fascinated with pelicans performing the aerobatic feat of "compression gliding" in which they glide over great distances just above the water riding on a cushion of air passing between their wings and the water below. Richard has completed illustrations of pelicans, with one performing this aerobatic, rather than acrobatic, feat (Weatherly 2020, 68-69). Unlike 'F.R.'s description of the pelican as an "apparently clumsy bird," Hannaford (1860, 115) observed what he called "noble pelicans" in his chapter about rambling by the Hopkins River.

'F.R.' continues his ramble from Willaura to **Moyston**. He does not mention that Moyston was famously the birthplace in 1859 of Australian Football from the Aboriginal game of 'Marngrook' (Hocking and Reidy 2016). He describes how:

the road is a pretty one. It has a number of lakes on it. On one of these lakes I see dozens of duck, as well as a few teal. Along the road there is a good lot of birdlife. Goldfinches and starlings abound.

The Birdlife Australia (NDB) webpage for Starlings states that:

The Common Starling is a pest, both in Australia and overseas. In eastern Australia, Starlings have had a significant economic impact on agriculture and the environment. [In the case of agriculture] starlings cause severe damage to high-value fruit crops by pecking at fruit in the trees, damaging it and making it unsaleable. Soft fruits, especially cherries, peaches and apricots, as well as all varieties of grapes, are particularly susceptible to damage from Starlings. Apples and other fruit are also readily damaged in this way. They may also contaminate harvested grain, and have the potential to damage expensive, high-precision agricultural equipment and necessitate substantial changes to the infrastructure at grain receival points. Also often consuming feed for livestock, they may spoil it with their faeces, adversely affecting intensive production of beef and dairy cattle, pigs and poultry. The wool industry can be affected too, as Starlings may contaminate the fleece of sheep with their faeces while they perch on their backs. (In eastern Australia, there are several records of Starlings actually building their nests deep within the fleece of unfortunate sheep.) Starlings also disperse weeds by spreading their seeds.

'F.R.' continues his ramble by observing how "the pretty little goldfinch is now becoming quite common. Although it is a seed-eater it does not seem to interfere with the agriculturist. At any rate, I have heard no complaints." What about starlings? Did he hear any complaints? The Birdlife Australia (NDB) webpage for the European Goldfinch states that is was "introduced at numerous places in south-eastern Australia in the 19th century, and their populations quickly increased and their range expanded greatly." It was common in western Victoria in 1917 as 'F.R.' indicates.

'F.R.' continues by observing how "a few parrots flit across in front of me. Most of them are grass-parrots or rosellas. But now and then a red lory [lorikeet] follows" and by describing how from Great Western via Stawell to **Halls Gap**:

is the beauty spot of the beautiful Grampians. Two miles out of Stawell I dive into the forest. At once I was in the home of the birds. The official guide to the district says that there are not the number of birds that one would expect. Of course it all depends on what you expect. I expected a lot of birds, and I was not disappointed. The place was alive in the first place with honey-eaters.

I saw about a dozen varieties. I saw a regent honey-eater fly across the track. Its glorious colours flashed in the sun as he flew past, and he was gone. Tits, of course, and wrens were in hundreds. They were on every bush. I saw quite a lot of fantails. Two of the rarer brown sort flew round me as I sat at lunch in a very quiet part of the forest. I crossed the Mokepilly Creek, and a kingfisher flew past me like a flash. As I drew near the ranges bands of lories became more numerous. I expected to come across some gang-gangs and funereal cockatoos, but saw none. It was probably too early for the latter.

The funereal cockatoo is now called the "yellow-tailed black cockatoo (*Zanda funerea*)" whose name enshrines that it is dressed as if for a funeral. Weatherly has painted a picture of yellow-tailed black cockatoos flying in the Grampians (Weatherly 2020, 242-243). The original painting is hanging in the family room at Connewarran Station. He has also painted illustrations of many species of wrens, including for the definitive, scientific monograph on the family of fairy wrens (*Maluridae*). Many of these illustrations are reproduced in *A Brush with Birds* that also includes illustrations of wrens not included in the scientific monograph. Also included in *A Brush with Bird* are illustrations of honeyeaters.

'F.R' continues his ramble and describes how "an occasional bee-eater and mistletoe bird flashes past me from tree to tree. The work of the latter can be seen everywhere." Birdlife Australia webpage for the mistletoe bird describes how it is:

> the only Australian representative of the flowerpecker family, *Dicaeidae*, and is also known as the Australian Flowerpecker [...] Their preferred food is the berries produced by mistletoe. The seeds within these fruits pass intact through the birds' digestive system and are excreted in sticky strands that adhere to branches, where they germinate. In this manner, mistletoe is spread from tree to tree, providing extra habitat for the species which rely on it to survive. (Birdlife Australia, NDC)

The mistletoe bird and the mistletoe plant are in mutually beneficial bio-symbiosis, the normative relationship between animal and plant, people and planet (see Giblett 2011, chapter 12).

'F.R.' continues his ramble and describes how:

> As I got to Fyans Creek I kept a good look-out for waders, but did not see many. An odd blue crane and a few ternlets sum them up. As I turned eastward, and skirted the great range, I saw above me the wedge-tailed eagle. He looked especially noble in this place. The great granite crags of the Grampians seem to me to be an ideal setting for the bird. Lonely, serene, and unmolested, they soar above

the massive peaks of the ranges. The ranges are their home.

'F.R.' could have been describing the scene of Eugene von Guérard's landscape painting on the front cover of the present volume (and figure 3.1) that depicts Fyans Creek in flood and an eagle flying magisterially above this watery place with the Grampians in the background. Eagles for 'F.R.' are unlike pelicans as they are not "a puzzle."

'F.R.' concludes his ramble at Halls Gap describing how:

> It was evening as I drew near the Gap. At the little rest-house where I stayed for the night there were a couple of thrushes, calling. A pair of whistlers were singing away as if for a wager near them. In a group of pines below the house some magpies were commencing their evening carol, and I sat and watched the sun set over the hills.

And evening was the end of his ramble.

This is not the end of the ramble of the fourth chapter of the present volume, though, as it continues by backtracking in time and space to **Wickliffe** in the 1880s with the story of members of the Burdett family who live on a bend on the Hopkins River on a farm called, naturally and unsurprisingly, 'River Bend.' The present chapter then moves forward to the recent past and present with the stories of Ayesha Burdett and Howard Brandenburg. Ayesha grew up on this farm and she, Howard and their two daughters now live there. Her grandparents bought the farm, so she is the third generation to live here. Her grandfather moved to the area as a teenager, but her grandmother (nee Grimmer) grew up at Wickliffe. Her great-grandfather came here from England and was one of the original Europeans in the area, probably working on Narrapumelap Station. There is an old gum tree across the river from Wickliffe that was planted by the Grimmers when they first arrived and set up a home. It's still standing today (email to author September 16, 2021). Ayesha and Howard visited it recently when they canoed down the Hopkins to the town of Wickliffe.

The Burdetts and Howard are all 'riverkeepers' of the upper Hopkins. Ayesha's parents, Barbara and George Burdett, completed extensive plantings across the farm. Howard describes how "everywhere are pockets and shelterbelts of trees, and native ground covers are also found throughout the farm. With low stocking rates of sheep these native groundcovers have persisted along the banks of the river" (email to author October 1, 2021). Building on their extensive plantings, Ayesha, Howard and their daughters have completed some extensive native tree and shrub plantings on the farm since they have arrived in late 2018.

Ayesha went to Primary School in Wickliffe, High School in Lake Bolac, and boarding school in Ballarat. She studied a double BA/BSc at the

University of Melbourne and later completed a PhD in Environmental Science at Charles Sturt University in Wagga Wagga in New South Wales. From there she gained a Post-Doctoral Fellowship and travelled to New Mexico where she worked on food webs in the Rio Grande at the University of New Mexico. She became the Curator of Bioscience at the New Mexico Museum of Natural History and Science. She met and later married Howard. After living and working for 13 years in New Mexico, she returned to Wickliffe with Howard and their two daughters.

Ayesha is a freshwater ecologist by training and profession. She continues to collaborate with colleagues in the USA. Howard and Ayesha work together on local ecology research projects and science outreach and communication. She took over the role of Landcare Facilitator for the Upper Hopkins Land Management Group in 2019. She says that working in this position enables her to engage with the local community, re-discover the environment and landscape, and learn about the priorities for natural resource management in the region (email to author September 14, 2021). She is a leading ecologist and conservationist of the Upper Hopkins catchment.

Part of Ayesha's current role with the Upper Hopkins Land Management Group is to publish its online newsletter for members of the group and interested supporters. Under the heading of 'Protecting the Environment,' the Spring 2021 edition covered many topics including:

- Managing serrated tussock in winter
- Wildlife cameras used to record livestock and biodiversity
- Galaxias making the most of spring flows
- Victorian Volcanic Plains Biosphere
- Planting trees is only part of the solution
- Andrews Lane Reserve Flora Survey
- Sallow Wattle - the golden invader
- Leaky Landscapes: Biolinks Alliance 2021 annual symposium
- Australasian Bitterns
- Frogging on the Victorian Volcanic Plains
- Button Wrinklewort recovery
- Water monitoring results. (Burdett 2021b)

Part of Ayesha's role is to facilitate some of the listed programs and works of the Landcare Group on the ground and in the water in the Upper Hopkins catchment.

Ayesha also writes descriptive and evocative pieces about the Upper Hopkins, its wetlands and the catchment. In the Spring 2021 edition of the newsletter under the heading of 'Meanderings and Reflections' she writes:

All of the little creeks and tributaries in the Upper Hopkins are flowing! It's been a long, wet winter and it was great to see so much water in our catchment. Lake Buninjon and Lake Bolac are brimming full, and there is still more water coming from upstream. All of the recent rain means that water was quite turbid across the Upper Hopkins as sediment was carried off the paddock and downstream. As we Landcarers know, planting trees and fencing waterways can help reduce the amount of erosion from streambanks. It's always fortifying to see areas with remnant vegetation holding soil together and creating habitat for riparian and in-stream fauna. I have also noticed that a lot of vegetation that has been planted in the last few years is really starting to take off and flourish in biodiversity corridors and fenced-off waterways. Thanks to everyone who has been working on their own land for so many years – you're really making a difference to the whole region! (Burdett 2021b)

Living on the Hopkins gives Ayesha and Howard the opportunity to "float a river," as he puts it, which he takes whenever possible. In August 2021 he wrote:

we just did a whole slew of short trips down the Hopkins River with the recent pulse of high flows. I kayaked from Halfway Gully (Major Mitchell Road) to the farm a few times. I saw a few platypus on those trips. When the river inundated our little bridge last week, we all paddled to the Glenelg Highway bridge. It takes a pretty good pulse of water to easily navigate through the stands of Phragmites. I am always looking for an opportunity to float a river. (email to author, August 7, 2021)

Floating a river, especially when it pulses, sounds like a very Thoreauvian thing to do as it suggests that a river is a natural highway and that water is the lifeblood of the body of the earth though which it circulates, as Thoreau maintains in *A Week* (as we saw in the first chapter of the present volume). Floating a river also sounds like a Pascalian thing to do to. Floating "a road that moves" downstream with the flow requires little effort; going upstream against the flow requires more effort.

The platypus for Bob McKenzie (2001, 7) is "Australia's most wonderful creature" and his favourite. He found them on his walk "down the Hopkins" (McKenzie 2001,128-130), as did Wheelwright (1861, 52-54) on his ramble, but not by 'F.R.' on his. McKenzie and Wheelwright go into great detail in describing the features of the platypus, including its bill and web feet like a duck that propel it like a mole, who lives for most of its time underwater like a fish and is a mammal (Wheelwright 1861, 53-54). The index to Wheelwright's book refers to the "duck-billed platypus" (Wheelwright 1861, 269). So peculiar was the platypus to the first Europeans to see it that it was regarded as a paradox, or as a stitched-together compilation of bits of other animals designed to mislead the unwary and confirm the suspicion that Australia was a strange place with weird animals. This peculiarity is enshrined in its Latin name of *Ornithorhynchus paradoxus* (meaning "paradoxical bird-snout"). Wheelwright (1861, 54) concludes that "we are hardly justified in regarding as monstrosities any peculiarities in the works of nature which we cannot understand." Indeed. The same applies to black swans, alligators and crocodiles, all of which have been regarded as monstrosities at some time or another, in one place or another.[42]

Phragmites is the name for the common reed. I asked Howard for more information about them and he kindly obliged:

> *Phragmites australis* are native to Australia. Invasive in New Mexico. They are native to the Hopkins River and are ecologically significant plants, providing food and cover for wildlife, preventing erosion, and are excellent at filtering nutrients from water. They are a pain in the ass to paddle through but a lovely plant to have growing in the river. (email to author September 12, 2021)

Howard is a native New Mexican and an artist who, like Carole Mules, exhibited at the Willaura Modern art gallery from December 2020 to March 2021. He also had a solo exhibition of paintings there in 2019. Howard's paintings often target concepts around environmental transformations attributed to human proliferation, including proliferation of humans (i.e. population) and proliferation of human activities. In an 'Artist Statement' he writes:

> My paintings weave a narrative about the human species and the causal effects of our proliferation. I am interested in what makes our species so successful and what that success means for the balance of nature. I am fascinated by human ingenuity, creativity, lack of foresight, and our destructive nature. My paintings often target concepts around environmental transformations attributed to human activities and economies. Visual art provides me the latitude and freedom to explore and communicate these concepts, using a visual language which conveys disparate perspectives: universally and individualistically. This duality is what I strive for in my work; producing an image that not only speaks a truth from a global perspective but its interpretation may also have differing meaning for individual viewers. I place a lot of emphasis on development of concept. I try to steer the content of each painting to a place that is simply an observation of the world. I explore and express these ideas using metaphors, motion, and space. I use geometry to build an idea into a composition, finding a way to move the viewer in and around the canvas and inviting them to linger on important passages.

Movement and energy is always visible in my work, using repetition and ghost images to reverberate key concepts while creating a sense of motion on the surface of the canvas. My work is loose and constructed with many thin washes of paint. The final finish of the work is a combination of detail and outlines of what could be.

Howard's artwork includes scientific illustrations of fish. He relates his training and years of field work in his native New Mexico:

I studied art and science at the University of New Mexico (UNM). I started working on endangered fish species during college when I was employed by the Museum of Southwestern Biology at UNM and spending my summers living solo along the banks of various desert rivers documenting the reproductive efforts of a number of species. Living alone in some very remote areas certainly shaped who I am today. Along with the research, there was time to explore, read, and create art. That job soon led to the full time research that I did on endangered fish for the next 20 years. (email to author September 12, 2021)

He also relates his artistic practice from field work, through sketchbook, to finished artwork:

I have been keeping sketchbooks since high school. They are way better than journals for me as I only need to see a sketch to be reminded of exactly what I was experiencing at that time. They are also the launching points for my paintings. (email to author September 12, 2021)

As a result of these field trips, research, and sketches, Howard illustrated all the native fish species in the rivers of New Mexico, including the larval development phases of minnows (*cyprinidae*) in the Pecos and Lower Rio Grande. His illustrations have been used in larval fish identification guides for researchers and in numerous books and science education material. He is currently working on fish illustrations and figures for a book about Murray Cod written by fish biologist Dr Paul Humphries and the larval descriptions and illustrations of the Southern Purple-spotted Gudgeon (*Mogurnda adspersa*). Howard is also illustrating some of the lesser known, non-game species that inhabit the Hopkins River and its tributaries, such as the male and female Little Galaxias (*Galaxiella toourtkoourt*), River Blackfish (*Gadopsis marmoratus*), Flathead Gudgeon (*Philypnodon grandiceps*), Southern Pygmy Perch (*Nannoperca australis*) and a less scientifically rendered illustration of the larva of the Short-finned Eel (*Anguilla australis*).

It's hard for a city-dweller, especially for one with conservationist convictions and living in a lock-downed city, not to idealise Howard's and Ayesha's lives and lifestyle as living a rural idyll on a farm on the Hopkins

River with them as a kind of latter day environmental Adam and Eve tending Mitchell's Eden and suspended in time in ongoing perpetuity (eternity) with no fall from grace and no expulsion. Idealising a rural idyll is part and parcel of the pastoral tradition in poetry, prose and music that was developed in the city to promote, celebrate and commodify escaping from the city to the country that has since become big business in real estate and tourism. Alternatively (in several senses) doing worthwhile environmental work by living bio- and psycho-symbiotic livelihoods in bioregional home habitats of the living earth, as Ayesha and Howard do, is applicable and possible in the city as all cities are located in bioregions and so all city-dwellers live in one too. It is also something that Richard and Jenny Weatherly have done on their farm further down the Hopkins west of Mortlake by practicing the principles of regenerative farming and following the 'conservation commandments' of a land ethic (as we will see in the following chapter).

5.

PEOPLE AND PLACE OF HISSING SWAN: WETLANDS ON THE MIDDLE HOPKINS

20 And God said, Let the waters bring forth abundantly the moving creature that hath life, and fowl that may fly above the earth in the open firmament of heaven. 21 And God created great whales, and every living creature that moveth, which the waters brought forth abundantly, after their kind, and every winged fowl after his kind: and God saw that it was good. 22 And God blessed them, saying, Be fruitful, and multiply, and fill the waters in the seas, and let fowl multiply in the earth. 23 And the evening and the morning were the fifth day. *Genesis* 1

The history of two cultures and the two life-stories of two remarkable men in the same locality in mid-western Victoria spanning two centuries are also connected by a common concern for Country, with learning to love and look after the abundant land and waters on the middle Hopkins River. Kaawirn Kuunawarn, an elder of the Girai wurrung peoples, was born at Lake Connewarren on the Hopkins River in *c.*1820, was removed in 1865 to Framlingham Aboriginal reserve further south on the Hopkins and died there in 1889. His life-story is retold by Jan Critchett in several places. The Weatherlys are a prominent pastoralist family of western Victoria who arrived on the Hopkins in 1895 and still live there. This discontinuous history of these people and this place with a three decade gap between them spans two centuries in total. Richard Weatherly was born in 1947 near to what is now called Lake Connewarren on *Woolongoon* station, grew up there and later spent 30 years from 1985 farming with his wife Jenny on nearby *Connewarran* station on the Hopkins River where they engineered and rehabilitated wetlands and regenerated drylands, as well as him becoming an internationally noted bird artist.

The Connewarren area on the Hopkins River near Mortlake in mid-western Victoria is rich in Aboriginal history, the archaeology of Aboriginal culture and Aboriginal story of Country, which underpins the statement that Australia 'always was, always will be, Aboriginal country'. The present chapter engages in mutually respectful, cross-cultural dialogue for caring for Country by indigenous and non-indigenous peoples. There will be no equitable reconciliation in Australia between its indigenous owners and everyone else unless and until truth-telling takes place with the stories of people and place as outlined in *The Uluru Statement from the Heart*. The present chapter explores the relationship to Country of the Aboriginal elder Kaawirn Kuunawarn who gives his name to, or took his name, from Lake Connewarren. Both give it to *Connewarran* station. The present chapter then discusses the Weatherly family who have run *Connewarran* since 1895, especially Richard and Jenny Weatherly who practised regenerative farming at *Connewarran* for 30 years from 1985 to 2015. As we saw in the previous chapter of the present volume, Richard Weatherly is also a noted bird artist, deepening his relationship to land. Relating both lives of both remarkable men interweaves Aboriginal, colonial and environmental history of people and place, as well as engages in truth-telling and aims for reconciliation.

Kaawirn Kuunawarn and Lake Connewarren

Kaawirn Kuunawarn was born at Lake Connewarren about 1820 and rose to become a key elder of the Girai wurrung people after the death of his father in 1841. He is depicted in a famous photograph taken in about 1880 holding a boomerang and stone axe, which graced the frontispiece of James Dawson's *Australian Aborigines. The Languages and Customs of Several Tribes of Aborigines in the Western District of Victoria* (Dawson 1881, frontispiece) and has been reproduced since (Clark 1990, plate 14, 198; Museums Victoria ND) (see figure 5.1).

The origin of the photo and how he got the name 'hissing swan' are related in Jan Critchett's entry for him in the *Australian Dictionary of Biography*:

> Kaawirn Kuunawarn (c.1820-1889) [...] was born at Lake Connewarren [...]. The youngster was later named after the noise the swans made when he robbed their nests. A young adult when Europeans moved into the area, Kaawirn Kuunawarn became clan leader on his father's death in May 1841. [He became known as 'King David.' He] was one of the chief informants for—and a photograph of him appeared in—James Dawson's *Australian Aborigines: The Languages and Customs of Several Tribes of Aborigines in the Western District of Victoria, Australia* (1881). [...] Impressive looking, with white hair, moustache and beard, his image was often reproduced in the nineteenth century, featuring in an album of Victorian kings and on cartes de visite [visiting cards. He] was also the inspiration for the main Aboriginal character in Louis Bayer's opera about colonial life, *Muutchaka or The Last of his Tribe,* an individual who showed all the superior qualities of human nature that the composer believed to be widespread among the Aborigines before the destructive effects of European invasion. (Critchett 2005)

Figure 5.1: 'Kaawirn Kuunawarn (Hissing Swan) Headman of the Kirroe Wuurong Tribe [Girai Wurrung Clan], Victoria, c.1881.' Federation University Australia Historical Collection.

The colonial settlers represented Kaawirn Kuunawarn in both the opera about him and the photograph of him as 'a noble savage.' This representation was a romanticised, imaginary indigenous figure who is seen as living in harmony with nature free of the corruptions of white society. The 'noble savage' is produced by what Stephen Muecke (1992) "the romantic discourse of Aboriginality." This discourse is one of a number of what he calls "available discourses of Aboriginality," that also include the anthropological and the racist.

Colonial settlers called Kaawirn 'King David' which might hark back to the biblical King David who is most famous for stunning Goliath with a stone from a slingshot, then beheading him, and for writing most of the book of *Psalms*. His reign was later looked on as a golden era. He also planned the construction of the Jewish temple in Jerusalem, but did not live to implement it. His son Solomon did. Colonial settlers calling Kaawirn 'King David' might also hark back to King David I of Scotland, the son of Queen Margaret, the patron saint of motherhood. This is perhaps the more likely as Margaret Kiddle (1961, 14, 517 n1) calculates that "at least two-thirds of the pioneer settlers of the Western District were Scottish," which led them to build Presbyterian churches (as we have seen in the previous chapter).

The Scottish colonists had a similar social structure of clans to the local Aboriginal people (and both peoples practiced grazing and hunting), but this did not lead to any sense of solidarity or empathy between the two cultures (Wilkie 2020, 21-22). Rather, it lead to clan rivalry. It is a cruel irony of history that some Scottish colonists of mid-western Victoria who had been subjected to "the clearing of the estates" in Scotland later "enacted their own brutal clearances on Indigenous [Aboriginal] peoples" (Wilkie 2020, 46). This was an act of repetition and displacement, of repeating dispossession and clan antagonism against Aboriginal clans. Clearance of Aboriginal from their clan estates culminated in this area in the massacres of the Girai Wurrung as documented by Ian Clark (1995, 129-133). Rather than following 'The Golden Rule' of "do unto others as you would have them do unto you" (*Matthew* 7: 12), it was a case of the Scottish colonists of mid-western Victoria following the colonial rule of 'do unto others what has been done to you,' thus perpetrating the cycle of violence. Banjo Clarke, an elder of the Girai wurrung who lived for many years at Framlingham on the Hopkins River, explicitly followed 'The Golden Rule' and refused the colonial rule (as we will see in the following chapter of the present volume).

Kaawirn Kuunawarn is also commemorated and memorialised in the current names of *Connewarran* and Lake Connewarren. These are an instance of the memorialist discourse of Aboriginality that in the words of Daisy Bates (1985, 34) "smooths the pillow" of a supposedly "dying race." This is a disavowing device for colonization that forgets the past and its people while preserving their names in placenames, sometimes in the wrong place (as we will see shortly). The meaning of these names often fades among colonists, and the connection between people and place is lost. Kaawirn Kuunawarn needs to be acknowledged in the present and his connection to this place in the past the home of the Girai wurrung in mid-western Victoria, restored.

In the language of the local Girai wurrung people, his name means 'Hissing Swan', the noise black swans make as their nests are robbed of eggs. Ian Clarke (1990, caption to plate 14, 198) informs us that Kaawirn Kuunawarn was "the clan-head of the Gunaward gundidj at Lake Connewarre [*sic*] and considered [...] to be the most eminent clan-head of the Girai wurrung." 'Connewarran' (and variant spellings) means 'hissing swan' in the local Aboriginal language of the Girai wurrung people, the traditional owners, users and inhabitants of this land. It was applied widely to lakes in central and western Victoria (as we have seen previously). Ian Clark's (1990, figure 8, 208; table 11, 209) map and table of the "clan estates" in the lands of the Girai wurrung people show the Gunaward gundidj clan located approximately at what is now called Lake Connewarren and the Gular gundidj clan located approximately at 'Konawarren' (now *Connewarran*) station on the Hopkins River due west of the present-day township of Mortlake (see figure 5.2). This place is the place of the hissing swan.

Figure 5.2 Girai wurrung Language Area and Clans. Clark 1990, figure 8, 208. Reproduced with the kind permission of Ian Clark.

The Girai wurrung were a wetlands people. Clark (1990, caption to plate 14, 198) goes on to relate that "in 1838, immediately prior to the occupation of their lands by Europeans, Kaawirn Kuunawarn summoned 1000 people to a meeting at a favourite swamp and camping place called 'Kuunawarn' (presumably Lake Connewarre [*sic*])." Phillip Chauncy in the 1870s sketched several oven mounds at "the outlet of Lake Connewarren, about five miles south-west from Mortlake" (Chauncy 1878, 233; see figure 5.3).

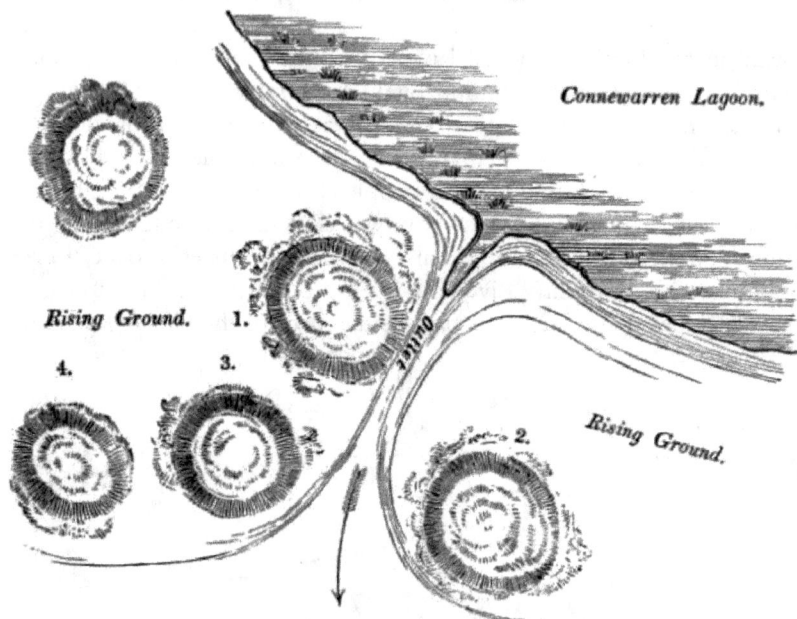

Figure 5.3 Phillip Chauncy, 'Diagram of *Mirnyongs* [Oven-mounds] which occur at the outlet of Lake Connewarren, Victoria, Australia.' Accessed February 6, 2021.

Chauncy (1878, 233) noted that these *mirnyongs* "must be of great antiquity" and that "the adjacent lagoon abounds with large eels." In the 1880s the Reverend Peter MacPherson (1884-85, 56-57) wrote that "the large oven-mounds [...] are numerous about Mortlake". He observed that "the necessity for water accounts at once for so many oven mounds being situated near creeks, rivers, lagoons, and lakes [which] abound with water-fowl, fish, and eels."

A century later the Victorian archaeologist observed of Aboriginal settlement in mid-western Victoria that "the most significant features of the area are the large numbers of perennial and intermittent lakes, swamps, streams and rivers which attract abundant wildlife and provide favourable environments for aquatic plants" (Coutts 1985, 23). Coutts emphasised "eels and the daisy yam". In September 1836, Major Mitchell remarked on a "yellow flower abundant on the plains of Australia Felix", believing it was a sign of reaching "the good country." Mitchell may not have been aware that the yam daisy's root was a staple food for Aboriginal people (as we have seen previously). Coutts (1985 23, 63 n2) concluded of this region that "such wetlands were potentially [sic] rich and reliable sources of food for the Aborigines and were the focus of much economic activity during […] the period immediately prior to the European invasion, circa 1830 CE." He added that no greater evidence for the abundance of wetlands as food sources for Aboriginal people is the number of oven mounds constructed around them dating back five thousand years (Coutts 1985, 31-38).

The wetlands of mid-western Victoria had, as Harry Lourandos (1987, 298) describes them, "a high capacity for annual regeneration. Their resources included both local and migratory species: fish (especially eels), birds, eggs and a range of edible plants. The location of wetlands also allowed access to a diverse range of neighbouring environments, such as the fertile open plains and forests. Plants were staple items of diet." Wetland plants were not only foraged and collected, but also cultivated; eels and fish were not only hooked and gathered, but also trapped; and birds were not only hunted, but also netted. Cultivation, trapping and netting required artifice and labour with the tending of plants, the building of traps and the weaving of nets. Lourandos (1987, 293) calls the Aboriginal peoples of mid-western Victoria "swamp managers" who "practised intensive gathering, hunting and fishing economies that included the management and manipulation of plants, animals and fish. They established semipermanent base camps and their ceremonial and political life involved large social networks." Lake Connewarren would also have been a case in point as "a favourite swamp and camping place" (as Ian Clark put it) for Kaawirn Kuunawarn and the Girai wurrung.

More than intensive hunters, gatherers, fishers and foragers, and more than merely managers and manipulators of plants, animals and fish, the Gunditjmara people of mid-western Victoria around Lake Condah were designers and builders of eel and fish traps, or "engineers of aquaculture" (Gunditjmara People (2010, 16-22), and cultivators of wetland plants (Gunditjmara People 2010, 7, 13-16, 67), or practitioners of paludiculture in their civilizations.

European Colonization and the Misnaming of Connewarren

Clark (1995, 125) later relates how, "throughout the early 1840s, organised groups of Girai wurrung people fought a sustained guerrilla war against the pastoralists." Part of that war has been a struggle against the official renaming of their country that is still ongoing to this day. Jan Critchett reveals the extent of this renaming and her own process of gradually becoming more specific about locations and their names. Initially she stated that "Kaawirn Kunnawarn (Hissing Swan), 'Chief' of the Kirrae Wurrong tribe, [...] was born in the area around Mt Shadwell [...] in 1822 or 1823" (Critchett 1990, 1). She is later more specific about Kaawirn Kunnawarn's birth place stating that he was born at Lake Connewarren, near [the town of] Ellerslie [on the Hopkins Highway], about five miles [eight kilometres] south-west of Mortlake" (Critchett 1998, 115). This is where Chauncy (1878, 233) said Lake Connewarren was and where it is indicated on this map of 1856 (see figure 5.4).

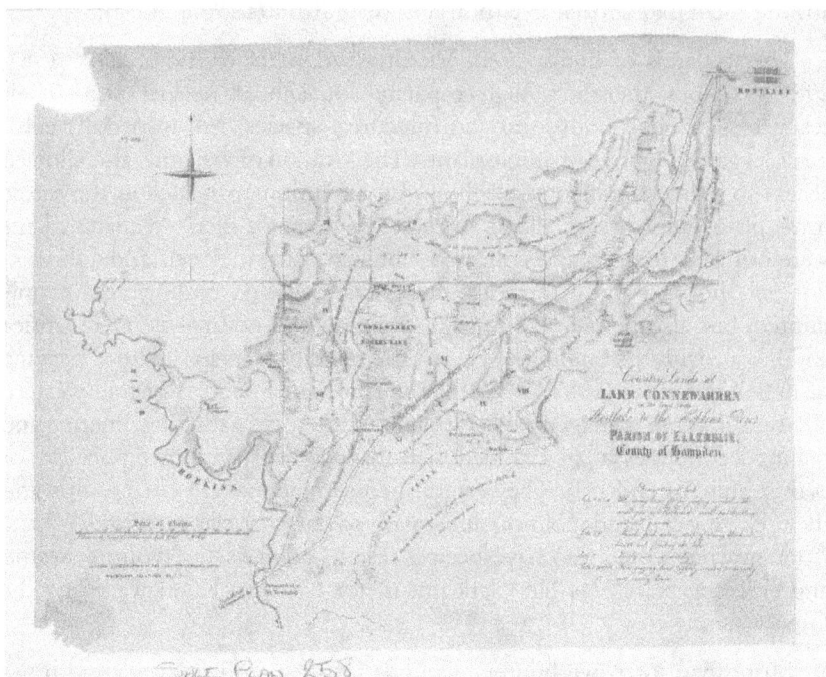

Figure 5.4: Lake Connewarren; Ainsworth; Ellerslie 1856 *Public Records Office Victoria* https://prov.vic.gov.au/archive/214BF07D-F844-11E9-AE98-A79F8D911E2A?image=1. Accessed September 8, 2021.

Present day Lake Connewarren is not located there, but about twelve kilometres to the north due west of Mortlake on Connewarren Lane. It is indicated as 'Salt Lake' on this undated map (see figure 5.5).

Richard Weatherly has elaborated that:

> the original Lake Connewarran, beside which Kaawirn Kuunawarn's indigenous settlement assembled [...] was in a different place [to what is now called 'Lake Connewarren.' The original Lake Connewarran was] close to Ellerslie [a town south-west of Mortlake], and the drainage of it is well documented. The Mortlake Historical Society possesses photographs of it prior to its drainage

by a hand dug trench some twelve feet deep and fourteen feet across [see figure 5.6]. The *Woolongoon* diaries record the earliest crops of wheat being grown on its drained bed in 1895. The drain is clearly visible as it crosses Delaney's Lane just south of its junction with New Bridge Road before it drains into the Hopkins River north of Ellerslie; the old lake bed protrudes close to the Hopkins Highway north of its junction with McRaes Lane. [What the Weatherlys called] Lake Woolongoon [now the official Lake Connewarren] was an ephemeral swamp which was deepened by draining the surrounding country, particularly to its, west into it. This was complemented by an overflow drain dug from a sluice gate at the base of the wall of the Woolongoon dam along the hillside below the dairy and into the lake on its south-west corner in a paddock named the Firebreak. So, it appears that officialdom has rewritten the historical names to exclude the indigenous inhabitants from their earlier haunts, which I find sad. The original Lake Connewarran was a beautiful shallow wetland surrounded by Red Gums and full of waterfowl. The photographs of it are very evocative. I would [have] loved to have seen it. (email to author, March 5, 2021)

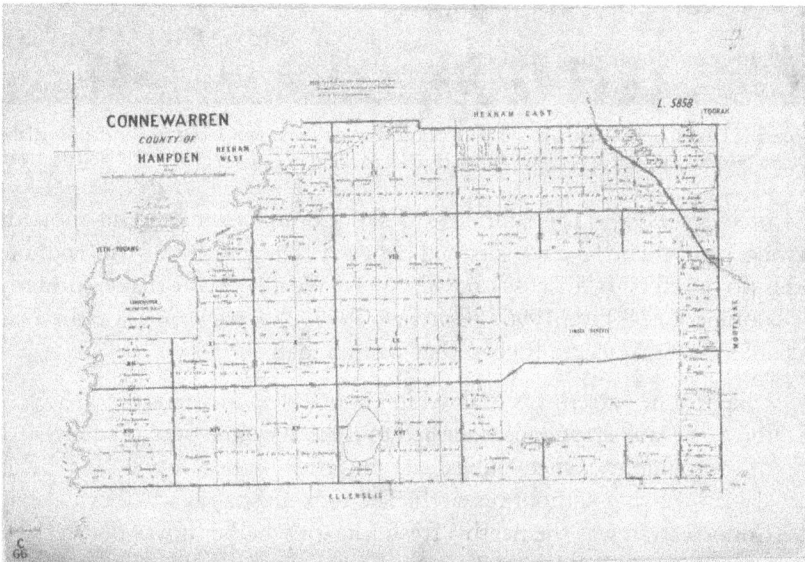

Figure 5.5: PROCC66; Connewarren (Undated) *Public Records Office Victoria* https://prov.vic.gov.au/archive/A69CEC47-F843-11E9-AE98-21A471EF7806?image=1. Accessed September 8, 2021.

It also appears that officialdom has rewritten the names of the home-places of the indigenous inhabitants to exclude them from history. In the present case Aboriginal history is being rewritten back into history as the pre-history of colonial history and as a shared history of place and peoples.

Figure 5.6: Lake Connewarren, *circa* 1860s, photographer unknown. Courtesy of the Mortlake and District Historical Society. Reproduced with kind permission.

Critchett (1998, 118) later says "Lake Connewarren and its mounds no longer exist. The lake was drained between 1890 and 1900." An endnote at this point refers to "discussion with Mr W. Weatherly, Mortlake, formerly of Woolongoon, 8 June 1996" (Critchett 1998, 258, n.21). W. Weatherly is Richard's father, William. Richard has written that:

> Lake Connewarren was drained in about 1895. In about the 1950's the name was erroneously applied to Lake Woolongoon as an error of cartography. Once published, the error was compounded by slavish copying without research. The only mystery is whether Lake Connewarran was the nearby 'fresh lake' or whether it was the fresh lake alongside Reishmans Lane about two or three miles south east of Lake Woolongoon and on the other side of the Blind Creek. This lake was also drained, I expect even earlier, but I have no information as to what date that occurred, merely a fairly good recollection of the area it occupied. (email to author, April 16 2021)

Critchett (1998, 118) goes on to state that "a few years earlier, in April 1884 twelve mounds at Connewarren were removed [and] the soil scattered "by means of plough and scoop" [...]." Richard Weatherly has written further that "while managing *Connewarran* and living at *Woolongoon*, we became intimately aware of the *mirnyongs* to which Chauncey refers, most of which have become degraded over my lifetime. Generally they were located along the slopes of the plateau country, well above the reach of floods, but the giant of them all commanded the junction of the Blind Creek and the Hopkins River. It must have been in use for centuries" (emails to author, March 5 and 10, 2021). These are all areas and sites of Aboriginal "cultural heritage sensitivity" (ACHRIS ND).

Connewarran and the Weatherlys

The first colonial settler of *Connewarran* was Jemima vans Robertson in 1839. Evidently she kept an elephant on the property (Hamish Weatherly, pers. comm.). William Weatherly was born in Scotland in 1839, travelled with Andrew Chirnside to Australia with his share of the proceeds of the sale of the family farm in Scotland and arrived in Australia in 1860. He mainly spent the next 35 years working for the Chirnside family managing or overseeing their pastoral properties in Victoria and New South Wales in which he also had a financial interest until 1912. A brief visit took him back "home to Scotland" in 1878 when and where he got married. Back in Australia he and his wife had three children, including the eldest, Lionel, Richard's grandfather.[43] Richard Weatherly, farmer and bird artist, relates in his memoir, *A Brush with Birds,* that in 1895 William "bought two adjoining properties watered by the Hopkins River and Blind Creek called Connewarran and Woolongoon" (Weatherly 2020, 74). They also had large lakes (as we have seen previously).

Lionel Weatherly's son and Richard's father was called William, but known as 'Bill' or 'WW' (Hamish Weatherly, pers. comm.). Richard was born in 1947 on *Woolongoon* with a large wetland that the Weatherlys called Lake Woolongoon and is now called Lake Connewarren. Lake Connewarren became for him, as it did for Kaawirn Kuunawarn, a significant place. Richard relates how he grew up "next door" to *Connewarran* on *Woolongoon* "with the extensive wetland [now called Lake Connewarren, or Hissing Swan Lake] that was a part of my life from when I was a baby" (email to author December 28, 2020). The "large lake," as he also calls it, had a formative influence on him (Weatherly 2020, 5). Like Thoreau and Walden Pond for whom it was "one of the oldest scenes stamped on my memory" (Thoreau 1982, 405), Richard remembers the lake well (as his emails cited previously in the present chapter indicate).

After early, successful home-schooling, Richard seems to have gone off the rails a bit, at least academically, so he was sent off to 'Timbertops,' the school in the bush of Geelong Grammar made famous by including among its alumni King Charles III. Richard says 'Timbertops' "was the saving of me" as he had become "a problem child." It is located over 200 kilometres north-east of Melbourne where it is "nestled in a secluded valley in the foothills of the Victorian Alps," as its website puts it. A boy who had spent his life "on the grassland plains of western Victoria" now found himself "in the bush [...] The birds were different, the trees were different, the plants were different and the topography was different." Timbertops "challenged us, physically and mentally, which was just what I needed" (Weatherly 2020, 8).

From Timbertops Richard went to Cambridge University in the late 1960s where he studied history (Weatherly 2020, iv, 10-11). I imagine it was a heady time to be there. The radical Raymond Williams, the patron saint of ecocultural studies, was teaching and writing there from the early 1960s.[44] After graduating from Cambridge, Richard moved to London where he began his training and development as an artist mentored by older artists (Weatherly 2020, 10-24). He met and married his wife Jenny in 1976 (Weatherly 2020, 75). After a decade of travel overseas and the production of the definitive book on fairy wrens, they settled at *Connewarran* in 1985 and started farming its 526 hectare (1300 acres). Over the following three decades Richard and Jenny Weatherly became exemplary regenerative farmers.

When they arrived at *Connewarran* in 1985 Richard says that "the land was bleak and flat, with poor pasture and low productivity" (Weatherly 2020, 78). In short, it was in a degraded state as described, documented and illustrated extensively elsewhere (Massy 2020, 217-229; Reid and Norton 2013, 320-332). Richard and Jenny "began by creating wetlands and planting trees to provide shelter for stock and protect the soil" (Weatherly 2020, 78). They gradually restored the land to health and financial viability through planting trees, rehabilitating wetlands, breeding and running livestock, and attracting birds and insects. Trees provide habitat for birds and insects (beneficial and detrimental), with the birds and beneficial insects ideally keeping the detrimental insects under control (Weatherly 2020, 81-82). Insects were important in "building the health of ecosystems," as Richard puts it (Weatherly 2020, 82). Birds became indicator species of the health of the land – dry and wet: fairy wrens in the case of bush-birds; brolgas in the case of waterbirds. Richard Weatherly's interest in and love for brolgas is documented and illustrated in *A Brush with Birds* (Weatherly 2020, 24, 96-99, 248-249) and for fairy wrens in the definitive scientific book on them (Schodde 1982), reprised in *A Brush with Birds* with more illustrations of the species (Weatherly 2020).

For 30 years Richard and Jenny worked cooperatively and symbiotically with wetlands by rehabilitating them, rather than draining and filling them, the standard agricultural practice of most colonial farmers, part of the cultural baggage they brought with them from Europe. The rehabilitated wetlands of *Connewarran* provide shelter belts and habitat for birds and insects, all of whom demonstrably improve the farm's financial bottom line, the health of the land and the mental and physical well-being of the farming family. Paralleling in some ways the land use of the Girai Wurrung, the Weatherlys became swamp farmers and engineers of wetlands for the provision of "ecosystem services" (Weatherly 2020, iv). They were also engineers of agriculture in drylands and wetlands for the regeneration of plants as habitat for animals – native and introduced.

In a recent article in a regional newspaper published to coincide with the launch of *A Brush with Birds* and an exhibition of his paintings in the book Richard tells how:

> his appreciation for the natural environment was nurtured from a young age thanks to a father who encouraged him to be curious about the world around him. 'You'd be going around the paddocks with your father and he would say 'oh, I wonder what all those birds are feeding on, let's go up and see',' Richard remembers. 'When you are on the land you tend to see a bird and want to know what it is. My grandfather kept a bird list and he had 111 species, my father had 148 species and we had 207 species by the time we left. Anything more than 200 is a lot.[45]' (Short 2020)

The parallels with Aldo Leopold teaching his children to look at, listen to and learn from the land and to identify species of plants and animals are striking. Drawing parallels with Leopold is also biographically justified as Richard Weatherly cited him in a speech he gave at a conference in 2009 (Massy 2020, 229). Leopold is the author of the conservation classic, *A Sand County Almanac* (Leopold 1949), the Moses of managing lands and the patron saint of marshes (Giblett 2020c, chapter 7). He is a more reliable guide than Major Mitchell for leading people in the promised land of 'Australia Felix.'

Aldo Leopold bought a degraded farm with his family in Wisconsin in the 1930s, planted trees, rehabilitated wetlands and attracted birds, such as sandhill cranes as creatures of the marsh and indicators of the health of the land (Leopold 1949, 95-101; Meine 1988, 329-330). The parallels between him and the Weatherlys are also striking as their farm was in a degraded state when they arrived and brolgas came to play a similar role to sandhill cranes as an indicator species for the Weatherlys of the health of the land as creatures of the wetland. Weatherly is the patron saint of the trinity of painting bird pictures, rehabilitating wetlands and regenerating farmland.

Other similarities are also striking. The Leopolds renovated an old shack on their Wisconsin property; the Weatherlys relocated a weatherboard cottage to their Victorian property (Weatherly 2020, 75). They later built a family house. A photo of Aldo Leopold checking the health of the trees he and his family planted (Lorbiecki 2016, 153) is remarkably similar to a photo of Richard Weatherly checking trees he and his family planted (Reid and Norton 2013, 324). The Weatherlys practice what Leopold (1949) called a land ethic in conjunction with soil conservation and a conservation aesthetic of appreciation for the sights and sounds of the drylands and wetlands, and their inhabitants. By using and working with the elements of earth and water in engineering and rehabilitating wetlands, by planting plants and thus making habitat for animals and conserving the soil, the Weatherlys created a farm that was an aesthetically pleasing composition to look at and a bodily and mentally enhancing environment to walk in, make observations about, live in and make a livelihood from, as described and documented in *A Brush with Birds* (Weatherly 2020, 74-87 and 96-111).

Land health is the conjunction of a land ethic, soil conservation and a conservation aesthetic. All three are vital and interdependent components of land health. Without a conservation aesthetic, a land ethic is an unpleasant set of dicta or rules; without soil conservation, a land ethic and a conservation aesthetic are theories divorced from practice; without soil conservation and a land ethic, aesthetics is a disembodied and disconnected artistic affectation or hedonistic pleasure. With a conservation aesthetic, a land ethic and soil conservation create a rich and rewarding way of life; with soil conservation, a land ethic and a conservation aesthetic are theories coupled with practice; with soil conservation and a land ethic, aesthetics is embodied, sensory pleasures experienced living in the land with its plants and animals. They are a set of 'commandments for conservation.' Leopold is the Moses of managing lands who codified these commandments and passed them on to all who care for land. Leopold as Moses leads land lovers to land and mental health.

The Weatherlys came to realise that they were practicing what Charles Massy in *Call of the Reed Warbler* calls "regenerative agriculture" based on Leopold's land ethic and the work of many others (Weatherly 2020, 83). Massy defines regenerative agriculture as "an ecologically and socially enhancing agriculture [...] based around revegetation and inculcating healthy, living soils [...] containing plants, insects, bacteria, fungi and other organisms" (Massy 2020, 4). Regenerative farming combines the principles and practices of traditional organic farming and gardening at the mid-scale of soil conservation with the macro-level of emergent holistic philosophy and ecology, based on recent scientific evidence from the micro-study of soil chemistry and physics (Massy 2020, 342, 357, 434). No longer involving the perhaps easily dismissed weird and wonderful prognostications and practices of whacky holistic and biodynamic do-gooders and permaculturalists, regenerative farming not only works, but Massy demonstrates how it works with a variety of different evidences — anecdotal, autobiographical, ethnographic, empirical and scientific.

Regenerative farming revolves around what Massy calls "five key landscape functions": the solar-energy cycle; the water cycle; the soil-mineral cycle; dynamic ecosystems; and the human-social component (Massy 2020, ix-x, 7, 48). Each of these functions is mutually interdependent on the others, as Massy (2020, 52, 183, 227) shows in his case studies of particular farms and farmers in widely separated regions of Australia with vastly different climatic conditions and soil profiles, such as *Connewarran* and the Weatherlys. Massy also shows that there is no right or wrong order in which to begin putting these functions into practice. It is better to begin somewhere than not begin at all.

Massy relates how Richard and Jenny Weatherly "focused initially on the fourth function of dynamic eco-system communities" on their property in the "swampy country" on the Hopkins River in the 'Australia Felix' of mid-western Victoria. Focussing on dynamic eco-system communities embraced the other functions. For the Weatherlys and Massy (2020, 68), "going down this path of regenerative agriculture unlocks an entirely new way of thinking, perceiving[,...] feeling [and acting] connected to a different set of values and ethics."[46] Thus embracing the human-social component.

The first three functions of the solar-energy cycle, the water cycle, and the soil-mineral cycle in Massy's account are vital components that underpin, make possible and generate the fourth function of a dynamic ecosystem that Massy (2020, 215) describes as "a complex community of organisms in any locality" in biogeographical regions of a catchment with its rivers, streams and wetlands — as Richard relates in the case of Connewarran (Weatherly 2020, 82-87, 96). For Massy (2020, 55) the fourth function of a dynamic ecosystem is "the keystone of the whole operation [of] our farm [as] a complex and dynamic series of ecological systems" that "constantly self-organize themselves towards resilient ecological health." Massy goes on to accept that he now realises he had "completely overlooked [this,] the most important of all factors." The fourth function of a dynamic ecosystem is the keystone to building the arch of regenerative farming. Without it, the whole structure collapses into isolated and futile practices, or abstract and useless theories. Without the other functions, the keystone is not supported by theory and practice. By beginning with this function the Weatherlys had not only *not* overlooked it, but also showed how it embraced the other functions of the solar-energy cycle, the water cycle and the soil-mineral cycle. It also embraced the human-social function, Massy's fifth function.

Richard relates how the Hopkins River was both a blessing and a curse with the water and soil-mineral cycles. On the one hand, and for the short term, "the Hopkins River flowing around two sides of our farm was periodically too saline for watering livestock or a hazard for young sheep, which frequently became bogged" (Weatherly 2020, 78). On the other hand, and for the longer term in the past and for the future:

> the Hopkins River was particularly helpful. It follows a geological fault line between two differing soil types, the old Tertiary sediments and the more recent basalt soils that were the legacy of volcanic activity possibly more than 30,000 years ago. This fault line marks a junction between habitat types: the red-gum woodland of the Tertiary soils to the east, and the grassland plains of the basalt soils to our west. We were fortunate to live in an area of natural diversity. (Weatherly 2020, 82)

Combined with relatively high rainfall, the proximity of the river, the abundance of sunshine, the lie of the land, the fertility of the soil, the drainage lines and the conservation of water in wetlands, this place was Australia the blessed indeed.

Conserving water in wetlands regenerates the soil. It can also help drought-proof the land. Drought-stricken farms are often more the result of poor land and water management, rather than of bad weather with no or little rain. Rather than droughts, Massy prefers the term "dry spells" (Massy 2020, 63, 130-131, 136, 139, 142). Dry spells are part and parcel of the weather and the cycle of the seasons in Australia exacerbated with wet spells in the age of global heating and climate catastrophe. Rehabilitating wetlands brings back the "chain of ponds" noted by early explorers, including Thomas Mitchell with the Cockajemmy Lakes in mid-western Victoria (as we saw in chapter 3 of the present volume). Massy relates how "these chain of ponds were located down the bigger water flow valleys (I hesitate to call them rivers). The chain-of-ponds pattern was a brilliantly evolved, self-organising system suited to Australia's unique physical and climatic environment" (Massy 2020, 130; see also 138, 383).

The most famous and visible of these chain of ponds is probably the Moonee Moonee Chain of Ponds in Melbourne (depicted in a map of 1838; Bertram and Murphy 2019, figure 63, 140). It is now Moonee Ponds Creek, a concrete-lined drain carving its way through the suburbs of Oak Park and Strathmore and then on through Pascoe Vale and its eponymous suburb beside the Tullarmarine Freeway and below the freeway in North Melbourne. It is a sad and sorry remnant and reminder of what it was when it was as a chain of ponds. Plans are afoot to restore parts of it at least to its former state in Oak Park and Strathmore (Melbourne Water 2021). Designs have also been prepared for rehabilitating Moonee Ponds Creek further downstream where it traverses North Melbourne beside the Upfield train line (Bertram and Murphy 2019, 124-151).

Rehabilitating remnant wetlands or creating artificial wetlands, or "engineered billabongs" as Massy (2020, 312) calls them, brings the land back to life. The Weatherlys engineered billabongs and a home lagoon. They created "a chain of ponds" with thirteen wetlands in total of various sizes. The largest is "a 78 acre (32 hectare) metre-deep, ephemeral wetland" that "we specifically created on a river flat [of the Hopkins] by erecting an earth wall 400 metres long by three metres high to retain floodwater" (Massy 2020, 228; Weatherly 2020, 97). It is also a seasonal habitat for waterbirds attracting hundreds of them (Massy 2020, 217, 219, 224, 227-228; Weatherly 2020, 96-111).

Coming to the realisation about the keystone role of the fourth function of a dynamic ecosystem involved Massy changing his thinking and shifting paradigms from the Mechanical Mind of industrial agriculture to the Emergent Mind of regenerative agriculture in the fifth function of the human-social, "*the* most influential and critical of all the landscape functional components" (Massy 2020, 278 his emphasis; 280). This "paradigm shift" for Massy (2020, 55, 110, 268, 277, 359, 363) means developing "ecological literacy," that is, "the ability to read a landscape, to appraise the state of its health and how it is functioning." Checking the health of trees, as both Richard Weatherly and Aldo Leopold did, is one way of doing so.

Massy (2020, 280; see also 359) came to realise that "the learnt concepts, understandings, inherited and trained beliefs, mental models and paradigms" farmers carry in their heads is "the key to farming behaviour." Without changing minds, it is impossible to change the land; without shifting paradigms, it is hard to shift habitual land practices. The fifth function is the biggest hurdle and the toughest challenge for most farmers. Developing a conservation aesthetic is one way of shifting paradigms The Weatherlys are again exemplary in this regard too. Richard Weatherly's education at Timbertops and Cambridge and his training and practice as an artist and Jenny Weatherly's training "making natural history programs with the Wildlife Unit for the ABC" (Weatherly 2020, 75) seems to have nurtured from the get-go a different human-social mindset, aesthetic sensibility and set of values from those of the standard farmer.

The Weatherlys' beginning with the fourth function of a dynamic ecosystem contrasts with Massy's scientific preference for beginning his discussion of the landscape functions at the level of the solar energy that powers the metabolism of the land, going on to the soil-mineral and water cycles of the land within its large scaler dynamic ecosystems and habitats, then considering the human farmer of the land within their social context and the overarching philosophical function of the farmer's mindset and making a paradigm shift, and concluding with transforming humans and the human-earth relationship.[47] The Weatherlys' mindset had been transformed and they had shifted paradigms before they began regenerative farming and practiced the landscape functions, including their embracing of a conservation aesthetic, all of which entailed self-transformation and the transformation of their relationship with the earth.

Like Aldo Leopold's practice of a conservation aesthetic on the land and in his nature writing, Richard Weatherly creates aesthetically pleasing compositions on the land and in his nature paintings. Richard depicts birds variously as individuals, as pairs and as communities in their home habitat, rather than only depicting birds abstracted as types of their species as in bird books, such as field guides. Richard insists that *A Brush with Birds* is "not a Bird Book. It is a book about birds, and animals and people" (Weatherly 2020, v). Similarly, *Middlemarsh* is not a book about the Hopkins River abstracted from its place and its inhabitants in it and along it, but a book about the river, animals, plants, people and wetlands. Richard's bird paintings include birds in situ at *Connewarran* on the Hopkins River, in Gariwerd (the Grampians), elsewhere in Australia, as well as in Africa and New Guinea.

Richard travelled and worked internationally for eight years illustrating the definitive scientific book on the fairy wrens (Schodde 1982). An article in *The Australian Women's Weekly* described how:

> Richard Weatherly has trekked across deserts and slogged through jungle, travelling by air, four wheels, horse and shank's pony during an eight-year pursuit of one bird. This traveller's tale, however, is no story of a long-distance romance but a wildlife artist's search for the Fairy Wren across the Australian continent and in the wilds of Papua New Guinea. Varieties of the bird can be seen hopping around most suburban gardens, but the entire family is scattered over thousands of square kilometres. Richard Weatherly has observed them all, at courtship, home-making, even sun-basking, and has captured them in detailed paintings for a large book on one of the smallest species in Australasia. Richard and his wife Jenny (who was a TV and radio producer's assistant in the Wildlife Unit of the ABC before her marriage) love the bush and plan to restore 2000 hectares of their lovely property, *Connewarran*, at Mortlake, Victoria, to its natural state. Richard was raised there as a child, and grew up with a love of the countryside and its fauna. 'I became tremendously interested in Fairy Wrens because they're bouncy, bright and trusting little birds,' said Richard, whose pursuit of the bird began at an ornithological conference, when wildlife writer, Dr Richard Schodde, decided to document the Fairy Wren for a definitive book [...] (Whitlock 1982, 22-23).

It won the Whitley medal in 1982, Australia's highest award for zoological publishing (Carruthers 2015).

Richard regards himself as equally a painter and a merino breeder (Carruthers 2015). Jenny and he could equally be regarded as "great conservationists" (as Carole Mules first described them to me in an email dated December 1, 2020), wetland rehabilitators (as Richard himself does; Weatherly 2020, 74-87 and 96-111) and as regenerative farmers (as Richard himself does; Weatherly 2020, 83; and as too does Massy 2020, 217-229). Restoring the land to health resulted in returning the farm to financial viability as a merino stud. Richard and Jenny's successful work with doing all three was recognised in 2018. An article in the regional newspaper related how:

> A lifetime commitment to Merino wool and the environment has been acknowledged with the choice of Mortlake wool producers Richard and Jenny Weatherly as representative woolgrowers to accept an international eco stewardship award presented to the Woolmark company. The Weatherlys, from Connewarran Merino Stud, joined fellow wool producers Matt and Vanessa Dunbabin, of 'Bangor', Tasmania, to represent the thousands of wool growers who contribute wool to the Woolmark company and its environmental credentials [...] The Weatherlys said they were 'very honoured and very proud' to accept the award. The pair said Australian wool growers had shown remarkable stewardship of their country. As well as producing merino wool, the Weatherlys have worked tirelessly to rebuild the ecosytem on their Connewarran property during their 35 year custodianship. They planted more than 1.5 million trees, fenced off rivers, created wetlands, and watched as bird, insect and plant numbers and diversity rebounded. They also built the Connewarren Merino Stud from scratch into a successful enterprise that sells more than 70 rams a year along with semen to clients in Australia and abroad. Mr Weatherly is also a noted artist, specialising in paintings of nature. (Himmelreich 2018)

He was the foundation president of the Society of Wildlife Artists of Australasia and was made an Honorary Associate in ornithology at the National Museum of Victoria (Short 2020).

Rehabilitating wetlands provides many benefits, such as flood mitigation to absorb and retain pulses water from high rainfall events (as depicted in a photo; Reid and Norton 2013, 321). A long family history on a farm such as *Connewarran* provides a longer historical perspective and creates the bigger context of the basin as the home habitat, rather than just the farm. In the aftermath of the flood of 2009, a regional newspaper described how:

> The clean-up effort is continuing after floods left a swathe of damage

across the south-west last week. Farmers were able to inspect their tracks, fences and dams as water levels receded in most areas. Council staff will assess roads today to determine if they can be reopened although some will remain closed indefinitely. With rivers and waterways still high above their banks, the fast-flowing water is pushing a large amount of debris and rubbish from upstream towards the ocean. People walking along the beach near the mouth of the Hopkins River yesterday reported seeing 'thousands of beer cans', a fridge, a pontoon and other debris. 'It's rather horrendous,' one woman said. The roads to the Hopkins Falls was lined with vehicles as people made their way to the car park and viewing area to watch the display which was reported to be the best for at least 15 years. The police helicopter patrolled the area around Lower Gellibrand and Chapple Vale after concerns that some residents may have been trapped by flood waters. Although there had been no distress calls made, the air patrols were carried out on Friday afternoon and again on Saturday after reports that the district was without power or telephone service. A police media spokeswoman said the areas affected included the Great Ocean Road and the Gellibrand River Road at Lower Gellibrand and Chapple Vale. 'A number of people were sighted, but no-one signalled for assistance and there was no winching required,' the spokeswoman said. Mortlake farmer Richard Weatherly described last week's heavy rain as 'fabulous'. 'I've had a grin on my face ever since it started,' Mr Weatherly said. 'I think it's just brilliant.' Mr Weatherly's historic property Connewarran sits on the Hopkins River west of the town. 'Compared with the big floods it's not a big flood. It's like the old times but it's easy for me because I've grown up along the river and I know what to expect.' He said the 1946 flood was the biggest he was aware of while the 1983 event was the biggest he had witnessed, particularly because it took a long time to disperse. (Alexander 2010)

Richard and Jenny Weatherly's work is a rich, rewarding (in several senses) and unique combination of artistic creativity, soil and water conservation, and regenerative farming. They have lived an exemplary life by gaining a livelihood living and working bio- and psycho-symbiotically with the land in their home habitat on the banks of the Hopkins River in the bioregion of the volcanic plains in mid-western Victoria. Richard and Jenny retired from *Connewarran* in 2015. They now live in Wallington on the Bellarine Peninsula overlooking the Barwon River estuary east of Geelong and close to Lake Connewarre (Weatherly 2020, 263). Richard's life has gone full circle from Lake Connewarren to Lake Connewarre around the widespread Aboriginal naming of the lakes in central and western Victoria (as we saw in the second chapter of the present volume). Richard continues to paint and exhibit his paintings. He held an exhibition of his paintings in December 2020 at a local gallery in conjunction with the launch of *A Brush with Birds* (Short 2020). It was also launched in December 2020 in the bookshop in Dunkeld south of Gariwerd (the Grampians) attended by 80 people (Roz Greenwood, pers. comm.).

The Weatherlys' work demonstrates that it is possible, desirable and feasible for farming and wetland conservation to work hand-in-hand cooperatively for the mutual benefit—economic, environmental and psychological—of all concerned, human and non-human, for land and mental health, as well as financial well-being. Rather than having naturalists and wetland conservationists trying to wrest control from farmers of wetlands on their property in order to rehabilitate them, Richard and Jenny adopted a style of farming that works with, rather than against, wetlands. They demonstrate by example what can be achieved. It is an object lesson for farmers, bird enthusiasts and wetland conservationists alike.

The Weatherlys' work takes place in a unique place that is a hotspot of Aboriginal and colonial history with two eminent elders from both cultures featuring prominently in its life-stories of living and working with wetlands over the past two centuries beginning with the birth of Kaawirn Kuunawarn in *c.*1820 and coming up to the recent past with the publication of Richard Weatherly's *A Brush with Birds* in 2020. With its grasslands and wetlands and their plants and animals, this unique place is also a hotspot of biodiversity and bioregional richness on the Victorian volcanic plains whose geological history spans thousands of centuries dating back five million years ago. The life-stories of this place and its peoples introduced and interwoven in the present chapter engage in mutually respectful cross-cultural dialogue between indigenous and non-indigenous peoples, nurture caring for Country by both and advocate for equitable justice and reconciliation between them. With their shared history in the wetlands and fertile plains of mid-western Victoria, indigenous and non-indigenous peoples may be able to dis-enclose and re-common water and riparian rights in this area for the common good. In the best of all possible worlds, there is a strong case for (re-)commoning these waters (rivers, creeks and original wetlands). Long may this place and its peoples live!

6.

FRAMLINGHAM AND HOPKINS FALLS: ABORIGINAL PLACES AND PEOPLE ON THE LOWER HOPKINS

> 24 And God said, Let the earth bring forth living creatures after their kind, [...] and God saw that it was good. [...] 27 So God created humankind [...] male and female created he them. 28 And God blessed them, and God said unto them [...] 29 Behold, I have given you every herb bearing seed, which is upon the face of all the earth, and every tree, in the which is the fruit of a tree yielding seed; to you it shall be for meat. 30 And to every beast of the earth, and to every fowl of the air, and to everything that creepeth upon the earth, wherein there is life, I have given every green herb for meat: and it was so. 31 And God saw everything that he had made, and, behold, it was very good. And the evening and the morning were the sixth day. *Genesis* 1

The long, continuous and often traumatic history of the Aboriginal people and place of Framlingham on the Hopkins River marks it as a special site of struggle for their rights and against colonialism, the Anglican Church, the state government and recently against a proposal for a quarry on the other side of the river from Framlingham. Opposition to the quarry and campaigning for the conservation of the river is being led by the 'Save the Hopkins River - Stop the Quarry' group (STHR-STQG). The history of the naming of the place from Framlingham forest, through Framlingham Aboriginal Mission, to 'Framlingham Aboriginal community' (Critchett 1998, 108) marks the history of the place on the river known today simply as 'Framlingham,' or 'the Mish.' This place has also been the home of some remarkable Aboriginal people, including Kaawirn Kuunawarn whose story began in the previous chapter and continues in the present chapter, and later with the stories of both Banjo Clarke and Robert Lowe of living on 'the Mish.'

The 'Victorian Places' (NDC) webpage for 'Framlingham' states that:

> Framlingham is a rural district and village in western Victoria, 25 km north-east of Warrnambool. In addition to the farmlands, there are the Framlingham Aboriginal Reserve and Forest to which the Aboriginal community secured freehold titles in 1971 and 1987. The second title came 126 years after a mission station was established there. White settlement of the Framlingham district first occurred

about 1840 and the village began with the Brefnay Hotel in about 1848. A store was opened during the next decade and a Presbyterian church was built in 1870. Settlement picked up during the 1870s and a school was opened in 1872. Farming involved a considerable amount of tree clearing, but grazing and dairying were successfully taken up. When there was a census population of as few as ten people, the Warrnambool Anglican church obtained a reservation of 1416 ha for an Aboriginal mission to 'ameliorate the present wretched conditions of the Aborigines'. The reservation adjoined the north bank of the Hopkins River west of the village. In 1890 the reserve was reduced by about five-sixths, the Aboriginal community only keeping an area by a persistent refusal to move elsewhere.

This refusal led to an early 'land rights' battle that the Aboriginal community fought and won with the help of some perhaps unlikely allies, such as the then local Federal MP for Wannon and Prime Minister Malcolm Fraser (Clarke 2003, ix, 198; Broome 2005, 235-257).

Ian Clark fleshes out the early history when he relates that:

In 1861, at the request of the Aboriginal mission formed by the Church of England in Warrnambool, 1400 hectares of land were gazetted beside the Hopkins River. This became the Framlingham reserve, which was occupied from 1865 until October 1867, when the central board appointed to watch over the interests of the Aborigines closed Framlingham and attempted to relocate its Aboriginal residents to Lake Condah, where a new station was to be opened. Some Girai wurrung refused to go to Lake Condah and those who were taken quarrelled with the Aborigines there and returned to Framlingham. In September 1868, the Girai wurrung actively sought the re-establishment of the Framlingham station. From this time, the history of the Girai wurrung becomes the history of Framlingham. From 1877 until 1890, a campaign was waged in Warrnambool to take the Framlingham reserve from the Aborigines and make it the site of an experimental agricultural farm. In 1894, the reserve was reduced to 222 hectares, and the majority of the reserve was given to the Council of Agricultural Education as the site of an Agricultural college. Ironically, these plans were never realised, and Framlingham Forest stands on the reclaimed land. (Clark 1995, 125, 127; see also Critchett 1998, 79-106)

Today:

Framlingham Forest, approximately 1130ha in area, is the largest remaining remnant of native vegetation within approximately a 150 km radius of Warrnambool city. It is located 25 km north-east of

Warrnambool and bounded on the east by the Hopkins River, and by cleared farmland to the north, south and west [...] This section of the river is the most natural and least modified for the whole of the river's length and it is one of the very few sections of river where bankside vegetation has not been cleared for agriculture and where the riverbanks are relatively free of erosion. (STHR-STQG 2020, 28)

Framlingham Forest is a special Aboriginal place as:

The Framlingham Aboriginal community is situated on Gunditjmara country on the western plains of Victoria. It is one of only two discrete Aboriginal communities in Victoria where Aboriginal people live on Aboriginal land. The people of this community have retained continuous occupation of this land, despite many attempts to move them. For thousands of years the Gunditjmara people have thrived using their ingenious methods of channelling waterflows, harvesting fish (River Blackfish) and eels. By farming and smoking them, they produced a year round supply of food and goods to trade in one of Australia's first aquaculture ventures. (STHR-STQG 2020, 32)

The Australian short-finned eel (*Anguilla australis)* is common in the state of Victoria and is one of only two species found in the state. In the local Aboriginal language it is called *kooyang* or *kuuyang*. The local Aboriginal people catch eels "using stone traps. Nets called *ngarrappeens*, are set in the gaps of the stone traps" into which the eels swim (Glenelg Hopkins Catchment Management Authority 2005, 25) and are then speared. The local Aboriginal name for the nearby Hopkins Falls is "Tangang punhart" or "Tung'ung buunart" meaning "eels bite the stones" (Clark 2009, table 8.1; citing Dawson 1881, p.lxxxii). This is a graphic rendition of the fact that eels jump up the falls. The force of the water is immense. Banjo Clarke and Robert Lowe tell stories of spearing eels in the Hopkins (as we will see in the present chapter).

The Falls have been depicted in painting and photography, including by Frank Hurley, Australia's most famous early-twentieth century photographer for photographing the wastewetlandscape of World War I and Shackleton's ill-fated expedition to Antarctica. Hurley's photographs of the Hopkins Falls are now held in the National Library of Australia. Unlike the Seine, this is the only stretch of the Hopkins deemed worthy of photographic depiction, probably because it is the most spectacular part of the river in accordance with conventional landscape aesthetics inherited by mainstream tourists.

The history of the Girai wurrung becoming the history of Framlingham includes the individual life-story of Kaawirn Kuunawarn from 1865 until his passing in 1889. Jan Critchett began his story in chapter 5 of the present volume and continues his story in the present chapter:

> Kaawirn Kuunawarn moved to Framlingham Aboriginal station when it opened in 1865. On 4 September 1889 the Board for the Protection of the Aborigines reaffirmed its decision to close Framlingham Aboriginal station, despite the desire of the Aborigines to stay on at least part of the land. Predeceased by his daughter, Kaawirn Kuunawarn died there on 24 September. William Goodall, Framlingham's manager, notified [James] Dawson by telegram: 'Old Davie (Hissing Swan) dead. Idea of his leaving home killed him. Buried on Thursday.' Dawson reproduced the wording in the *Camperdown Chronicle,* adding: 'my faithful friend of forty years, as honest a man as ever breathed, sacrificed to the greed of a race of men, who, not satisfied with having deprived him and his friends of their hunting grounds, now seek to turn them, in their old age, out of their established homes and associations.' To the *Hamilton Spectator*'s Warrnambool correspondent, however, Davie was a 'very violent old rascal . . . and a few broken heads were saved, to his womenkind especially, when the gin-soddened, possum-gorging old warrior was laid *hors de combat.*' Appalled at this final 'kick at the dying lion,' Dawson responded that King David [Kaawirn Kuunawarn] had been an exemplary worker on Kangatong for over twenty years and that there was little need to defend his character, given that 'his enemies and slanderers' were 'straining every nerve' to rob the Aborigines of the little they had left. (Critchett 2005; see also Critchett 1998, 107-136)

Kaawirn Kuunawarn died of a broken heart from being (re)moved from his home land of Connewarren to Framlingham.

The history of the Girai wurrung (Kirrae Whuurong) people becoming the history of Framlingham continues there thirty years later with the story of Banjo Clarke who was "born in a bark hut on Framlingham Mission" (Clarke 2003, 7, 132) in the early 1920s, a hundred years after Kaawirn Kuunawarn was born at Lake Connewarren. Clarke was an elder of the Girai wurrung (Kirrae Whuurong) too and died at Framlingham in 2000 (as related by six of his sons and daughters; Clarke 2003, xii-xiii). They relate later that he is "buried on his tribal land, at a point we all called 'the pretty place,' on the brow of a hill overlooking the Hopkins River" (Clarke 2003, 246). This term is taken up and preserved in the lyrics of a Paul Kelly song who pays homage to Clarke in this song and another, 'Smoke Under the Bridge' (Clarke 2003, 270).

Beginning in 1975, he told the story of his life to Camilla Chance, a fellow member of "the Baha'i Faith [that] is so like the Aboriginal way of life" for

Clarke (2003, 216). He became an active Baha'i as "I was very interested in it all" (Clarke 2003, 181). He "went to a great many conferences and met different nationalities from all over the world. It wasn't how I'd understood religion to be" (Clarke 2003, 181). Similarly, Thoreau's understanding of religion as "where our love is" isn't how a lot of people might understand religion to be either. Clarke's life journey is a story of what he understood religion to be changed and grew. His spirituality of "love, compassion and wisdom" (Clarke 2003, xiii) isn't how a lot of people might understand religion to be either, nor is 'Aboriginal' a category on the Australian census form to answer the now optional question of 'Religion' (nor is Baha'I for that matter).

The place where one was born, lives, walks, learns and dies was important for both Thoreau and Clarke as their homeland and as a place of religion and story. Clarke told his story to Chance beside a waterfall on the Hopkins River at (Clarke 2003, xiii). Framlingham is "the place where I was born" (Clarke 2003, 54), where he lived most of his life and where he died. Framlingham is also the place where he walked in the forest and where "there are story places. They give us feelings and they give us dreams" (Clarke 2003, 241; see also 242). Clarke attended school for two days because he "didn't like how the teacher would hit the little kids. So I went back to the bush. The bush was my school [...] I grew up in the bush school where I learnt all that I know today" from it and "the Old People" (Clarke 2003, 13, 240). Thoreau lasted for about two days too as a teacher because he was supposed to cane the kids. The woods, meadows and swamps of Concord where he was born, lived, walked, learnt and died was his school too where he learnt from them and from a few old and new books.

Clarke's story was published in 2003 as *Wisdom Man*. In the 'Preface' to *Wisdom Man* six of Clarke's sons and daughters write that "it is appropriate that this book stems from an oral account [...] in accordance with Aboriginal custom" (Clarke 2003, xiii). It is also appropriate that the book stems from the stories told in and about a particular, special place in accordance with Aboriginal custom that a place is vitally connected to the earth and "all the life it supports" (Clarke 2003, xii). Clarke was dubbed 'Banjo' after Banjo Paterson, "Australia's most famous poet." Paterson is depicted on the current Australian $10 polymer note. Henry Lawson, Australia's other famous poet and storyteller, was depicted on the original Australian $10 paper note.

The oral account transcribed in the book also stems from an eternally present moment in time that has no past in accordance with Aboriginal custom. The 'Preface' relates that "to a large extent, the spiritual life to an Aboriginal person means living in the eternal present, with the past, present and future all experienced as one and simultaneously." As a case in point,

Clarke retells what his mother told him about his great-great grandmother, Truganini, the so-called 'Last Tasmanian' as proclaimed in the controversial film of that title, "but we know that's not right" (Clarke 2003, 57) (as he is living proof to the contrary). Clarke's mother told him that Truganini "could feel the future in the depths of her being" (Clarke 2003, 59). And it was not pleasant, as Clarke goes on to retell a story his mother told him about Truganini and her daughter Louisa, including kidnapping, rape and "a terrible massacre" (Clarke 2003, 58-65). The storyteller retells stories and keeps them alive as Clarke demonstrates here and later. For Clarke "the Aboriginal way" is that "there is no past. Everything is still happening" (Clarke 2003, 175) in the place here and in the eternal now. "Our connection with the forest links both our past and our future" (Clarke 2003, 243).

For Clarke (Clarke 2003, 7), "the Hopkins River below my place is sacred." Not only is a place on the river sacred, but also life itself. Clarke learnt from "the Old People" that "life should be looked upon as a sacred thing" (Clarke 2003, 55). The sacredness of place and life extended further as:

> everything was sacred to us. We looked on the land as a mother who knew how to care for us, and we knew how to care for her [...] Our sacred bush transforms us for the better when we go into it! [...] We've got to protect the land where we were born [...] The land is like a mother to us. (Clarke 2003, 188, 235).

Aboriginal people practiced conservation, sacrality, mutuality and symbiosis with their home habitat in a bioregion of the loving and living "mother earth" a long time before these terms were invented or taken up in other cultures. As Clarke says, "we've been conservationists all the time. Before white people ever *thought* about it" (Clarke 2003, 238). The sacredness of life and place on the Hopkins flows through his story and the story of the place of Framlingham that "was all more or less forest when I was a little fellah" (Clarke 2003, 7). The place is known today as 'Framlingham Forest,' but it was more forest, or had more forest, when it was 'Framlingham Mission' (Clarke 2003, 7), later 'Framlingham Aboriginal Settlement' (Clarke 2003, xi).

Clarke tells how "the Old People knew when it was time to put the fish traps in" the river "where there's rocks" and spear fish and eels (Clarke 2003, 13). Clarke relates how he learnt to make eel traps:

> I would watch the Old People weave long, narrowing shapes out of grass, with a hoop and then a funnel, which the eels could get in but not out of. We'd build stones up around the finished nets and wait for the floods, which usually came in May, at the end of autumn. Us kids used to love this time. (Clarke 2003, 26-27)

Clarke learnt how to read and appreciate the signs of the seasons with their changes in the weather. For Clarke, "people living with nature have to know when the weather's going to change. We know when a storm's coming up, or when there's going to be a long dry or a wet season. You live with all them things" (Clarke 2003, 200). Through the seasons[48], "the land provided everything for them, and she looked after them [...] The bushland was always very important to us – it was work, it was shelter in the winter; there was plenty of wood for our fires" (Clarke 2003, 213, 242).

Clarke and the other kids would have fun hunting and killing eels and fish in "the rocky river [that] was like a smooth highway to us" (Clarke 2003, 230). A river is a highway, as Thoreau said. Childhood on the Hopkins was a time and place of "great laughter!" (Clarke 2003, 13). Clarke laments that "when I look down over that gully these days, there's no more laughter, and all them things are gone, but I like that place because that's a spiritual sort of place to me" (Clarke 2003, 13). After Clarke's house burnt down, he had a new house built "overlooking the big gully and beautiful bend in the river where I used to roam when I was a little kid, hunting and spearing fish and eels" (Clarke 2003, 230).

The sound of children's laughter "playing by the river would ring through the hills and the valleys" (Clarke 2003, 211). This sound is a recurring expression of joy in Clarke's life story (Clarke 2003, 210, 230, 242). Sounds are strongly associated with his sense of place that is not only landscape, the surface of the land for visual appreciations, but also soundscape, the sound of the land for aural delight, such as when he could "hear wind singing in the trees, the beating of birds' wings" (Clarke 2003, 28). Sounds are also strongly associated with his sense of loss of people from this place and his spiritual sense of place, as they are for Brett Clarke (as noted in the first chapter of the present volume). Sounds, or the lack of them, were also noted by colonists. The rambler 'F.R.' in 1917 remarked how "the country is very quiet" with "a deadly and oppressive stillness" (as we saw in chapter 4 of the present volume). Aboriginal people from this area had been removed to Framlingham where they contributed to the soundscape there.

One place in particular that Clarke misses is Wangoom Lake west of the Hopkins Falls where the Old People would take him when he was a child to:

> get duck and swan eggs. We'd always behave ourselves. We understood that we were keeping a custom alive which makes the bird families strong, and which had gone on for thousands of years. Wangoom Lake used to be three and a half miles in circumference. The Government of Victoria sold it to some landowners whose properties reached its banks, and they have now drained it. That's sad, because in those days thousands of swans used to settle on the mud and shallow water. They would pull up the reeds to make nests

[...] When we arrived at Wangoom Lake we'd see nests everywhere and we'd start collecting eggs for our tribe. We'd gently lift one or two from each nest of five, being careful not to leave human scent. We'd never even think of removing a whole clutch of eggs [...] We were kind as we could be to nature, and nature was kind to us. (Clarke 2003, 20-21)

Clarke later says, "we felt that the bush was our soul. We belonged to its creatures and had to give them a chance to breed" (Clarke 2003, 41). The creatures of the bush did not belong to them. Clarke talks later about the Aboriginal 'environmental ethic' or 'land ethic' in which "native animals are entitled to live here, same as anyone else. We've got to share our hospitality with the animals, and be their friend" (Clarke 2003, 200).

Aboriginal people practiced this ethic as Clarke relates with a specific example that he remembers from when he was a child about Lake Bolac (as we saw in chapter 2). The white men from Ararat, as Clarke goes on immediately to relate (as we also saw), were not only stealing land and food from Aboriginal people and preventing the continuation of their lifeways, but also enclosing the wetland owned by one tribe and shared in common with other tribes into their own private property in "the madness of greed," as Clarke (32) puts it later, with "the destruction of land for money" (Clarke 2003, 203).

Clarke relates how:

my dad and other Old People used to sit around the campfires in the night, talking about how all the land was disappearing and there was no more hunting ground left. How they was put on the mission and not allowed to go anywhere. Talking about all the bad things what's going on, and the massacres. (Clarke 2003, 30)

Clarke goes on to tell how he was 'taught' about a particularly horrific massacre of Aboriginal children on the beach near Killarney between Port Fairy and Warrnambool. Squatters buried them up to their necks in the sand and used their heads for a game of polo, too awful to describe in any more detail. He was also taught about the later poisoning of Aboriginal people by a Killarney squatter. The place is Killarney by name, 'kill-arney' by nature. Poisoning is massacring by other means, both amounting to genocide. The Killarney massacre and poisoning of "about 1861" (Clarke 2003, 33) are not documented by Ian Clark (1995) in his atlas of massacre sites in western Victoria. The oral stories of the massacre and poisoning were seared on Banjo Clarke's memory. The storyteller retells stories and keeps them alive. Clarke "became a storyteller" (Clarke 2003, 84) who is "speaking from the heart" and who tells "our stories from the heart" (Clarke 2003, 145, 190).

The memory of massacres and stolen children for Clarke is "a living one, always present. Whatever happens to us at any time is there forever" (Clarke 2003, 145). So much for civilization beginning and barbarism ending in the last quarter of the eighteenth century.

The land was disappearing and becoming farmers' land, "but we wanted our land too" (Clarke 2003, 32). Aboriginal people were being "disappeared" from their land and hunting grounds by brutal slaughter and fatal poisoning. Not only Aboriginal people, but also "native animals were massacred" (Clarke 2003, 213). Although they "not allowed to go anywhere" else, on Framlingham "we kept a lot of our tribal law well into the twentieth century, and a lot of our language too" (Clarke 2003, 35). Speaking in the late twentieth century, Clarke lamented that "a lot of our language has been lost now" (Clarke 2003, 227).

Clarke kept a connection to country when he was a kid in the city during the Great Depression beginning in 1929. Clarke tells how, even though:

> the buildings blocked my view of my Dreamtime tribal home [...,] I still longed for my homeland. All I wanted to do was get back in the bushland, go walkabout, walk along the gullies, look into the rivers, and find a fish and eels and make a spear. (Clarke 2003, 46, 236)

The smell of gum-tree tips on the wood that he would deliver in the city during this time "would take me back to my homeland" (Clarke 2003, 50). Home was not a house, but land, his place and the place of his people. The smell of gum-tree tips was the means or vehicle for conveying him from the city to the country of his "homeland in the bush" (Clarke 2003, 242) with its living beings of plants and animals, rocks and rivers. "My heart and spirit will never leave the bush" (Clarke 2003, 244).

Homeland is "a spiritual place to us [...] That's my homeland. That's my spiritual home" (Clarke 2003, 239). Clarke points to the Irish, Italian and Scottish immigrants to Australia who "pay homage to their homeland [by returning to them for a visit]. Just like we do in Australia — we pay homage all the time to our tribal land here" (Clarke 2003, 214). When Aboriginal people "were shifted from one mission to another like cattle getting drafted here and there [...,] all they wanted to do was come back to their land where they was [sic] born" (Clarke 2003, 215). When Clarke "used to travel around as a young man looking for work, I tended to move in a circle because my forest homeland was calling and pulling me back to hard. You always come back to your homeland. You always come back" (Clarke 2003, 244). These are his final words in *Wisdom Man*.

Clarke declares earlier that:

we won't ever leave our land. That's our spirit-land [...] It's our spiritual home [...] We never forsook it or left it vacant. Somebody always remained here like a guardian of the spiritual sites where our ancestors roamed. That's what our bush means to us — a spiritual place where we can come and go. It's not just a tree or a river, it's something sacred what money can't buy from you. It's something there forever [... K]nowing that we are connected to the spiritual world makes us Aboriginal [...T]he land still belonged to us because it had never been taken from us [...] We loved the land because it was our spiritual home. [...] Everything spiritual has its physical part, and everything physical has its spiritual part. (Clarke 2003, 144, 171, 175, 197, 218)

For Clarke there is no hard and fast divide here between the spiritual and material worlds, and so no such divide between life and death. Death is a part of life. Clarke says that "from birth, we [Aboriginals] live with death" (Clarke 2003, 171). Being disconnected from the spiritual world of sacred land makes many city-dwellers into modern secularists who are disconnected from nature and place, including place of birth, unlike Aboriginal people: "*We* know where we come from and where we belong. That's the Aboriginal way of life. That's part of your living, to know where you're from" (Clarke 2003, 235).

Clarke mourns the fact "all the bush is being cut down now, and the rivers are being polluted. Everything is going wrong because people don't love nature. She can't provide for her children now. She's trying to fight back but everyone's too greedy" (Clarke 2003, 211). Clarke goes on to refer as a case in point of greed and the destruction of land for money to the specific example of the uranium mine at Jabiluka in the Kakadu National Park in the Northern Territory, a World Heritage Site (Clarke 2003, 211-212). Local Aboriginal tribal elders "have been talking about 'the monster in the ground' for thousands of year [...] The Aboriginal people knew all about the good things and the bad things in the earth [...] They loved and respected the land where they lived" (Clarke 2003, 212). Mining the monster in the ground leads to the making and dropping of atom bombs, and to the death and destruction of people and place. Clarke cites the example of "the poor Japanese" (Clarke 2003, 212) at the end of World War II as a dangerous instance of letting the monster out of the ground and not heeding the warnings of Aboriginal people about its destructive power. Nature is not only be a good, providing mother, but can also be a bad, destructive monster created by the greed of mining.[49]

Clarke says his elders "can see the white man destroying himself, so there's no need for *us* to take revenge. They've done so much damage to Aboriginals and to the country – leave them to it, because they'll destroy themselves in the end" (Clarke 2003, 214). Clarke believes that "I can see it would save the world if people got back to Aboriginal principles" (Clarke 2003, 218). Doing so would mean "keeping the peace" as Aboriginal people did for "sixty or seventy thousand years" (218). First and foremost among Aboriginal principles for Clarke is "love – great love – [which] is Aboriginals' strength. Aboriginals have respect for all people, no matter where they come from or how poor or how bad they are [...] We treated other people the way we wanted to be treated" (Clarke 2003, 219). When Aboriginal people gather for a funeral of someone they know, their love and respect for each other lead to "the deep sense of unity we all have for each other" (Clarke 2003, 219).

The story of Framlingham becoming the story of one person continues with the life-story of Uncle Robert Lowe who was born in Melbourne in 1947, grew up on Framlingham and who retells his life-story in *The Mish* (Lowe 2002). It won the David Unaipon Prize in 2001. One of the natural features that Robert describes is the preponderance of swamps in the area of the Framlingham Aboriginal community (Lowe 2002, 23, 27, 41-42). A map of the nearby town of Framlingham (not to be confused with the Aboriginal community) shows the town surrounded by swamps (see figure 6.1).

One of Lowe's stories is about one of his elders teaching him how to spear eels using nets, poles and rocks placed in the Hopkins to create a small channel into which the eels swam and where they were trapped and speared (Lowe 2002, 24-31). He relates that "spearing eels was the traditional way to catch them" (Lowe 2002, 25). Lowe's teacher made spears with hooks from the tines of old pitchforks that had been discarded by farmers. These hooks were lashed to saplings. He also relates how the small eels crawl up the Hopkins Falls and up the creeks to grow to more than a meter before heading back downstream "towards the end of January" (27) and out to sea to spawn, possibly as far away as the Coral Sea in the Pacific Ocean. On one occasion he speared an eel that was so big that "I couldn't get him out from between the rocks [...] I finished up having to let him go 'cause I couldn't get him out" (26). Lowe masculanises this eel as 'him' and has an interpersonal relationship with the eel as 'I-him,' rather than objectifying the eel as 'it,' as a thing, as non-indigenous anglers would tend to do, though Izaak Walton in the seventeenth century feminised the European eel (as we will see in the following chapter of the present volume).

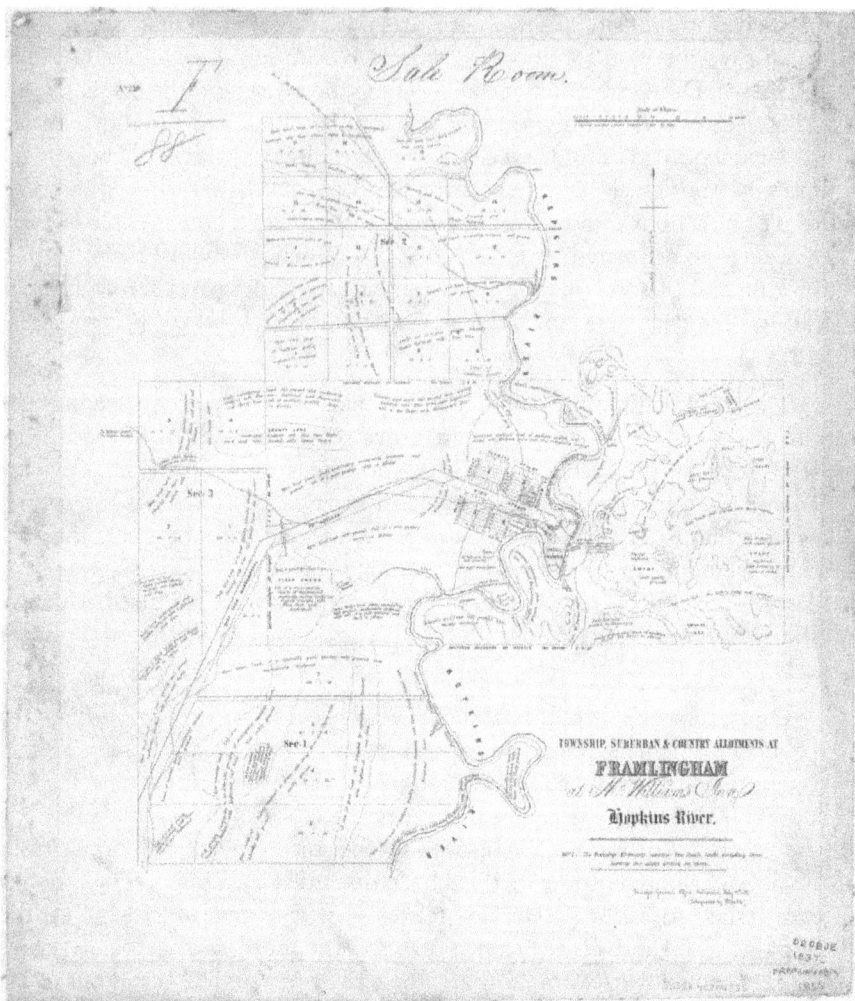

Figure 6.1 Framlingham Township, Hopkins River and Swamps. National Library of Australia. https://nla.gov.au/nla.obj-230662066/view. Accessed September 8, 2021.

The Framlingham Aboriginal community is a watery place, not only due to the fact that "the Hopkins River runs right around the Mish. and the swamps go right through the bush," as Lowe (2002, 42) puts it, but also because Mt Emu Creek meets the Hopkins at what Aboriginal people called "the Junction" (Lowe 2002, 29), not far downstream from "the Mish." The influx of water from the creek, the longest in Victoria, into the river, the longest in Victoria, creates the voluminous flows downstream for the cascading Hopkins Falls. The confluence of the creek and the river also created deep holes (or vice versa) in the water that were good fishing spots

(Lowe 2002, 29). Further upstream in the Hopkins River at the Little Falls and Picnic Grounds in Framlingham is "a big hole that channels over a big flat rock so when the eels are travelling they come out and lay on that rock" (Lowe 2002, 28). The banks of the river are steep here which makes it difficult to get down to the water so Robert and his mates would tie a rope to a tree to get down to the river.

The lower Hopkins River in the Framlingham area is threatened by the proposed development of a basalt quarry at Panmure on the other side of the river from Framlingham. The proponents for the quarry commissioned a report in which they state that the proposal "represents an acceptable planning outcome" for a number of reasons including:

> The Proposed Quarry can be established with no impacts on the environmental values of Subject Land, the surrounding area and the Hopkins River. Officers from the Department of Land Environment Water and Planning (DELWP) have inspected the Subject Land and have confirmed that there is no native vegetation within the proposed work authority area and there will be no potential for offsite impacts to flora and fauna, including any species present in the Hopkins River […] The Proposed Quarry will not impact groundwater, with the water table estimated to be found at least 20 metres below the proposed floor[…] The Work Authority boundary and extraction area of the Proposed Quarry operations have been sited outside of any identified areas of Aboriginal cultural heritage sensitivity and will not have any impact on other nearby areas of Aboriginal cultural heritage. (Equipe Lawyers 2020, 6-7)

The Report does not go into any detail about "the environmental values of […] the surrounding area [including Framlingham] and the Hopkins River," such as the ones already described by Banjo Clarke and Robert Lowe in the present chapter. The Report also plays down the hydrogeological features of the site, including that "there is a fall of about 35 metres across the Subject Land from the Ellerslie-Panmure Road to Hopkins River to the west" (Equipe Lawyers 2020, 8). Any surface water run-off from the proposed quarry would flow directly down into the Hopkins River that forms the western boundary of the site, on the other side of which is Framlingham (as the maps in the Report show; see figure 1, 8; figure 3, 15; there is no figure 2 for some strange reason).

The Report later states that:

> The extraction area will be located at least 200 metres from, and 30 metres above the Hopkins River and will not be visible from the River or the Kirrae Whurrong Aboriginal Corporation land [Framlingham] further to the west. (Equipe Lawyers 2020, 8)

In fact, Framlingham is on the other side of the Hopkins River, and so not so far "further to the west." The Report plays down the proximity of the site to the river and to Framlingham. It also reduces the possible impacts of the proposed quarry on the people and place of Framlingham to a visual one.

The Report goes on to state that:

> All water used and captured within the extraction area will be retained on site in the sediment dam, which will be approximately 650 metres from the Hopkins River. (Equipe Lawyers 2020, 11)

The fall of the land is still 30 to 35 metres from the site to the river and surface water can easily flow across 650 metres with that amount of fall. Sediment dams on mining sites have a tendency to burst with devastating environmental impacts. There is no contingency plan outlined in the Report if a dam were to burst. If it did in this case, there would be only one way and one place to which the water would flow – straight into the Hopkins River – with devastating environmental impacts locally and downstream on water quality and riparian vegetation, and so the quarry would impact visually from the Framlingham side of the river.

Sediments from a dam-burst would flow into the Hopkins River, either directly to the west or indirectly from the north as a creek forms the boundary on the north side of the site and it flows into the Hopkins River (though the Report does not say so):

> To the north, the extraction area will be approximately 50 metres from the unnamed creek running adjacent to the northern boundary of the Subject Land. All water used and captured within the extraction area will be directed to the sediment dam, which will be 200 metres from the creek to the north. (Equipe Lawyers 2020, 12)

The site is thus bounded to the west by the Hopkins River and to the north by a creek that is a tributary of the Hopkins as indicated in figure 3 (15). It also sits above both waterways topographically as indicated in the contour mapping of figure 1 (8).

The 'Bushfire Management Overlay' (Equipe Lawyers 2020, figure 4, 16) indicates that there is bush on both sides of the river at this point. In fact, this is a beautiful, tree-lined stretch of the river with rocky outcrops and gently flowing water. Banjo Clarke and Robert Lowe write poignantly about this stretch of the river. I was there in May 2021 with Robert Lowe as my guide. When I asked him what he thought about the quarry, he said, "it will kill the river." Both sides of the Hopkins River at this point are an area of 'Aboriginal Cultural Heritage Sensitivity' (as we have seen previously with other areas along the Hopkins). The Report acknowledges "that parts of the Subject Land are within such an identified area" (figure 5, 21). This is one reason for locating the proposed quarry away from this area along the river.

Another reason is the presence of native vegetation along the river. The Report goes on to state that:

> No native vegetation removal is required for the Proposed Quarry and no threatened or endangered native fauna will be at risk due to the Proposed Quarry operations. (Equipe Lawyers 2020, 11)

All fauna and flora along the river and creek would be at risk in the event of a dam-burst and it would have a high visual impact for Framlingham. It is arrogance for the Report to state categorically that "there will be no potential for offsite impacts to flora and fauna" (Equipe Lawyers 2020, 6). All sediment dams have the potential for "offsite impacts" to flora and fauna. Built into a dam is the potential for an accident, either through mismanagement or an extreme rainfall event, or both, a perfect storm.

This site seems like a crazy place to propose locating a quarry. It is too close (horizontally and vertically) to the Hopkins River and to Framlingham. It sits above the Hopkins River and a creek that is a tributary of the river; it is on the other side of the Hopkins to Framlingham. The proposal seems like a continuation of colonization on neighbouring Aboriginal land. The conservation battle over the proposed quarry seems like a continuation of the struggle of the Framlingham community to have their neighbours respect them and their lands. For the reasons that the Report assembles in text and figures in different places, but does not bring together into a single picture as it would problematise the proposal, it is highly disputable that "the Proposed Quarry can be established with no impacts on the environmental values of […] the surrounding area [including the area of 'Aboriginal Cultural Heritage Sensitivity'] and the Hopkins River." There is only one conclusion: 'Save the Hopkins, Stop the Quarry.'

This is the same conclusion reached by the 'Save the Hopkins – Stop the Quarry' group. They have prepared and presented an impressive array of well-researched and substantiated documentation to support their case and cause. The group is chaired by Geoff Rollinson, also the Landcare Coordinator of the Heytesbury District Landcare Network. In September 2020 the group lodged an 'Objection to Planning Application' with Moyne Shire Council and respectfully requested that the Council *not* issue a planning permit for the proposed quarry (STHR-STQG 2020, 3).

Their first objection is "the most outstanding aspect of the applicant's submission[:] the lack of a cultural heritage management plan (CHMP)" (STHR-STQG 2020, 3). Consequently and in response the group engaged Amanda Boucher, Principal Cultural Heritage Advisor from A. B. Heritage Consulting, to assess whether a CHMP might be required. After considering the proposal, the site and relevant legislation, she concluded that in her professional view a CHMP is required and recommended that a CHMP be prepared (Boucher 2020, ii, 12).

Boucher reported in her "heritage due diligence assessment" many reasons for recommending that the preparation of a CHMP be required, including the fact that:

> approximately 15 ha of the subject land is located within 200 m of the Hopkins River and is included on the Victorian Aboriginal Heritage Register (VAHR) as a place of Aboriginal cultural heritage sensitivity, which means that use and development of this land is subject to Victorian Aboriginal Heritage Legislation. The VAHR was established by the *Aboriginal Heritage Act* 2006 (Act) and the *Aboriginal Heritage Regulations* 2018 (Regs) and provides statutory protection for all Aboriginal cultural heritage places, areas or relics, and private collections of relics in Victoria. (Boucher 2020, 3, 4, 5).

Besides the known areas of Aboriginal cultural heritage, Boucher also points out in her assessment that there is the potential for the discovery of currently unknown areas and relics of Aboriginal cultural heritage on the site of the proposed quarry. This is an additional reason for a CHMP, as Boucher (2020, ii, 13) argues:

> The preparation of a CHMP is recommended as a control measure to manage the 'Very High' and 'High' level of risk associated with harming any unknown Aboriginal cultural heritage that may exist within the subject land, since it is an indictable offence to harm Aboriginal cultural heritage, both tangible and intangible, under the Act (s. 27 Act).

The precautionary principle to minimise harm or risk should apply by preparing a CHMP.

Boucher emphasises that:

> *it is important to note that the risk of harming intangible Aboriginal cultural heritage is not assessed as part of this heritage due diligence assessment because it can only be determined in consultation with the Eastern Maar Aboriginal Corporation* (EMAC), the Registered Aboriginal Party (RAP) with responsibility for the subject land. Consultation with EMAC will be necessary during the preparation of any future cultural heritage assessments. (Boucher 2020, ii, 8; her emphasis)

Whether or not the proponent will be required to prepare a CHMP will be determined by a full hearing of the Victorian Civil and Administrative Tribunal (VCAT) in February 2022.

In addition to the preparation of a CHMP, the 'Objection to Planning

Application' prepared and submitted by the 'Save the Hopkins – Stop the Quarry' group concluded that the following "background reporting" should have been completed by the proponent as part of their proposal for the quarry:

- An Environmental Effects Statement (EES) based on the potential off-site impact of the proposed quarry;
- Flora/Fauna (Biodiversity) Assessment to map threatened species on site;
- Emergency Management Plan – fire, chemical spill, blasting accidents, sediment dam failure, etc;
- Dust Management Plan (including analysis via modelling using meteorological data to managepotential project risk);
- Noise Management Plan (including analysis via modelling using base noise management on variable topography to assess potential influence to managing noise and dust impact;
- Environmental Management Plan – incorporating a Weed and Pest Management Plan;
- Viewshed modelling and impact to neighbouring properties, Framlingham Forest IndigenousProtected Area [FFIPA], and cultural/ecotourist uses, including eel-trapping;
- Land Capability Assessment for onsite wastewater use on site (site office building amenities);
- Site Stormwater and Drainage Plan - incorporating intense rainfall events and sediment damcontingencies;
- Comprehensive Decommissioning Management Plan; and
- Geotechnical investigation (to include impact of blasting, extraction etc., on site stability). (STHR-STQG 2020, 3, 9)

In the absence of adequate reporting on these matters the group submitted that "the application does not contain sufficient information to make a decision and therefore [Moyne Shire] Council cannotbe expected to seriously entertain the application" (STHR-STQG 2020, 3).

The group also noted later the potential for intense and irregular weather events to carry vegetation-covering dust and contribute to increased turbidity in the watercourses (STHR-STQG 2020, 14), including the creek on the northern boundary of the site and the Hopkins River into which the creek flows. Groundwater flow would most likely be in this direction too and into the river. The group engaged consultants to undertake a desk top literature review of the hydrogeology of the site. It concluded that "waterways within the region are likely to be groundwater fed, such that the local flow of groundwater will be towards rivers and drainage lines [...] Groundwater flow, while within a regional context is to the south, locally will be from the site towards Hopkins River, driven by changes in topography " (CDM Smith 2021, iv, 10).

The group noted that the area has immense Aboriginal significance as "the Hopkins River features in song lines, which is how the indigenous community relates to, mind-maps and moves through the landscape" and that "the short-finned eel (Kuuyang) is an example of an important species culturally that may be impacted by degraded water quality" (STHR-STQG 2020, 11). In keeping with Brett Clarke's proposition presented in the first chapter of the present volume that "water is Aboriginal Culture on the Hopkins River" (Hughson, 2011), the group point out in their 'Objection' that:

> Anglo-Celtic land management and environmental planning processes have struggled with the notion that the natural environment has cultural values. For Aboriginal people, the entire landscape encompasses both archaic and living cultural dimensions and creation stories that provide a context within which the form of the country is understood, including totems existing in the form of plants and animals, and the six seasons that provide a natural rhythm. (STHR-STQG 2020, 33)

The nature-culture binary is problematic and damaging. It is historically contingent and culturally constructed. It privileges a masculinised active culture over a femininized passive nature and creates a hierarchy between them. The binary needs to be deconstructed and decolonized (as we have seen throughout the present volume). Reconstructing "cultures of natures," in which there is not one unitary or timeless nature or culture, is one way of doing so (see Giblett 2011). Aboriginal country leads the way.

Besides its significant fauna, the area contains significant flora as the group points out in their 'Objection':

> Vegetation bordering the Hopkins River and Forest area to the east contains an endangered EVC Riparian Woodland (FFG Act), with the entire site subject to increased Biodiversity Conservation Significance (DELWP2020). The Forest represents two threatened Ecological Communities: *Grassy Eucalypt Woodland and Natural Temperate Grassland of the Victorian Volcanic Plain* and two corresponding Ecological Vegetation Classes (EVCs): *Herb-rich Foothill Forest* (EVC23 – Vulnerable, Vic) and *Riparian Woodland* (EVC641 – Endangered, Vic). The Forest contains significant *Herb-rich Foothill Forest* (Vulnerable FFG Act) vegetation which includes stringybark and manna gum savannah that once dominated the landscape across much of southwest Victoria. (STHR-STQG 2020, 28)

The grasslands of the Victorian Volcanic Plain are a vital habitat of the bioregion (as we have seen on many occasions previously).

The same conclusion to stop the quarry and save the Hopkins is also reached by Jess Chatfield who grew up and lives at Framlingham. She is a proud Gunditjmara woman, part of the Maar nation. She tells a moving story on video about the importance of Country, the power of the magnificent Hopkins River, the connection to the Framlingham bush, and the safety and security of 'home':

> I have never campaigned before, but when I found out about this proposed quarry that will basically be in my backyard, I could not be silent. This will affect my community's whole way of life and I have made a video story about what is at stake and my fight so far. (Chatfield 2020).

Many conservationists start off as 'NIMBYs' ('Not in my Backyard') when their local area is threatened with ruination. NIMBYism can lead to a wider appreciation for the home of a bioregion and support for conservation there and elsewhere in the earth home ('Not in Anyone's Backyard').

Jess's video has some stunning aerial footage of the Hopkins River in the Framlingham area where the quarry is proposed. In the video she speaks passionately about her connection to country and voices her opposition to the proposed quarry. She points out that the noise and dust created by a quarry would impact severely on the cultural heritage and environmental values of the surrounding area, including the area of 'Aboriginal Cultural Heritage Sensitivity' of and along both sides of the Hopkins River. Her video is called *Leenyaa Merreeng: Grandmother Land*. Who would blast a quarry in a grandmother's land?

7.

WHERE THE RIVER MEETS THE SEA: THE HOPKINS ESTUARY

1 Thus the heavens and the earth were finished, and all the host of them. 2 And on the seventh day God ended his work which he had made; and he rested on the seventh day from all his work which he had made. 3 And God blessed the seventh day, and sanctified it: because that in it he had rested from all his work which God created and made. *Genesis* 2

The serpentine Hopkins River departs from its largely north to south course on its journey from its source near Ararat to the sea through the city of Warrnambool and does a series of abrupt westerly turns near the town of Allansford. At this point the river becomes an estuary where fresh water from the natural land drainage of the Hopkins River basin, including its creeks and wetlands, merges and mixes with salt water from the ocean. The water of the Hopkins basin comes to rest in its estuary ('restuary' for short). Yet unlike the end of the biblical story of creation, the Hopkins Estuary continues to do creative work.

This place is where the present volume comes to rest and reaches its end in this, the seventh and final chapter. It is also where the good ship *Middlemarsh* reaches its destination on its journey or voyage from source to sea. This chapter gives a guided tour of the intertwined natural and cultural history of the estuary for Aboriginal and colonial settlers. It also focusses on its fishes, anglers and birds, as well as on its environmental history and development pressures. The conclusion to the chapter finally considers recent Aboriginal artwork about the area and makes a plea for looking after the country of the Hopkins basin from source to sea as bioregional home habitats of the living earth for humans, plants and animals. *Middlemarsh* is coming to an end, but the work of caring for and looking after Middlemarsh, inspired and guided by the remarkable people who live and work, or lived and worked, in it is ongoing and continuous.

Warrnambool on the Estuary

Going downstream, the exit from the Hopkins River, or going upstream, the entrance to the river is located in the regional city of Warrnambool on the coast of the Bass Strait between the states of mainland Victoria and island Tasmania. Warrnambool was founded, developed and lives today on the banks of the Hopkins River. Warrnambool was made by the river.[50] It was also made on the coast. Warrnambool thinks of itself as more of a coastal city, than a riverine or estuarine one. Warrnambool has been spruiked as "a vibrant coastal city in southwest Victoria, the heart of a prosperous and diverse region and the fifth largest provincial city in Victoria" (Bantow, Rashleigh and Sherwood 1995, 1). The residents of Warrnambool are among the over 75% of all Australians who live on the coast (Bantow, Rashleigh and Sherwood 1995, 3). All the Australian state capital cities and Australia's most populous cities – Sydney, Melbourne, Brisbane, Perth/Fremantle, Adelaide and Hobart – were founded and developed on the coast, as were many large regional cities, such as Warrnambool. Coastal zones, "the area where land and sea meet, are ecologically very dynamic areas" (Bantow, Rashleigh and Sherwood 1995, 3). This dynamism is especially the case with Warrnambool in south-west Victoria as "it faces the world's most energetic ocean [—] the Southern Ocean" (Bantow, Rashleigh and Sherwood 1995, 60).

Most of these coastal Australian cities, including Warrnambool, are also located on an estuary. At the heart of the vibrant city and in the biodiverse bioregion of the Warrnambool plains lies the vital estuary of the Hopkins River, a fertile womb, or more precisely cloaca, next to which the city was born and grew. The Hopkins Estuary is also the creative place that helped Aboriginal people make environmental artwork celebrating its natural and cultural values (as we will see in the conclusion to the present chapter). The Hopkins River and its estuary helped make Warrnambool what it is today.

Estuaries are areas where land, river and sea meet and mix. They are liminal zones where fresh water and salt water mix, as with the Hopkins Estuary. It is like the Thames Estuary, "an ambiguous place" (Ackroyd 2009, 393), "an in-between space, neither one thing nor the other" (Crampton 2019, 11). Estuaries are "highly productive ecosystems [that] can be 20 times more productive than the open ocean" (Bantow, Rashleigh and Sherwood 1995, 9). Coastal zones are very dynamic and estuaries are very productive. An estuary has been defined as "a semi-enclosed body of water having a free connection with the open sea and within which sea water is measurably diluted with fresh water derived from land drainage" (Officer cited by Bantow, Rashleigh and Sherwood 1995, 19). An estuary is thus a body of water located between other bodies of water, such as a river, sea and wetlands, with a passageway between them through which fresh and salt water move and mix. A sand bar across this passageway can periodically open and close. The sand bar may rest on an underlying rock bar.

Such is the case with the Hopkins Estuary where a sand bar lies across the rocky 'mouth' of the river. Minor blasting took place at the entrance/exit to the Hopkins in the early twentieth century to create a more permanent opening (John Sherwood, pers. comm). The bar has been opened artificially on many occasions since, with often disastrous consequences such as when "during the […] sampling of bream larvae in the Hopkins Estuary in December 2003, an estimated total of 26,000 larvae per day were swept out to sea as a result of the estuary mouth being open." Opening the bar artificially is a vexed and contentious topic to which the *Hopkins Estuary Management Plan* devotes several pages trying to resolve without success (Glenelg Hopkins Catchment Management Authority 2005, 33-35).

The extent of the Hopkins Estuary is indisputable as its upstream extent is clearly marked by a basalt rock bar and it is contained within rocky banks. It is unlike the famous Thames River artificially embanked in London and the extent of whose estuary downstream of London is debatable (Lichtenstein 2017, 6-7). Also unlike the Thames Estuary where land and water mix in marshes creating "liminal areas […] neither water nor dry land" (Ackroyd 2009, 394), the Hopkins Estuary is not marshy, but rocky. Unlike many cities founded in, by or near wetlands, including most of the Australian capitals,[51] Warrnambool was founded on a rocky estuarine headland. London is a case in point of a city founded among wetlands that developed downstream into the Thames Estuary comprised of shifting, tidal sandbanks and salt marshes where land mixes with fresh and sea water, whereas in the Hopkins Estuary these waters mix in a series of pools "confined by a rock-walled canyon for much of its length" (Sherwood cited by Glenelg Hopkins Catchment Management Authority 2005, 13). Warrnambool, like many other cities, has developed and spread into its wetlands elsewhere, sometimes resulting in flooding, most recently in January 2021. Warrnambool has become a wetland city.

The 'mouth' of the Hopkins has not been developed as a port, unlike many estuarine cities with tidal marshes that made them more amenable for the development of docks. Probably the most famous of these is also London and the Thames Estuary that has a chequered history with development, dredging, conservation and rehabilitation at various points and places along its course. *Not* being developed as a port has meant that the Hopkins Estuary today is relatively unmodified, undeveloped and unpolluted, unlike the Thames Estuary.[52] Yet the Hopkins Estuary is like the Thames Estuary in one important respect. The delta of the Thames Estuary (Lichtenstein 2017, 297), or more precisely reverse delta of the Thames (Leardini, Ozgun and Mouils 2019, 241), is like the Hopkins Estuary in which salt water wedges upstream into the 'mouth' of the river from the coast of Bass Strait carrying sand and creating a reverse delta. It is also like the reverse delta of the Brisbane River in the city to which it gives its name. The 'mouth' of the Hopkins is both a salt wedge and a reverse delta.

The Victorian Fisheries Authority webpage for the estuary explains how the 'salt wedge' has:

denser sea water sitting on the bottom and fresh water flowing over the top. Sea water is denser because of its salt content. Mixing of the two layers is only slight and the seaward movement of river water pushes the salt water into a 'wedge' shape. At any point in the estuary you may be fishing in the fresh or salt water. The two water layers also tend to differ in temperature and dissolved oxygen levels. During a typical year the river experiences floods in winter and spring and only slight flows in summer and autumn. The salt wedge moves up and down the river as the flow changes. During years of low flows the entire estuary may become salty. Alternatively in years of extensive flooding the estuary may become entirely fresh with all seawater being flushed out. (Victorian Fisheries Authority, ND)

These waters of various depths and degrees of salinity create niche habitats for a variety species of fish that rely on their specific chemical composition (Bantow, Rashleigh and Sherwood 1995, 7-9, 25, 27-28).

The Victorian Fisheries Authority webpage for the estuary goes on to describe how:

salinity can affect the distribution of different species. The advancing salt wedge will assist the movement of bream and mulloway upstream, while freshwater inflows can push them closer towards the mouth or even out to sea during the wetter months. Short-finned eels and estuary perch are tolerant to freshwater and can be encountered well upstream of the estuary. (Victorian Fishers Authority, ND)

Gross disturbance of this fluctuating regime would have devastating consequences for the variety of fish species in the estuary who inhabit its niche habitats, for the anglers who frequent and fish in its waters and for the Aboriginal people who live in the region and spear or trap its eels.

The Hopkins River estuary and its coastal environs are an important area for Aboriginal people, and have been for tens of thousands of years. The *Hopkins Estuary Management Plan* states that:

The estuary marks the tribal border [or boundary] of the Kirrae Whurrong, Gunditjmara and Tjap Whurrong peoples and was a place for gatherings and trade. The wealth of natural resources provided by the river and estuary were, and are still, highly important to the Indigenous community. (Glenelg Hopkins Catchment Management Authority 2005, 1, 25)

The Victorian Fisheries Authority website concurs (Victorian Fisheries Authority ND). Both this website and the *Management Plan* do not mention that the estuary is also culturally significant for the Pik Wurrung peoples and marks their eastern tribal border or boundary (Dawson 1881, 1-2). Both do not also mention that the area also includes "sites of spiritual significance and the resources necessary for [sustaining] semi-permanent residence[s] along the banks" of the river (Bantow, Rashleigh and Sherwood 1995, 33). These residences are indicative of Aboriginal settlement of the area and of their civilization in the area.

The traditional Aboriginal name for the 'mouth'/cloaca (outflow and inflow, exit and entrance) of the Hopkins River near Point Ritchie is *'moyjil'* (Clark 2009, table 8.1). A midden at Moyjil "has been dated as 60,000-80,000 years old" (Bantow, Rashleigh and Sherwood 1995, 37). It may be as old as 120,000 years (John Sherwood, pers. comm.). John showed me this midden in May 2021. I was shocked and amazed that it had no physical protection and no interpretative signage, unlike other sites in the area.

The 'Tooram Stones' south of Allansford are one of several flows of basalt that once crossed the subsurface of the earth at various depths and create varying depths of water in the Hopkins Estuary, including 'plunge pools' with the one at Tooram Stones up to ten metres deep and shallows, such as at 'The Pass' at Jubilee Park with water about a metre deep (Sherwood, 1982; Bantow, Rashleigh and Sherwood 1995, iii; figure 2.2, 21). John Sherwood's (1982) *Angler's Map of the Hopkins River Estuary* fold-ups to an A5 pocket size map and folds out to a double-sided A3 size sheet. It shows the length, breadth and indicates the water depths at mid-tide and the dangers of the estuary. These waters of varying depths comprise waters of varying degrees of salinity and freshness with an intermediary 'mixing zone' between the overlying layer of fresh water and the 'salt wedge' of a underlying layer of salt water (as illustrated in a vertical profile and longitudinal cross-section of the estuary; Sherwood, 1982; Bantow, Rashleigh and Sherwood 1995, 20; figure 2.2, 21; figure 2.4, 24).

Maps of the Hopkins River Catchment and the estuary (Bantow, Rashleigh and Sherwood 1995, iii; figure 1.1, 2; figure 1.2, 4; figure 2.3, 23) show the estuary as not too dissimilar in shape to that of the bowel or bladder in animal anatomy, and the cloaca in embryos (including humans), in anatomical illustrations at the bottom of the digestive tract (see, for instance, *Gray's Anatomy*, figure 977). The estuary is a cloaca (as discussed in the first chapter of the present volume). It is both an excretory and reproductive organ, an exit for, and entrance to, the life-giving water of the river and habitat for its living creatures. It is a vital part of the body of the earth. Traditional, pre-modern cultures figure the earth as body or the body as earth; modern cultures figure the body as machine (Giblett 2008).

The Hopkins River estuary is "a nursery" for eleven species of fish, eight of which are desirable catch for amateur anglers (Bantow, Rashleigh and Sherwood 1995, 9). The Victorian Fisheries Authority webpage for the estuary states that:

> Popular with both local and visiting anglers, it provides a premier fishing experience for highly valued recreational species such as black bream, estuary perch, mulloway, yellow eye mullet, Australian salmon, and short-finned eels. (Victorian Fisheries Authority, ND)

The presence and activities of two angling clubs on the river, one at Jubilee Park in the Allansford area and the other in Warrnambool, indicate the richness of the river's fish stocks and their popularity among local anglers. In total, thirty-nine species of fish are known to inhabit the estuary (Glenelg Hopkins Catchment Management Authority 2005, 1, 22).

The Hopkins River estuary is unlike the Murray River estuary in South Australia with its iconic and internationally important Coorong wetlands, its highly engineered water regime, its infamous pelican slaughter of the early twentieth century and its recent struggles over seals and carp between commercial fishers, state government and indigenous peoples (O'Gorman 2021, 3-5, 120-140, 168-193).[53] The Coorong is also a fascinating place for Richard Weatherly (2020, 66-71) who has painted its wetlandscape and some of its birds, including pelicans that we have encountered previously during our ramble along the river. The Hopkins is only open to recreational fishers with bag limits for catches, minimum size limits for different species and closed seasons for different species too (Victorian Fisheries Authority, ND). The Victorian Fisheries Authority has an office in Warrnambool where Fisheries Officers are stationed as a rule. Presumably they undertake regular patrols on land and water of the Hopkins River and its fishing spots and conduct inspections of catches to ensure compliance with these regulations.

Short-finned eels are among the noteworthy figures of spiritual significance and resources of physical sustenance associated with the Hopkins for local Aboriginal peoples. Eels are "a powerful cultural symbol for the local Gunditjmara people" (Victorian Fisheries Authority, ND). The estuary of "the Hopkins River is a major distribution river for eel migration in Western Victoria" (Bantow, Rashleigh and Sherwood 1995, 10). Like the short-finned Australian eel (*Anguilla australis, kooyang* or *kuuyang*), the European eel (*Anguilla anguilla*) is a powerful cultural symbol and source of sustenance for the local people of the English Fens (as related graphically, for instance, in Graham Swift's *Waterland;* Swift 1983, 197-206). In the seventeenth century Izaak Walton (2016, 121, 123) in *The Compleat Angler,* the classic book that celebrates the joys of fishing in England, relates how the European eel is *'The Queen of palat[e] pleasure.'* By contrast to Robert Lowe who masculinises the Australian eel (as we saw in the previous chapter), Walton feminises the European eel. He goes on to relate that "the European eel is bred in Rivers that relate to, or be nearer to the Sea." In other words, the European eel is an estuarine species of fish, like its Australian counterpart in the Hopkins Estuary.

The traditional Aboriginal name for the Hopkins Estuary is '*tuuram*' (Clark 2009, table 8.1; citing Dawson 1881, p.lxxxii) which translates as "salmon" (Glenelg Hopkins Catchment Management Authority 2005, 25). The Australian salmon (*Arripis truttagea*) is an estuarine species of fish like its English counterpart, the Atlantic salmon (*Salmo salar*). Walton (2016, 92) in *The Compleat Angler* "accounted [the Atlantic salmon as] the King of fresh-water fish, and is ever bred in Rivers relating to the Sea, yet so high or far from it as admits of no tincture of salt, or brackishness." Walton masculinises the Atlantic salmon. The Aboriginal name for the Australian salmon gives its name to the Hopkins Estuary as "the King" of its waters that is a home to "the Queen of [antipodean] palate pleasure," the Australian eel.

Walton's *Compleat Angler* is not just a classic book about fishing, but also a timely reminder about the importance of water for all life. Referring to *Genesis* 1: 2 (cited in the epigraph to the introduction to the present volume), Walton instructs his readers that "the *water* is the eldest daughter of the Creation, the Element upon which the Spirit of God did first move, the Element which God commanded to bring forth living creatures abundantly" (Walton 2016, 26; his emphasis). In Walton's gloss on the biblical verse, God the Father creates water the daughter upon which God the Spirit then moves. The daughter, in turn, gives birth to abundant living creatures. In Walton's account, God the Father is the primary creator, God the Spirit is the procreator, and water the daughter is the womb out of which new life springs.

In other than Walton's and biblical terms, swamps and other wetlands are the 'Great Mother' or 'Great Goddess' out of whose womb new life springs and into whose tomb old life dies to be reborn in the perpetual cycle of life, death, and new life (see Giblett 1996). Walton neglects this aspect of water, yet reminds his readers that water is "the chiefest [Element] in mixtion of all living creatures." He also points to the belief of some that "all bodies are made of *water*" (Walton and Cotton 2016, 26; his emphasis). The human body is mainly water and the body of the earth is mainly water too – more than 60% in both bodies and cases.

Fishing with Thoreau

On his river journey Thoreau (1998, 22) remembers 'the Walton' of the Concord River for whom "fishing was not a sport, nor solely a means of subsistence, but a sort of solemn sacrament and withdrawal from the world, just as the aged read their Bibles." Like Walton himself and Thoreau, the Walton of the Concord may have contemplated *Genesis* 1: 2 and the watery first day of creation. Like Walton, Thoreau and Thales, the Walton of the

Concord may have contemplated water as the first element. The white-fella Walton of the Hopkins may have contemplated the creativity of water in Mesopotamian mythology and the primacy of watery wetlands. The Aboriginal Walton of the Hopkins may have contemplated the Rainbow Serpent as a sacral being and river.

All these Waltons are complete anglers who "attend to the nature of fishes." Thoreau (1998, 22) continues on his river journey by contemplating that "whether we live by the seaside, or by the lakes and rivers, or on the prairie, it concerns us to attend to the nature of fishes, since they are not phenomena confined to certain localities only, but forms and phases of the life in nature universally dispersed." Attending to the nature of the fishes of the Hopkins shows that they are not confined to the estuary, nor in the upper river, but "universally dispersed" as the comparisons between Walton's discussion of eels and salmon and the Hopkins' eels and salmon shows. Howard Brandenburg certainly attends to the nature of fishes (as we have seen in a previous chapter of the present volume).

Attending to the nature of fishes for Thoreau is a means to the end of contemplating nature. It is not fishing, a means to the end of catching fish. He continues that:

> The natural historian is not a fisherman, who prays for cloudy days and good luck merely, but as fishing has been styled 'a contemplative man's recreation,' introducing him profitably to woods and water, so the fruit of the naturalist's observations is not in new genera or species, but in new contemplations still, and science is only a more contemplative man's recreation. (Thoreau 1998, 22-23)

The aim of science for Thoreau is not to discover and name new species or genera, nor to study nature as a job, but to contemplate as a recreation the economy of nature, or ecology, the processes of nature:

> It enhances our sense of the grand security and serenity of nature, to observe the still undisturbed economy and content of the fishes of this century, their happiness a regular fruit of the summer. (Thoreau 1998, 23)

Attending to the nature of fishes is locating them not only in space, here in this place, of this county or country, but also in time, now in the cycle of the seasons and in this century. Attending to fishes is contemplating the sacrament of nature.

Attending to the nature of fishes for Thoreau (1998, 46) is also more affective for contemplating nature than science:

> modern ingenious sciences and arts do not affect me as those more venerable arts of hunting and fishing, and even of husbandry in its

primitive and simple form; as ancient and honorable trades as the sun and moon and winds pursue, coeval with the faculties of man, and invented when these were invented.

Thoreau (1982, 351) wrote in *Walden* that "time is but the stream I go a-fishing in." There is plenty of time with the Hopkins River to go fishing in the stream of time from 30 million years ago with its geological formation, through human habitation 120,000 years ago to the present.

Thoreau fished in his own stream of time and wrote in his journal about his observations and own experience of fishing. On 26th January 1853 Thoreau (1962, *IV*, 480) wrote that:

> It is remarkable that many men will go with eagerness to Walden Pond in the winter to fish for pickerel and yet do not seem to care for the landscape. Of course it cannot be *merely* for the pickerel they may catch. There is some adventure in it, but any love of nature which they may feel is certainly very slight and indefinite. They call it going a-fishing and so indeed it is, though perchance their nature know better. Now I go a-fishing and a-hunting every day, but omit the fish and the game, which are the least important part. I have learned to do without them. They were indispensable only as long as I was a boy.

In adulthood Thoreau (1982, 459) wrote in *Walden* that "no humane being, past the thoughtless age of boyhood, will wantonly murder any creature which holds its life by the same tenure that he does. The hare in its extremity cries like a child."

Hunting and fishing for Thoreau (1982, 459) are:

> oftenest the young man's introduction to the forest, and the most original part of himself. He goes thither at first as a hunter and fisher, until at last, if he has the seeds of a better life in him, he distinguishes his proper objects, as a poet or naturalist it may be, and leaves the gun and fish-pole behind.

He left the gun behind as we saw in a previous chapter, though he concedes "I see that if I were to live in a wilderness I should again be tempted to become a fisher and hunter in earnest" (Thoreau 1982, 460). Thoreau became a poet *and* a naturalist whose "proper objects" of contemplative recreation and sacrament were not dead animals, but living beings. In *The Maine Woods* he wrote that "every creature is better alive than dead, men and moose and pine-trees, and he who understands it aright will rather preserve its life than destroy it" (Thoreau 1988, 164).

The Incomplete Angler

For most anglers on the Hopkins, fishing is a 'sport' and not a sort of solemn sacrament. One such angler was 'Pike' who penned a newspaper article in the nineteenth-century. He is not Thoreau of the Hopkins who cares for the landscape (except for when it conforms to conventional aesthetic norms) and loves nature (except for when it provides an abundance of fish). He is also not the Walton of the Hopkins who fishes for subsistence or physical sustenance, sacramental contemplation and spiritual nurture. He is unlike the Walton of the Concord. In 1871 'Pike' waxed lyrical in the pages of *The Australasian* weekly newspaper that:

> The Western District can claim precedence for many things — its beautiful scenery, incomparable arable land, yielding fabulous crops of the mealy potato [!...] and a steady-going, well to-do population much given to hospitality. But the thing which delighted me most on my arrival at Warrnambool was my first glimpse of the River Hopkins [...] There are very few rivers in the colony that would excel it from an angler's point of view, it being perfectly open to the sea, with good deep water, which can be fished anywhere from both banks for a distance of nearly nine miles. This is a great advantage to the majority of anglers, as it avoids the necessity of counting boat-hire as one of the items of expense. ('Pike' 1871)

'Pike' goes on to compare the pure air and water of the Hopkins River to the polluted air and water of the Maribyrnong River in Melbourne that:

> must play second fiddle when brought into contrast with the Hopkins. The latter is twice, and in many places four times, as wide as our river, and is bordered by the most beautiful scenery, without any drawbacks such as wool-washing, boiling-down, tannery, and other establishments, to taint the air and pollute the water. Those places no doubt are very useful; but it would take a better argument than I have ever heard yet to persuade me that they have any right to make a common sewer and a future source of pestilence of what should be an element of health and recreation. On the Hopkins it is just the opposite. The river is as pure as are the waters of the Southern Ocean, which sends its spray in thunder over the reef at its entrance.

Both the Maribyrnong and Yarra Rivers were polluted, open sewers at the time (Giblett 2020b, chapter 8).

After giving an accurate description of the physical features of the place, 'Pike' goes on to paint a rosy picture of a rural idyll with upper and lower classes living in blissful harmony with each other and with nature on the banks of the Hopkins River:

The scenery from its mouth up is lovely and varied. In some places it is hemmed in by precipitous rocks of yellow sandstone, out of the crevices of which shrubs and trees hang suspended; then beautiful slopes, like an English deer-park, dotted here and there with the substantial villa of the independent gentleman and the humble cot of the labourer, followed by fields under cultivation, which give place to the bush in a perfect state of nature; then sandy points and rugged-looking reefs, leading up to islands; and so on, as far as I went at least. These, indeed, are the scenes which are calculated to soothe and elevate the mind.

"Rugged-looking reefs" are Pike's description of the basalt rock flows across the estuary. "Beautiful slopes like an English deer-park" and "the bush in a perfect state of nature" were the product of Aboriginal fire practices. "The Islands" are located in the estuary opposite Jubilee Park. Hannaford (1860, 114-115) on his river-side ramble of the Hopkins estuary noted "a little picturesque island," which was "a burial site" for early colonial settlers and became "endeared" to them.

After two hours of unsuccessfully "plying the hickory" upstream "without even a nibble" in one of the plunge pools that was "a most romantic spot" and that looked "fishy" to his "unsophisticated eye," 'Pike' anchored downstream opposite the boathouse where:

> The water [...] was very shallow, not more than four or five feet. The boat being anchored close to the weeds, [...] in about a minute I had a bream about three quarters of a pound floundering in the basket [...] In less than five minutes I had a splendid run, and after some fine play, succeeded in landing a splendid fellow over 3lb. [pound] weight. Fish after fish was taken, but none so large as my second. By tea-time we had about 50 fish, from half a-pound to a pound-and-a-quarter. This I did not think a bad day's sport, taking all things into consideration; but it is not thought anything of here.

A local angler tells Pike he would never have caught anything at his first location if he fished there for three months. Pike concludes, "so much for not knowing the peculiarities of the river." Armed with local knowledge, "on the last morning I was there I killed 75 good fish, varying from half a-pound up to two pounds, in the short space of three hour." He is not fishing for subsistence, or for physical and spiritual sustenance. He is the incomplete angler.

Fishing relies on local knowledge of the peculiarities of the river and the good fishing spots along it. Fishing requires an appreciation for place, at least as fish habitat. Fishers tend to be focussed on fish and abstract them from the fish's habitat before extracting them from it where they cannot live for long. An appreciation for place could lead to an appreciation of the bioregion, including the estuary and its geology, hydrology and biology, such as other animals beside fish that live there. An appreciation for place could lead to an appreciation of the Aboriginal people who lived and gained a livelihood from the bioregion for tens of thousands of years.

No such appreciation was expressed either by the rambling Horace Wheelwright (1861, 243) who claimed in his guide to the "field sports" of 'Australia Felix' that:

> very little can be said respecting the angling, or river-fishing, in Victoria [… N]othing struck me more than the insignificance of the rivers in this part of the colony; they are, in fact, little more than creeks – many of them merely a succession of water-holes [chain of ponds?] during the summer choked with high reeds and bulrushes; the banks of others stony, steep and rugged, or grown up with small trees which overhang and nearly meet at the top.

While Wheelwright's description of rivers with "banks stony, steep and rugged" applies to much of the Hopkins Estuary, 'Pike's' praise for its accessibility in other places for fishing and its abundance of fish demonstrates that is not an insignificant river for angling.

Nor is it an insignificant river for birds, both upstream (as we have seen on our ramble along the river in chapter 4 of the present volume) and downstream in the estuary. According to the management plan for the estuary, at least thirty-three species of birds have been recorded in the area, ten of which are on the Threatened Wildlife of Victoria listing and two of which are listed under the China-Australia Migratory Bird Agreement (CAMBA) (Glenelg Hopkins Catchment Management Authority 2005, 1, 21). Logan's Beach on the eastern side of the mouth/cloaca of the Hopkins River is a noted whale-watching site (Bantow, Rashleigh and Sherwood 1995, 7). The presence and sight of charismatic megafauna is one of "some outstanding natural values" (6) of the area. The evidence of Aboriginal presence in the past is one of some outstanding cultural values of the area.

Environmental Writing

Tuuram is not only the Aboriginal name for the estuary of the Hopkins River and the "coastal environs" where the river meets the sea in the Bass Strait. It has also been used as the title of a book about these areas (Bantow, Rashleigh and Sherwood 1995). The present chapter has drawn extensively on *Tuuram* already as it is a valuable source book for many of the topics discussed previously. *Tuuram* presents the environmental and human history of this area from ancient Aboriginal times to the 1990s. It is an interdisciplinary study drawing on archaeology, anthropology, geology, geography, natural history and zoology. The book is also part of an exemplary multimedia project combining artwork, video and creative writing. The book and project presents "the environmental and heritage values of Warrnambool's Hopkins River estuary and coastal environs" (v). Both also arose out of an exemplary "university-community partnership" (v) between academic staff of the Warrnambool campus of Deakin University led by local scientist John Sherwood with local artists, librarians, musicians and writers (vi-vii). They aim for conservation of the natural and cultural values of the area and their proper management, especially in getting local residents to appreciate these values and look after the estuary.

Tuuram presents some of the outstanding natural history and values of the area before presenting the cultural history and values of the area, including the outstanding cultural history and values of the area for Aboriginal people. *Tuuram* gives far more weight to presenting a lengthy discussion of colonial heritage and imperial history than to discussing Aboriginal heritage and indigenous history. Its implied readership seems to be local non-Aboriginal people, especially amateur anglers, such as when it abstracts fish from their habitat by presenting the list of fish species who inhabit the estuary nearly 20 pages before the account of their habitat of the estuary (Bantow, Rashleigh and Sherwood 1995, 7-9, 25, 27-28). Fish cannot live out of water. Fish cannot breed, be nursed and grow big enough to be caught without the womb and cradle of the estuary. Amateur anglers should value and conserve the estuary.

Tuuram acknowledges that "the Hopkins Estuary area is a special place for Warrnambool. It is an aspect of what defines Warrnambool to its community and to others, an essential part of the city's culture and a favourite place for an enormous variety of passive and active recreation activities" (Bantow, Rashleigh and Sherwood 1995, 11). It is not a place for commercial activities. Two pages later *Tuuram* acknowledges that the Hopkins Estuary "holds deep historic value" for the Aboriginal people of the area who "have lived here for thousands of years" (13). It holds present day value too. Despite their longevity, residence and ownership, a more extensive discussion of them is relegated to the third chapter of 'People in the Area' (33-37). Aboriginal people are put on a par with European explorers and colonizers as mere "people in the area" and "regional inhabitants," rather than acknowledged as the first nations, the traditional owners, users and inhabitants of their lands who were dispossessed of them and who are still residents in them today. Belatedly *Tuuram* acknowledges that what it calls "the bond" between Aboriginal people of the area and the Hopkins River estuary is "created through interaction with one another" (77). It also continues to be maintained through interaction. This bond is maternal, mutually beneficial and symbiotic. It is a bond from which those current residents who parasitically live off the estuary could learn in how to care for country.

After the five-page presentation of the cultural history and values of the area for Aboriginal people, the following fourteen pages of chapter three of *Tuuram* are devoted to discussing the colonial cultural history and heritage values of the area, including a detailed account of 'European History' (37-38); 'Settlement' (38-39; that is, European settlement, and not Aboriginal settlement mentioned earlier (33)); 'First Subdivisions along the Coast and Estuary' (39-40); 'Commercialisation of the Estuary' (including three hotels; 40-42); 'Some Early Homes' (43-47; that is, colonial settlers' homes, rather than Aboriginal settlers' homes); 'Rowing and Angling' (47-48); 'Jubilee Park' (landscaped to celebrate Queen Victoria's 50th year of reign in 1887; 48-49); 'Artists on the River' (49-50; that is, European artists and photographers, such as Daniel Clark and George Webb, and not Aboriginal artists); and 'Tragedies on the River,' including the infamous sinking of the *Nestor* in 1921 in which 10 people drowned (50-51). By presenting first the outstanding natural values of the area before its outstanding cultural values (including Aboriginal ones), *Tuuram* foregrounds and privileges scientific knowledge over human experience, the sciences over the humanities, natural history over human history, European art over Aboriginal art. By giving a detailed and extensive account of colonial heritage and imperial history, including later of Proudfoots Boathouse (68-70), *Tuuram* privileges them over Aboriginal heritage and indigenous history.

Development Pressure

The banks of the Hopkins Estuary on both sides are under development pressure from suburban sprawl. A proposal in 1993 for an unsewered development "to create waterfront lots" opposite Jubilee Park on the south side was eventually rejected by the Victorian Administrative Appeals Tribunal (Bantow, Rashleigh and Sherwood 1995, 17). The successful appeal was led by John Sherwood (pers. comm.). The Motang Park development further downstream on the eastern side of the estuary with its 'Riverview Terrace' demonstrates Australians' love of a water-view, that banal feature of coastal suburban Australia. It also represents a token allocation of public space with access to the river held as 'common property' by a 'body corporate' versus the mercenary desire to cash in on the greater dollar value of private waterfront lots with river views (Bantow, Rashleigh and Sherwood 1995, 70-72). This is yet another instance of the tragedy of improvement of colonial settlers enclosing the commons into private property.

Warrnambool Cemetery on the western side of the river on the hillside above Proudfoot's Boathouse overlooks the river and provides excellent views of it. The dead have some of the best views of the tranquil lower Hopkins where they hopefully rest in peace. The cemetery is also "like an open air museum, full of stories and links to the past" (Bantow, Rashleigh and Sherwood 1995, 14). The estuarine cemetery is a link between the past and present of the river. On the north side of the estuary the eastward spread of Warrnambool's suburban development currently finishes at Mahoney's Road with Deakin University on the other side of the road. This is obviously an attractive development site for the university that could improve its bottom line by liquifying this solid asset. At present, there are no plans to do so (John Sherwood, email to author July 3, 2021).

After undertaking an extensive process of community consultation and research in 2004 for a management plan for the estuary, the Glenelg Hopkins Catchment Management Authority published the plan in 2005 in which it outlined:

Some of the most significant threats to the estuary's ongoing health include:

- residential development along the estuary's length with an associated increase in the volume of stormwater flowing into the system,
- the effect of poor water quality from the upper catchment,
- pest plants and animals, and,
- artificial river mouth openings. (Glenelg Hopkins Catchment Management Authority 2005, 1)

Recently and specifically, John Sherwood sees two major threats to the estuary:

(1) Climate change may act to change the estuary in several ways over the coming decades. A predicted decrease in rainfall is likely to see more frequent and longer mouth closure periods. This may interfere with seasonal fish migrations into and out of the estuary. A reduction in winter flood flows may also mean less flushing of aged, anoxic seawater from the estuary - essential for the successful breeding of some estuarine species.

(2) Increasing urbanisation along the estuary is a concern in the more immediate future. Urban runoff contains high concentrations of nutrients, oils and other domestic chemicals. If septic tanks become more common nutrient release into groundwater and then into the estuary may increase. The estuary may experience more serious algal blooms — particularly during closed mouth conditions over summer and autumn as it acts as a receiving water for this runoff. (email to author July 3, 2021)

The estuary is at the bottom (and is the bottom anatomically) of the Hopkins basin and receives water of whatever quality from it, whether it likes it or wants it or not.

Environmental Artwork

Revaluing and appreciating the Hopkins River, its water, wetlands, basin and estuary, and their connection to human bodies and the earth can be cultivated and nurtured through environmental artwork. A recent exhibition in the Warrnambool Art Gallery called 'Mirteetch Meering (Sea Country)' held from January to June 2021 goes a long way to foregrounding the outstanding cultural history and values of the area for Aboriginal people through the work of Aboriginal artists. The exhibition is introduced and described by the Gallery on its website as:

> Featuring new works that celebrate the South West Coastline by 'sand artist' Lowell Hunter 'Salty One' (Nyul Nyul/Bardi), along with works from the Warrnambool Art Gallery Collection by First Nations artists Fiona Clarke (Kirrae Whurrong) and Lisa Waup (Gunditjmara /Torres Strait Islander). *Sea Country* invites you to immerse yourself in our coastal wonders, ancient Aboriginal culture and traditions with a focus on Moyjil – at the entrance to [or exit of] the Hopkins River. (Warrnambool Art Gallery 2021)

John Sherwood supplied a timeline for the exhibition which, as the director of the Gallery put it in her 'Message' in the catalogue, "suggests that First Nations people gathered at the midden [at Moyjil] 120,000 years ago" (Gerrans 2021, 2).

One of Lisa Waup's works, 'Cradled,' is described on the accompanying title card as made of "screen printed bull kelp, emu feathers, upholstery cotton." Its materials express local, natural, indigenous and colonial history and culture; its title a reminder that 'Mirteetch Meering' is a cradle for nurturing the life of all four. 'Cradled' weaves together an individual indigenous life-story and colonial history by weaving a basket with "whatever material is available" (O'Gorman 2021, 35). The basket-like shape of 'Cradled' reminds me of Joanne Francis's womb-like baskets (Giblett 2021c, 126-130). Both artists' baskets express the reality that watery places, such as estuaries and wetlands, are wombs for the creation of new life. They are places of being born, or in a word, natality, a term coined by the twentieth-century philosopher, Hannah Arendt, in her thesis on love (Giblett 2021c, 17, 132-33, 188). Her philosophy of being born (and born again) counters Martin Heidegger's morbid, solipsistic philosophy of being towards death. Death is a part of life, but new life is born in an eternal return and cycle of birth, life, death, birth, etc., as in wetlands.

Another of Waup's (2021) works included in the exhibition is featured on the cover of the catalogue. 'Seaing Land,' is woven of emu and parrot feathers, kelp leaf, dyed pandanus and cotton, again using "whatever material is to hand" in an act of what the structural anthropologist Claude Lévi-Strauss called 'bricolage.' More than mere condescending 'craft,' bricolage is an act of story-telling and myth-making in the sense of telling stories to live by and make meaning, not in the sense of a false account. More than mere decorative 'textile art,' weaving is a case in point. Aboriginal weaving, as O'Gorman (2021, 26, 34) puts it, "is a way of being on and caring for Country." In Waup's case it is also a matter of being in and caring for sea Country. Country is the sea and the land (Webb 1996, 69-70). 'Seaing Land' weaves together the Hopkins River, the sea land, and the land under the sea of 'Mirteetch Meering' in disparate materials. Weaving and Country are not ways of seeing as in landscape painting, but ways of being on, in and with Country (see Webb 1996), of seaing land. Waup's bricolagic weavings decolonize colonial history and culture and affirm local, natural and indigenous story by cradling sea Country and seaing land. The Hopkins River is born from the womb of wetlands in and near the rugged mountains of Gariwerd, flows through and nurtures the fertile, sweeping plains of 'Australia Felix' and comes to rest cradled in the estuary of the sea country of Mirteetch Meering before issuing into the sea at Moyjil.

These two works with their kelp might still have a briny smell if the gallery-goer could get close enough to them to experience it. Such a smelly odour is a reminder that one of the denigratory qualities patriarchal societies have held against fertile places, such as estuaries and wetlands, is their uncanny odour that overcomes the mastery of sight and plunges the viewing subject into visceral and sensual intimacy with the viewed object in what Julia Kristeva called 'the abject' (Giblett 1996, 2021). The abject is neither subject nor object; it precedes and refuses the grammatical and philosophical distinction between them. It is associated with what Kristeva calls "powers of horror" (Giblett 1996, 2021). The uncanny odour of fertile spaces of natality is an abject of horror where the repressed and feminised monstrous resides in the mind of patriarchal men.

'Sand artist' Lowell Hunter's (2021) environmental artwork in the Mirteetch Meering exhibition is a performative piece that involved Aboriginal people dancing in the sand at Moyjil. The performance was filmed and photographed from the air using a drone to become a moving and still artwork displayed as part of the exhibition. It retells the story and song of the place traced in lines in the sand that are ephemeral and will be washed away by the next storm sea surge upstream or river outflow downstream, but that will live on in photographs and on film. This tracing in the sand decolonizes and deconstructs the inscription of the nearby city of Warrnambool on the surface of the earth. Traces in the sand are ephemeral and performative, whereas the inscription of the city on the surface of the earth is monumental and permanent. These differences align with two different cultural paradigms, the matrifocal and the patriarchal and with two different kinds of writing, the trace and the inscription (see Giblett 2011, figure 2, 32-34). They also align with the valuing of vital wetlands in indigenous and matrifocal cultures, or their denigration and destruction and the privileging of drylands in colonial agriculture, urban architecture and patriarchal culture generally.

Starting in November 2020, two months before the 'Mirteetch Meering (Sea Country)' exhibition, and closing a week before it, local artist Megan Nicolson (2021) created a mixed media and interactive installation and environment for the young and young-at-heart in the entry space to the Warrnambool Art Gallery. The installation was called 'Soggy Homes: the Wonder of Wetlands' and focussed on south-west Victorian wetlands. The sea and river country of the Hopkins River estuary was, and is, a soggy home for humans, plants and animals. The watery places of the Hopkins River basin and catchment from source to sea with its kindred wetlands are too. Please help look after them.

APPENDICES:

THREE REVIEWS OF RECENT BOOKS ABOUT WETLANDS, WETLAND HUMANITIES AND THE ENVIRONMENTAL HUMANITIES

Wetlands in a Dry Land: More-Than-Human-Histories of the Murray-Darling Basin. By Emily O'Gorman. University of Washington Press. Seattle. 2021. xviii + 261. US$30 paperback. ISBN: 978-0-295-74915-0.

Wetlands in a Dry Land (hereafter *Wetlands*) assembles a vast amount of valuable archival and ethnographic research into an interdisciplinary study and environmental history of some of the wetlands of the Murray-Darling Basin. Particularly valuable is its ethnography of Aboriginal weaving using native plants, such as sedge, and "whatever material is available," (p.35) such as raffia, as a means of connecting to and caring for Country in the present and for the future. Succeeding chapters are devoted to informative and valuable case studies of specific wetland sites and to issues with wetlands in the Basin, their use and the role of some "more-than-human" actors and agents, such as malaria, mosquitoes, ducks, pelicans and seals. Acknowledging the role of these actors and agents, and writing them back into history, is one of the invaluable contributions that *Wetlands* makes to the appreciation of wetlands and should make for their conservation, though *Wetlands* does not tie its colours too firmly to that mast. It makes the case for "reimagining wetlands" (pp.196, 197) more than for actually conserving them. The former may or may not lead to the latter. Conserving them relies on reimagined and real ecologies.

Despite its protestations about foregrounding gender among its "approaches," ecofeminism is absent from *Wetlands*, especially in relation to the feminisation of wetlands and the masculinisation of draining or filling them as discussed in the literature. Similarly, class is numbered among *Wetlands'* "approaches," but this does not lead to a Marxist ecology of wetlands and a critique of the enclosing of the wetlands commons into private property (and draining wetlands into drylands). Such a political critique is directly pertinent to chapter 5 in *Wetlands* on pelicans and carp. *Wetlands* neglects politics, especially the vital role Greens' politicians and wetland conservationists have played at the state and federal levels in the conservation of wetlands in Australia over the past 30 years, including the ones discussed in *Wetlands*, and their critical contribution to struggles over water politics and for wetland conservation in the Murray-Darling Basin.

Wetlands is firmly and resolutely placed within the disciplines of ethnography, environmental history, natural history and scientific ecology with many of their strengths and weaknesses. *Wetlands* demonstrates the strengths of environmental history, such as thorough and exhaustive archival research and assembling a vast array of descriptive and detailed data in accounts of important episodes in the environmental history of the wetlands of the basin.

Wetlands also demonstrates the weaknesses of environmental history. These include the wood not being seen for the trees, with the bigger picture, the longer historical view, the deeper environmental philosophy and the wider cultural context of wetlands in western cultures and struggles over their conservation. These are lost in the overwhelming attention to detail and the failure to theorise what is at stake here environmentally, culturally and politically, such as urban development, farming practices, wetland conservation, land health (including wetland health) and the future of human and more-than-human life on planet earth.

For instance, the chapter devoted to whether ducks are to blame for damage to rice paddies describes in great detail the irresolvable difference between farmers' anecdotes and scientists' data. These competing views are permitted to co-exist side by side as merely different "imagined ecologies" operating in implicit functionalism. Yet ducks and wetlands are sites of struggle for competing interests and investments, including ways of making meaning about them in discourses and stories.

The concept of 'wetland' is also a site of semiotic struggle. *Wetlands'* informative discussion of the history of the concept of 'wetland,' especially in relation to the Ramsar convention and its adoption by Australian governments, brings to the fore the conflict between scientists, politicians, bureaucrats and NGOs over the definition of wetlands. This invaluable discussion shows how 'wetland' entered into scientific discourse and history in the 1960s as a non-denigrative and umbrella term for swamps, marshes, etc. It was then taken up in governmental discourse by politicians and bureaucrats in the 1970s where it became a site of struggle between them, among themselves and with scientists and NGOs.

These, too, are "imagined ecologies," though *Wetlands* does not theorise them in these terms and what is at stake with them for wetlands, especially as habitat for more-than-human actors and agents, including on farms. Ducks, for instance, do not observe the boundary and distinction between wetlands in the conservation estate and rice paddies that are "a kind of wetland" (pp.16, 118) as *Wetlands* points out. What is a wetland is a mobile category and cannot be fixed in taxonomy or cartography. Ducks will decide with their feet and wings what is a wetland in ways that humans won't and can't. Some farmers are learning to live with ducks in their rice paddies and with the fluid definition of both them and wetlands as waterbird habitat (as *Wetlands* discusses briefly). An imagined ecology of wetlands could make some proposals for how the principles and practices of regenerative farming might apply to rice-growing.

An imagined ecology of wetlands could also show how cities are learning to live with wetlands by designing wetlandscapes for recreational spaces, water absorption and flood mitigation. *Wetlands* presents a case study of Toowoomba in south-east Queensland with its history of draining and filling wetlands, culminating in the devastating floods of 2011. This is where the story in *Wetlands* largely begins and ends, whereas the Toowoomba Regional Council has learnt lessons with the transformation of swamps into "park-like recreational areas," as photographed and briefly discussed in *Wetlands*, that include swales for flood mitigation not noted in *Wetlands*. A "reimagined ecology" of wetlands should imagine the future of living and working with wetlands in cities and on farms for their conservation and/or rehabilitation.

English Wetlands: Spaces of Nature, Culture, Imagination. By Mary Gearey, Andrew Church, and Neil Ravenscroft. Palgrave Macmillan. 2020. xiv + 175. 42.79 € eBook, 49.99 € hardback. ISBN 978-3-030-41305-7 ISBN 978-3-030-41306-4 (eBook)

The relationship between humans and wetlands has sometimes been vexatious. *English Wetlands* takes up the discussion of this general issue by foregrounding the dialectical and dialogical relationship between humans and wetlands, and the way they have shaped each other for better and worse. This relationship is mediated by both aesthetic and ecological perceptions and valuations that *English Wetlands* goes on to explore, especially in relation to writing about wetlands. It also situates these concerns in three case study sites in Bedfordshire, Somerset and the Humber Valley where it discusses human use, experience, value and perception of local wetlands. These studies are underpinned by, and are the result of, extensive social surveying and data collection and analysis.

Addressing these issues on site requires a multidisciplinary point of view and the willingness to draw from different disciplines as *English Wetlands* does, such as: palaeoenvironmental archaeology; landscape architecture and environmental planning; human geography; ecosystem services; eco-criticism; literary, cultural and critical theory; environmental history; and natural resources management. This multidisciplinarity creates a rich and diverse discussion, as is evident in the early pages of the book where it draws on humans' lived experiences of wetlands (as one might expect to find in an environmental humanities' approach) and where it discusses definitions of wetlands drawn from the scientific literature placed within inter-governmental and policy frameworks (perhaps to be expected of social scientists). The former is inductive, the latter deductive. Both are valid and valuable and *English Wetlands* interweaves them successfully here and throughout.

English Wetlands begins with recounting humans' lived, embodied experiences of wetlands as 'nether regions' both geographically and anatomically in a fine piece of 'new nature writing' that evokes poetically how wetlands are visceral and corporeal spaces and places linked to the nether regions of the human body, or 'the grotesque lower bodily stratum' as Mikhail Bakhtin called it, a place of carnivalesque inversion of the social hierarchy. It is contiguous and continuous with I call 'the grotesque lower earthly stratum' of wetlands.

This stratum is also a fertile and fecund womb, the place of what Hannah Arendt calls 'natality' (being born) in her early work on love that she countered to Martin Heidegger's being towards death. Wetlands are wombs of new life. Wombs are also watery spaces of new life. *English Wetlands* seems a bit squeamish about tackling this messy topic with its feminist and psychoanalytic implications. This squeamishness smacks of gender-blindness as wetlands are feminised places for good or ill: ill in misogynist patriarchy as places of disease, death, horror, the monstrous and tombs of dead matter; good in matrifocal ecofeminism, especially French feminism, as place of life, death, health, the maternal and wombs of new life. Dredging, draining and reclaiming wetlands is a quintessentially masculinist thing to do. It was certainly the kind of war the Fascist Mussolini liked to fight and win, at least in the short term. Floods in wetland cities, such as New Orleans and New York, suggest that in the longer term the war was never won, never could be and at best only a truce can be achieved.

English Wetlands then goes on address "the slippery definition" of wetlands in science and the sad and sorry history of wetlands in England from commons, through drainage and enclosure to conservation. It also discusses the ways in which wetlands have been represented and mediated in and by art, story and literature, beginning with a poem by Seamus Heaney, 'the patron saint of bogs,' and gesturing towards the poetry of John Clare, the 'patron saint of the Fens,' as I call them.

Addressing the reader directly, *English Wetlands* "ends on a positive note" and invites the reader to wade into wetlands in one way or another. The great achievement of *English Wetlands* is that it is not only a well-researched and -written study of the history and culture of English wetlands with case studies of specific sites in Bedfordshire, Somerset and the Humber Valley and a discussion of wetlands in culture, but that it is also a call for conservation that engages with contemporary and local issues of recreation and tourism in English wetlands. The fact that it does both within the constraints of a limited word-count required by the series in which it is published is even more praiseworthy. It should receive a wide readership in its own and other countries among anybody who cares for human and more-than-human life on earth. After all, wetlands are wombs of new life.

Introduction to the Environmental Humanities. By J. Andrew Hubbell and John C. Ryan. Routledge. London. 2022. xi + 302. ISBN 9781351200356. US$69.99 Paperback, US$56.69 eBook.

Hubbell and Ryan are heroes, pioneers and trailblazers for going boldly into the vast and varied field of the Environmental Humanities where no two authors have been brave enough to venture before them and to survey its prominent contours, map some of its borders and botanize its growths. _Introduction to the Environmental Humanities_ is a great achievement and an exemplary transdisciplinary study. It is a vital and valuable introduction to the Environmental Humanities for teaching undergraduate students and for mapping the field for graduate students and teachers. It provides contemporary case studies with appropriate pictorial illustrations and accompanying learning tools, such as "waypoints" with definitions of key terms and "exercises" for further study and reflection.

The annotated bibliographies, links to online resources and copious references for each chapter of _Introduction to the Environmental Humanities_ provide suggestions for further research and reading that give ample scope and plenty of opportunities for readers to continue exploring the vast area of the Environmental Humanities, to traverse many well-trod and not so well-trod avenues and to discover many new delights. The book is what it says is, an _introduction_ to the Environmental Humanities. It is not the be all and end all, the final word, nor even _the_ introduction to the Environmental Humanities. _Introduction to the Environmental Humanities_ and my review of it gives me the opportunity to point towards its absences, such as ecocultural studies, and to continue the dialogue it generates. This review is an ecocultural introduction to _Introduction to the Environmental Humanities_ for those who haven't read it, or an ecocultural conclusion for those who have.

Given the ambitious scope and vast range of what Hubbell and Ryan discuss and present in their book, an approach, aspect, feature or figure in the Environmental Humanities was bound to have been overlooked, or not receive the consideration it deserves. Such is the case with ecocultural studies and the pioneering, transdisciplinary work of Raymond Williams as the founder of this field. Ecocultural studies is not mentioned and Williams's work gets scant attention, despite its transdisciplinarity, a desideratum for Hubbell and Ryan (1, 3, 4). Transdisciplinarity in the Humanities is demonstrated in the work of Williams on nature, culture, landscapes, livelihood and resources for a journey of hope that cuts across the disciplines of geography, history, economics, cultural studies and literary studies.

Subsequent work in ecocultural studies following in Williams' footsteps, such as Alexander Wilson's classic *The Culture of Nature* (Wilson 1992), is not discussed either. Later work in ecocultural studies following in both Wilson's and Williams' footsteps, such as on landscapes, livelihood and cultures of natures (Giblett 2011), is also not discussed. Ecocultural studies is a way of knowing nature.

Psychoanalytic ecology is another notable absence from *Introduction to Environmental Humanities*. Psychoanalytic ecology diagnoses the symptoms of environ-mental illness in psycho-geopathology and prescribes the talking cure for them. It also promotes environmental health to prevent the manifestation of those symptoms in the first place by nurturing psycho-symbiosis (Giblett 1996; 2019). The work of Walter Benjamin, "the patron saint of cultural studies" as Rebecca Solnit calls him (see Giblett 2020, chapter 6), is also absent from *Introduction to Environmental Humanities*. It is pertinent to the discussion of history, especially the history of cities and swamps briefly touched on by Hubbell and Ryan (265). The lost swamps on or in which many cities were founded are present "by virtue of their very oblivion" in Benjamin's terms (see Giblett 2016, chapter 2). Benjamin has a foot in both camps of ecocultural studies and psychoanalytic ecology. The Green Benjamin has not been taken up much in the Environmental Humanities with some exceptions (see Mules 2014).

Of course, authors are always constrained by the word limits imposed by their publishers. Yet in an introductory book, such as *Introduction to the Environmental Humanities*, one would expect that classic texts and pioneering writers would be given due attention, rather than concentrating on more recent developments and contemporary manifestation as the classic texts and pioneering writers tend to get lost in the mists of time and in the obsession with the current and fashionable.

Introduction to the Environmental Humanities devotes individual chapters to most of the disciplines of geography, history and literary studies that Williams worked across, with the additions of environmental anthropology, environmental philosophy, ecological religious studies, as well as environmental theater, film and journalism. Emerging theoretical areas, such as critical animal and plant studies, gender and queer studies, indigenous studies, and energy studies are also introduced. Re-emerging theoretical areas, such as class, critique of political economy and socialist ecology, are not introduced to all of which Williams contributed. Ryan is eminently well-qualified to introduce plant studies as he is the author or editor of many books in this field (for Ryan as "the patron saint of plants" see Giblett 2021a, chapter 40).

Williams' work on nature, culture, landscapes, livelihood and resources for a journey of hope qualify him as "the patron saint of ecocultural studies" (Giblett 2020, chapter 10). He is arguably both *a* founder of cultural studies and the transdisciplinary Environmental Humanities, as well as *the* founder of ecocriticism and ecocultural studies, though of course he did not use these terms, nor make these distinctions between them, but that is the point. Williams is exemplary in this respect in that he just got on and did the eco and this is no more the case than in his development of the concept of livelihood. This concept is included in a glossary of "Keywords in Space and Place Studies" in *Introduction to the Environmental Humanities* (Hubbell and Ryan 77). Williams developed a socialist ecology around the concept and practices of livelihood in the essays he wrote in the last years of his life and his last book, *Towards 2000* (Williams 1985; 1989). Livelihood deconstructs the culture/nature binary and decolonizes the commodification and aestheticization of land as landscape. It reinstitutes nature as ordinary, as the stuff of work and everyday life. Nature, like culture for Williams, is ordinary too.

The integral role of nature to the development of cultural studies and the Environmental Humanities is particularly evident in Williams' discussion of the politics and aesthetics of landscape, especially the commodification and aestheticization of land as landscape, in *The Country and the City* (Williams 1973). *The Country and the City* is mentioned briefly in *Introduction to the Environmental Humanities,* strangely in the annotated bibliography to a chapter on 'Environmental Anthropology' (86) and not discussed elsewhere in the chapters on environmental art and literary studies.

By organizing the chapters of *Introduction to the Environmental Humanities* according to the traditional disciplines – Anthropology, Philosophy, History, Literary Studies, etc. – Hubbell and Ryan run the danger of inadvertently reinforcing their hegemony, despite their admiration for transdisciplinarity. Overlooking or neglecting ecocultural studies and giving the work of Williams scant attention, as well as not foregrounding its transdisciplinarity, seem like a missed opportunity to strengthen the case for the transdisciplinary Environmental Humanities and advance its cause. By not doing so, they have given me the opportunity to do so, for which I am grateful. Certainly gaining a solid grounding in the core disciplines is desirable as Hubbell and Ryan (1) argue (and I certainly benefitted from studying English, History and Philosophy as an undergraduate), but at some stage it's time to move on and work across the disciplines with environments and environmental issues that rarely stick within one disciplines. Hubbell and Ryan devote the final page of *Introduction to the Environmental Humanities* (265) to a brief discussion of what they call "the wetland humanities" that has been transdisciplinary from the get go twenty five years ago (Giblett 1996) and still is (Giblett 2021c).

As the publisher's blurb for *Introduction to the Environmental Humanities* says, "in an era of climate change, deforestation, melting ice caps, poisoned environments, and species loss, many people are turning to the power of the arts and humanities for sustainable solutions to global ecological problems. *Introduction to the Environmental Humanities* offers a practical and accessible guide to this dynamic and interdisciplinary field." Indeed it does. Many readers would do well to follow it with the supplement of this review for additional guidance and its references that are suggestions for further reading in the rich and fertile field of the Environmental Humanities that embraces ecocultural studies as a way of knowing nature and psychoanalytic ecology as the talking cure for environ-mental illness and health.

BIBLIOGRAPHY

AAP. 2019. 'Budj Bim Indigenous Eel Trap Site Added to World Heritage List.' *The Guardian,* July 7. Accessed July 7, 2020. https://www.theguardian.com/australia-news/2019/jul/07/budj-bim-indigenous-eel-trap-site-added-to-world-heritage-list.

ACHRIS (Aboriginal Cultural Heritage Register and Information System). ND 'Lake Connewarren,' *Map.* Accessed February 8, 2021. https://achris.vic.gov.au/#/onlinemap.

Ackroyd, Peter. 2009. *Thames: The Biography.* New York: Anchor Books.

Allam, Lorema. 2020. 'Australian Researchers Find Native Grasses could be Grown for Mass Consumption.' *The Guardian,* November 10. Accessed November 14, 2020. https://www.theguardian.com/australia-news/2020/nov/10/australian-researchers-find-native-grasses-could-be-grown-for-human-consumption.

Alexander, Mary. 2010. 'Flood Clean-Up Continues but Hopkins Falls a Highlight.' *The Standard,* August 15. Accessed November 30, 2020. https://www.standard.net.au/story/783833/flood-clean-up-continues-but-hopkins-falls-a-highlight/.

Andrews, Alan E. J., editor. 1986. *Stapylton: With Major Mitchell's Australia Felix Expedition, 1836: Largely from the Journal of Granville William Chetwynd Stapylton.* Hobart: Blubber Head Press.

Anonymous. NDA. 'An Evolving, Resilient Ecosystem.' *Chatsworth House Pastoral.* https://chatsworthhouse.com.au. Accessed March 28, 2021.

Anonymous. NDB. 'Lake Bolac Eel Festival: Kuyang Lapakira – Plenty Eels.' http://www.eelfestival.org.au/about.html. Accessed July 22, 2021.

Antos, Mark and Nicholas S.G. Williams. 2015. 'The Wildlife of our Grassy Landscapes,' in Nicholas S.G.Williams, Adrian Marshall and John W. Morgan (editors), *Land of Sweeping Plains: Managing and Restoring the Native Temperate Grasslands of South-Eastern Australia.* Clayton South, Victoria: CSIRO Publishing, 87-114.

Arthur, Bill and Frances Morphy, editors. 2019. *The Macquarie Atlas of Indigenous Australia. Second Edition.* Sydney, N.S.W.: Macquarie Dictionary/Pan Macmillan.

Ash, Eric H. 2016. 'Reclaiming a New World: Fen Drainage, Improvement, and Projectors in Seventeenth-Century England.' *Early Science and Medicine,* 21, 445-469.

Ash, Eric H. 2017. *The Draining of the Fens: Projectors, Popular Politics, and State Building in Early Modern England.* Baltimore, MD: Johns Hopkins University Press.

Ashton, Rosemary. 1994. 'Introduction,' in George Eliot, *Middlemarch,* vii-xxii. London: Penguin Classics.

Bakhtin, M. M. 1984. *Rabelais and his World,* trans. Hélène Iswolsky. Bloomington: Indiana University Press.

Banfield, Lorna. 1986. *Like the Ark: The Story of Ararat.* Revised edition. First published 1955. Melbourne: Longman Cheshire.

Bantow, Jennifer, Mark Rashleigh and John Sherwood, editors. 1995. *Tuuram: Hopkins Estuary and Coastal Environs.* Warrnambool: Deakin University, Australia Felix Series, Centre for Regional Development.

Bates, Daisy. 1985. *The Native Tribes of Western Australia,* edited by Isobel White. Canberra: National Library of Australia.

Bertram, Nigel and Catherine Murphy. 'The Swampy Lowlands of Melbourne.' In *In Time with Water: Design Studies of 3 Australian Cities,* edited by Nigel Bertram and Catherine Murphy, 79-153. Crawley: University of Western Australia Publishing, 2019.

Birdlife Australia. NDA. 'European Goldfinch.' Accessed August 24, 2021. https://www.birdlife.org.au/bird-profile/european-goldfinch.

Birdlife Australia. NDB. 'Impact of Starlings.' Accessed August 24, 2021. https://www.birdlife.org.au/projects/starlings-in-western-australia/impacts-of-starlings.

Birdlife Australia. NDC. 'Mistletoebird.' Accessed August 24, 2021. https://www.birdlife.org.au/bird-profile/mistletoebird.

Bird, Rod. 2014. *A Short History of Wetlands in SW Victoria: The Landscape at Settlement, Impact of Agriculture, Major Wetlands near Hamilton, and Wetland Restoration.* Hamilton, Victoria: R. Bird.

Blackbourn, David. 2008. "'Time is a Violent Torrent': Constructing and Reconstructing Rivers in Modern German History', in C. Mauch and T. Zeller (eds), *Rivers in History: Perspectives on Waterways in Europe and North America,* 11–25. Pittsburgh: University of Pittsburgh Press.

Blass, Tom. 2022. *Swamp Songs: Journeys Through Marsh, Meadow and Other Wetlands.* London: Bloomsbury.

Bode, Carl. 1982. 'Epilogue by the Editor.' In *The Portable Thoreau,* edited by Carl Bode, 683-696. New York: Viking Penguin.

Boucher, Amanda. 2020. *1690 Ellerslie-Panmure Road, Panmure, Vic, 3265: Save The Hopkins – Stop The Quarry: Heritage Due Diligence Assessment.* Highett, Victoria: A. B. Heritage Consulting.

Brady, Danielle and Jeffrey Murray. 2020. 'The Cultural Significance of Wetlands: Perth's Lost Swamps to the Beeliar Wetlands.' In *Australian Wetland Cultures: Swamps and the Environmental Crisis,* edited by John C. Ryan and Li Chen, 175-194. Lanham, MD: Lexington Books.

Bride, Thomas Francis, editor. 1898. *Letters from Victorian Pioneers: Being a Series of Papers on the Early Occupation of the Colony, the Aborigines, etc. Addressed by Victorian Pioneers to his Excellency Charles Joseph La Trobe, Esq., Lieutenant Governor of the Colony of Victoria.* Melbourne: Trustees of the Public Library of Victoria.

Broome, Richard. 2005. *Aboriginal Victorians: A History Since 1800.* Crows Nest, NSW: Allen and Unwin.

Burdett, Ayesha. 2021a. 'A Community Approach to Gorse in Ararat and the Upper Hopkins.' *Victorian Landcare Magazine,* 81. Accessed October 14, 2021. https://www.landcarevic.org.au/landcare-magazine/winter-2021/native-bee-forums-buzz-with-questions-2/.

Burdett, Ayesha. 2021b. *Upper Hopkins Land Management Group Spring 2021 Newsletter.* Accessed September 15, 2021. https://upperhopkins.org.au/newsletter/spring-2021-newsletter/?mc_cid=8ff2bd0c7b&mc_eid=45a9fdf05a.

Burdett, Ayesha. 2021c. *Upper Hopkins Land Management Group Summer 2021 Newsletter.* Accessed December 7, 2021. https://upperhopkins.org.au/newsletter/summer-2021-newsletter/?mc_cid=e54ef2e869&mc_eid=45a9fdf05a.

Cahir, Fred. 2018. 'Shelter: Housing,' in Fred Cahir, Ian D. Clark and Philip A. Clarke, *Aboriginal Biocultural Knowledge in South-Eastern Australia: Perspectives of Early Colonists,* 151-172. Clayton South, Victoria: CSIRO Publishing.

Cahir, Fred, Ian D. Clark and Philip A. Clarke. 2018. 'Conclusion: The Future of Aboriginal Biocultural Knowledge,' in Fred Cahir, Ian D. Clark and Philip A. Clarke, *Aboriginal Biocultural Knowledge in South-Eastern Australia: Perspectives of Early Colonists,* 281-284. Clayton South, Victoria: CSIRO Publishing.

Cahir, Fred and Sarah McMaster. 2018. 'Fire in Aboriginal South-Eastern Australia,' in Fred Cahir, Ian D. Clark and Philip A. Clarke, *Aboriginal Biocultural Knowledge in South-Eastern Australia: Perspectives of Early Colonists,* 115-131. Clayton South, Victoria: CSIRO Publishing.

Carter, Paul. 1987. *The Road to Botany Bay: An Essay in Spatial History.* London: Faber.

Carruthers, Fiona. 2015. 'Richard Weatherly, Merino Breeder and Painter.' *The Australian Financial Review Magazine,* August 23. Accessed December 14, 2020. https://www.afr.com/life-and-luxury/richard-weatherly-merino-breeder-and-painter-20150721-gih3dm.

Cathcart, Michael. 2010. *The Water Dreamers: The Remarkable Story of our Dry Continent.* Melbourne: Text.

CDM Smith. 2021. *Hopkins Quarry Groundwater Investigation.*

Chamberlain, Matt. 2015. *Proposed Subdivision Green Hill Estate, Ararat Cultural Heritage Management Plan*. Kensington, Victoria: Heritage Insight.

Chatfield, Jess. 2020. *Leenyaa Merreeng: Grandmother Land*. Accessed October 22, 2021. https://www.facebook.com/Save-the-Hopkins-River-Stop-the-Quarry-106357197825830.

Chatsworth House Pastoral. ND. *An Evolving Resilient Ecosystem, Interconnected Farming for a Better Future*. Accessed March 12, 2021. https://chatsworthhouse.com.au.

Chauncy, Phillip. 1878. 'Appendix A: Notes and Anecdotes of the Aborigines of Australia,' in R. Brough Smyth, *The Aborigines of Victoria: With Notes Relating to the Habits of the Natives of Other Parts of Australia and Tasmania / Compiled from Various Sources for the Government of Victoria, Volume II*. Melbourne: John Ferres, Govt. Printer, 221-284.

Clark, Ian D. 1990. *Aboriginal Languages and Clans: An Historical Atlas of Western and Central Victoria*. Melbourne: Department of Geography and Environmental Science, Monash University.

Clark, Ian D. 1995. *Scars in the Landscape: A Register of Massacre Sites in Western Victoria 1803–1859*. Canberra: Aboriginal Studies Press.

Clark, Ian D. 2007. 'The Djab wurrung: The First Peoples of Ararat and District,' in Danny and Judy Barry, editors, *Ararat 1857-2007: Ararat 150th Committee*. Ararat: Ararat Rural Council.

Clark, Ian D. 2009. 'Reconstruction of Aboriginal Microtoponymy in Western and Central Victoria: Case studies from Tower Hill, the Hopkins River, and Lake Boga.' In *Aboriginal Placenames: Naming and Re-Naming the Australian Landscape,* edited by Harold Koch and Luise Hercus. ANU E Press and Aboriginal History Incorporated, Aboriginal History Monograph 19. Accessed April 14, 2021. http://press-files.anu.edu.au/downloads/press/p17331/html/ch08.xhtml?referer=xxxxxx&page=1.

Clark, Ian D. 2018a. 'Trade,' in Fred Cahir, Ian D. Clark and Philip A. Clarke, *Aboriginal Biocultural Knowledge in South-Eastern Australia: Perspectives of Early Colonists*, 229-245. Clayton South, Victoria: CSIRO Publishing.

Clark, Ian D. 2018b. 'Water,' in Fred Cahir, Ian D. Clark and Philip A. Clarke, *Aboriginal Biocultural Knowledge in South-Eastern Australia: Perspectives of Early Colonists,* 95-113. Clayton South, Victoria: CSIRO Publishing.

Clarke, Banjo (as told to Camilla Chance). 2003. *Wisdom Man*. Camberwell, Victoria: Penguin.

Clarke, Patricia. 2008. *The Rainbow Serpent of the Hopkins River*. Camberwell East, Victoria: One Day Hill.

Clarke, Philip A. 2018a. 'Animal Food,' in Fred Cahir, Ian D. Clark and Philip A. Clarke, *Aboriginal Biocultural Knowledge in South-Eastern Australia: Perspectives of Early Colonists,* 73-93. Clayton South, Victoria: CSIRO Publishing.

Clarke, Philip A. 2018b. 'Plant Food,' in Fred Cahir, Ian D. Clark and Philip A. Clarke, *Aboriginal Biocultural Knowledge in South-Eastern Australia: Perspectives of Early Colonists,* 55-71. Clayton South, Victoria: CSIRO Publishing.

Clarke, Philip A. 2018c. 'Space,' in Fred Cahir, Ian D. Clark and Philip A. Clarke, *Aboriginal Biocultural Knowledge in South-Eastern Australia: Perspectives of Early Colonists,* 247-263. Clayton South, Victoria: CSIRO Publishing.

Clarke, Philip A. 2018d. 'Time,' in Fred Cahir, Ian D. Clark and Philip A. Clarke, *Aboriginal Biocultural Knowledge in South-Eastern Australia: Perspectives of Early Colonists*, 265-280. Clayton South, Victoria: CSIRO Publishing.

Clarke, Philip A. 2018e. 'Totemic Life,' in Fred Cahir, Ian D. Clark and Philip A. Clarke, *Aboriginal Biocultural Knowledge in South-Eastern Australia: Perspectives of Early Colonists,* 1-18. Clayton South, Victoria: CSIRO Publishing.

Clarke, Philip A. 2018f. 'Water Spirit Beings,' in Fred Cahir, Ian D. Clark and Philip A. Clarke, *Aboriginal Biocultural Knowledge in South-Eastern Australia: Perspectives of Early Colonists,* 35-53. Clayton South, Victoria: CSIRO Publishing.

Cook, Margaret. 2019. *A City with a River Problem: A History of Brisbane Floods*. St Lucia, Queensland : University of Queensland Press.

Coutts, Peter J. F. 1985. 'An Archaeological Perspectives of the Western District, Victoria,' in *Settlement of the Western District: From Prehistoric Times to the Present*, Proceedings of a Public Lecture Series held in Warrnambool, 3 November 1984, edited by J. Sherwood, J. Critchett and K. O'Toole, 21-64. Warrnambool: Warrnambool Institute Press.

Cowley, Jason. 2008. 'Editor's Letter: The New Nature Writing,' *Granta: The Magazine of New Writing: The New Nature Writing, 102*, 7, 9-12.

Crampton, Caroline. 2019. *The Way to the Sea: The Forgotten Histories of the Thames Estuary*. London: Granta.

Critchett, Jan. 1990a. *A 'Distant Field of Murder': Western District Frontiers 1834-1848*. Carlton: Melbourne University Press.

Critchett, Jan. 1990b. *Our Land Till We Die: A History of the Framlingham Aborigines*. Australia Felix Series No.1. Warrnambool: Warrnambool Institute Press.

Critchett, Jan. 1998. *Untold Stories: Memories and Lives of Victorian Kooris*. Carlton South: Melbourne University Press.

Critchett, Jan. 2005. 'Kaawirn Kuunawarn (1820–1889),' in *Australian Dictionary of Biography*. Melbourne: Melbourne University Press. Accessed January 26, 2021. https://adb.anu.edu.au/biography/kaawirn-kuunawarn-13018.

Curr, E. M. 1883. *Recollections of Squatting in Victoria: Then Called the Port Phillip District (from 1841 to 1851)*. Melbourne: George Robertson.

Dalley, Stephanie, editor and translator. 2000. *Myths from Mesopotamia: Creation, the Flood, Gilgamesh and Others*, Revised Edition. Oxford: Oxford University Press.

Dawson, James. 1881. *Australian Aborigines: The Languages and Customs of Several Tribes of Aborigines in the Western District of Victoria, Australia*. Melbourne: George Robertson.

Department of Environment, Land, Water and Planning (DELWP). 2019. *Wetlands of the Greater Grampians*. Accessed March 25, 2020. https://www.water.vic.gov.au/waterways-and-catchments/our-catchments/ococ/projects/wetlands-of-the-greater-grampians.

Dugdale, William. 1662. *The History of Imbanking and Drayning of Divers Fenns and Marshes, both in Forein Parts and in this Kingdom, and of the Improvements thereby Extracted from Records, Manuscripts, and Other Authentick Testimonies*. Accessed September 16, 2022. https://quod.lib.umich.edu/e/eebo/A36795.0001.001?view=toc.

Eastern Marr Corporation. 2020. 'Media release – Fiddle back tree and Western Hwy.' Accessed October 31, 2020. https://easternmaar.com.au/media-release-fiddle-bark-tree-and-western-hwy/.

Eliot, George. 1994. *Middlemarch*. London: Penguin Classics. First published in 1871-1872.

Equipe Lawyers. 2020. *Planning Report: Proposed Basalt Quarry 1690 Ellerslie-Panmure Road, Panmure*. Accessed September 4, 2021. https://www.moyne.vic.gov.au/

Fanon, Franz. 1967. *The Wretched of the Earth*, translated by Constance Farrington. Harmondsworth: Penguin Books. First published in French in 1961.

Flagship Farmers. ND. *David and Nick Allen, Mortlake, Victoria, Australia*. Accessed October 14, 2021. https://www.flagshipfarmers.com/media/1187/flagship-farmer-case-mcdonalds_ff_case-study_david-nick-allen-australian_071019.pdf.

'F.R.' 1917. 'The Naturalist: Bush Notes: A Ramble to Stawell.' *The Australasian*, Saturday June 23, 44. Accessed August 21, 2021. http://nla.gov.au/nla.news-article140190852.

Gammage, Bill. 2011. *The Biggest Estate on Earth: How Aborigines made Australia*. Sydney: Allen & Unwin.

Gearey, Mary, Andrew Church, and Neil Ravenscroft. 2020. *English Wetlands: Spaces of Nature, Culture, Imagination*. Cham, Switzerland: Palgrave Macmillan.

Gerrans, Vanessa. 2021. 'Director's Message,' *Warrnambool Art Gallery January-June 2021*, Exhibition Catalogue, 2-3.

Giblett, Rod. 1996. *Postmodern Wetlands: Culture, History, Ecology*. Edinburgh: Edinburgh University Press.

Giblett, Rod. 2006. *Forrestdale: People and Place*. Bassendean: Access Press.

Giblett, Rod. 2008. *The Body of Nature and Culture*. Basingstoke: Palgrave Macmillan.

Giblett, Rod. 2009. *Landscapes of Culture and Nature.* Basingstoke: Palgrave Macmillan.

Giblett, Rod. 2011. *People and Places of Nature and Culture,* Bristol: Intellect Books.

Giblett, Rod. 2013. *Black Swan Lake: Life of a Wetland.* Bristol: Intellect Books.

Giblett, Rod. 2014. *Canadian Wetlands: Places and People.* Bristol: Intellect Books.

Giblett, Rod. 2016. *Cities and Wetlands: The Return of the Repressed in Nature and Culture.* London: Bloomsbury.

Giblett, Rod. 2018. *Environmental Humanities and Theologies: Ecoculture, Literature and the Bible.* London: Routledge.

Giblett, Rod. 2019a. *Environmental Humanities and The Uncanny: Ecoculture, Literature and Religion.* London: Routledge.

Giblett, Rod. 2019b. *Psychoanalytic Ecology: The Talking Cure for Environmental Illness and Health.* London: Routledge.

Giblett, Rod. 2020a. 'Artist and Swamp: Wetlands in Australian Painting and Photography,' in *Australian Wetland Cultures: Swamps and the Environmental Crisis,* edited by John Charles Ryan and Li Chen, 51-70. Lanham, MD: Lexington Books.

Giblett, Rod. 2020b. *Modern Melbourne: City and Site of Nature and Culture.* Bristol: Intellect Books.

Giblett, Rod. 2020c. *New Lives of the Saints: Twelve Environmental Apostles.* Lanham, MD: Hamilton Books.

Giblett, Rod. 2020d. *Odds and Ends of a Writer's Life 2014-2019.* Champaign, IL: Common Ground.

Giblett, Rod. 2020e. 'Rainbow Serpent Anthropology, or Rainbow Spirit Theology, or Swamp Serpent Sacrality and Marsh Monster Maternity?' in *Australian Wetland Cultures: Swamps and the Environmental Crisis,* edited by John Charles Ryan and Li Chen, 33-50. Lanham, MD: Lexington Books.

Giblett, Rod. 2021a. *Black Swan Song: Life and Work of a Wetland Writer.* Lanham, MD: Hamilton Books.

Giblett, Rod. 2021b. 'The Nature and Culture of the Seasons: Homage to Henry David Thoreau,' in *The Seasons: Philosophical, Environmental and Literary Perspectives,* edited by Luke Fischer and David Macauley, 223-242. Albany, NY: State University of New York Press.

Giblett, Rod. 2021c. *Wetlands and Western Cultures: Denigration to Conservation.* Lanham, MD: Lexington Books.

Giblett, Rod. 2022. *Swamp Deaths: Collected Cold Cases and Other Marshy Mysteries.* London: Europe Books.

Giblett, Rod and Hugh Webb, eds. 1996. *Western Australian Wetlands: The Kimberley and South-West.* Perth, Western Australia: Black Swan Press/Wetlands Conservation Society.

Giblett, Rod and John Charles Ryan, eds. 2018. *Forest Family: Australian Art, Culture and Trees.* Boston and Leiden: Brill.

Glenelg Hopkins Catchment Management Authority. (2005). *Hopkins Estuary Management Plan.* Accessed 9 February 2021. https://info.ghcma.vic.gov.au/wp-content/uploads/2017/05/management_plan_FINAL.pdf.

Grasslands Biodiversity of South-East Australia. ND. *Mortlake Common Flora Reserve.* Accessed 9 February 2021. https://grasslands.ecolinc.vic.edu.au/grassland/mortlake-common-flora-reserve.

Gunditjmara People, the, with Gib Wettenhall. 2010. *The People of Budj Bim: Engineers of Aquaculture, Builders of Stone House Settlements and Warriors Defending Country.* Heywood, Victoria: em PRESS Publishing for the Gunditj Mirring Traditional Owners Aboriginal Corporation.

GWM Water. ND. *Lake Wartook.* Accessed March 25, 2020. https://www.gwmwater.org.au/using-lakes-and-reservoirs/our-reservoirs/lake-wartook.

Hannaford, Samuel. 1860. *Sea and River-Side Rambles in Victoria: Being a Handbook for those Seeking Recreation during the Summer Months.* Geelong: Heath & Cordell.

Heritage Council Victoria. 2005. 'The Grampians, Southern Grampians Shire.' *Victorian Heritage Database.* Accessed March 27, 2020. https://vhd.heritagecouncil.vic.

gov.au/places/70397

Himmelreich, Everard. 2018. 'Local Wool Growers Receive Sustainability Award.' *The Standard*. September 26. Accessed November 30, 2020. https://www.standard. net.au/story/5668733/green-carpet-milan-and-cate-blanchett-a-big-day-out-for-mortlake-wool-producers-video/

Hocking, Jenny and Reidy, Nell. 2016. 'Marngrook, Tom Wills and the continuing denial of indigenous history: On the origins of Australian football', *Meanjin*, Winter. Accessed 1 March 2017. https://meanjin.com.au/essays/marngrook-tom-wills-and-the-continuing-denial-of-indigenous-history/.

Hoskins, Ian. 2020. *Rivers: The Lifeblood of Australia*. Canberra: National Library of Australia.

Hubbell, J. Andrew and John C. Ryan. 2022. *Introduction to the Environmental Humanities*. London: Routledge.

Hughson, Colleen. 2011. 'Water is... Aboriginal Culture on the Hopkins River.' *ABC Local*. Accessed June 8, 2021.
    https://www.abc.net.au/local/stories/2011/12/06/3384686.htm

Hunter, Lowell. 2021. 'Mirteetch Meering (Sea Country).' *Warrnambool Art Gallery January-June 2021*, Exhibition Catalogue, 11. Accessed June 6 2021.
    https://www.thewag.com.au/exhibition/mirteetch-meering-sea-country.

Keaney, Magdalene. 1998. 'Eugene von Guérard 1811-1901: 'Mount William from Mount Dryden, Victoria, 1857'.' In *New Worlds from Old: 19th Century Australian and American Landscapes*, edited by Elizabeth Johns, Andrew Sayers and Elizabeth Kornhauser, 155. Canberra: National Gallery of Australia/Hartford, CT: Wadsworth Atheneum.

Kiddle, Margaret. 1961. *Men of Yesterday: A Social History of the Western District of Victoria 1834-1890*. Melbourne: Melbourne University Press.

Koori Heritage Trust. 1991. *Massacre Map*. Accessed April 8, 2020.
    https://cv.vic.gov.au/media/oldmedia/5755/massacre_File0001.jpg.

Leardini, Paola, Kaan Ozgun and Antony Mouils. 2019. 'The Reverse River Delta of Brisbane.' In *In Time with Water: Design Studies of 3 Australian Cities*, edited by Nigel Bertram and Catherine Murphy, 217-290. Crawley: University of Western Australia Publishing.

Leopold, Aldo. 1949. *A Sand County Almanac and Sketches Here and There*. New York: Oxford University Press.

Lichtenstein, Rachel. 2017. *Estuary: Out from London to the Sea*. London: Penguin Books.

Lorbiecki, Marybeth. 2016. *A Fierce Green Fire: The Life and Legacy of Aldo Leopold*. New York: Oxford University Press.

Lourandos, Harry. 1987. 'Swamp Managers of Southwestern Victoria,' in *Australians to 1788*, 292–307, edited by D. J. Mulvaney and J. P. White. Sydney: Fairfax, Syme and Weldon. Accessed February 18, 2021. https://socialsciences.org.au/library/australians-to-1788-chapter-15/.

Lowe, Robert. 2002. *The Mish*. St Lucia: University of Queensland Press.

MacPherson, Peter. 1884-85. 'On the Oven-Mounds of Aborigines in Victoria,' *Royal Society of New South Wales*, XVIII, 49-59. Accessed February 6, 2021. https://nla.gov.au/nla.obj-344468367/view?partId=nla.obj-344480395#page/n9/mode/1up.

Martin, Daniel Jan and Geoffrey London. 2019. 'The Deep Waters of Perth.' In *In Time with Water: Design Studies of 3 Australian Cities*, edited by Nigel Bertram and Catherine Murphy, 157-215. Crawley: University of Western Australia Publishing.

Massola, Aldo. 1968. *Bunjil's Cave: Myths, Legends and Superstitions of the Aborigines of South-East Australia*. Melbourne: Lansdowne.

Massy, Charles. 2020. *Call of the Reed Warbler: A New Agriculture, A New Earth*. St Lucia, Queensland: Queensland University Press.

Mauch, Christof and Zeller, Thomas. 2008. "Introduction," in *Rivers in History: Perspectives on Waterways in Europe and North America*, edited by Christof Mauch and Thomas Zeller, 1–10. Pittsburgh: University of Pittsburgh Press.

Mayes, Christopher. 2018. *Unsettling Food Politics: Agriculture, Dispossession and Sovereignty in*

Australia. Lanham, MD: Rowman & Littlefield.

Mbembe, Achille. 2019. *Necropolitics,* translated by Steven Corcoran. Durham, NC: Duke University Press.

McDowall, Carolyn. 2014. 'Eugene Von Guérard – Colonial Artist, Nature Revealed.' Accessed September 6, 2018. https://www.thecultureconcept.com/national-gallery-eugene-von-Guérard-nature-revealed

McKenzie, Bob. 2001. *Down the Hopkins.* Mortlake: Robert J. McKenzie.

McPhee, John. 2004. 'Introduction,' in Henry David Thoreau, *A Week on the Concord and Merrimack Rivers,* ix-xlvi. Princeton: Princeton University Press.

Meine, Curt. 1988. *Aldo Leopold: His Life and Work.* Madison, WN: University of Wisconsin Press.

Melbourne Water. 2021. *Reimaging Your Moonee Ponds Creek.* Accessed October 29, 2021. https://www.melbournewater.com.au/building-and-works/projects/reimagining-your-moonee-ponds-creek.

Mitchell, Thomas. 1839. *Three Expeditions into the Interior of Eastern Australia: With Descriptions of the Recently Explored Region of Australia Felix...* Accessed April 8, 2020. http://gutenberg.net.au/ebooks/e00036.html#CHAPTER%203.14.

Muecke, Stephen. 1992. 'Available Discourses on Aborigines,' in *Textual Spaces: Aboriginality and Cultural Studies,* 19-35. Kensington, NSW: University of New South Wales Press. Accessed 26 January 2021. https://www.austlit.edu.au/austlit/page/C828136.

Mules, Warwick. 2014. *With Nature: Nature Philosophy as Poetics through Schelling, Heidegger, Benjamin and Nancy.* Bristol: Intellect Books.

Museums Victoria. ND. 'Kaawirn Kuunawarn (Hissing Swan) Headman of the Kirroe Wuurong Tribe [Girai Wurrung Clan], Victoria, *c.*1881.' *Victorian Collections.* Accessed 26 January 2021. https://victoriancollections.net.au/items/592e2039d0cdd31744d28c26.

National Gallery of Victoria. ND. 'Eugene von Guérard, 'Tower Hill,' 1855.' Accessed September 6, 2018. www.ngv.vic.gov.au/essay/eugene-von-guerard-nature-revealed/3/.

Nature Conservancy Australia. 2020. 'Exploring Gayini - Nari Nari Country.' Accessed April 6, 2020. https://www.natureaustralia.org.au/what-we-do/our-priorities/ land-and-freshwater/land-freshwater-stories/gayini/.

Nicolson, Megan. 2021. 'Soggy Homes: The Wonder of Wetlands.' *Warrnambool Art Gallery January-June 2021,* Exhibition Catalogue, 8. Also available online and accessed June 6 2021. https://www.thewag.com.au/exhibition/megan-nicolson-soggy-homes-wonder-wetlands

Obeng-Odoom, Franklin. 2021. *The Commons in an Age of Uncertainty: Decolonizing Nature, Economy, and Society.* Toronto: University of Toronto Press.

O'Gorman, Emily. 2021. *Wetlands in a Dry Land: More-Than-Human-Histories of the Murray-Darling Basin.* Seattle: University of Washington Press.

Otto, Rudolf. 1950. *The Idea of the Holy: An Inquiry into the Non-Rational Factor in the Idea of The Divine and its Relation to the Rational, second edition,* translated by John W. Harvey. Oxford: Oxford University Press.

Parks Victoria. 2003. *Grampians National Park Management Plan.* Accessed March 25, 2020. https://www.google.com/search?client=safari&rls=en&q=grampians+national+park+management+plan&ie=UTF-8&oe=UTF-8.

Parliament of Victoria, Legislative Council e-Petitions. 2020. 'Save the Hopkins.' Accessed May 29, 2021. https://www.parliament.vic.gov.au/council/petitions/electronic-petitions/view-e-petitions/details/12/220.

Pastoreau, Michel. 2001. *Blue: The History of a Color.* Princeton: Princeton University Press.

Peck, H. Daniel. 1998. 'Introduction,' in Henry David Thoreau, *A Week on the Concord and Merrimack Rivers,* vii-xxi. New York: Penguin.

Perkins, Miki. 2020. ''Devastated': Anger after 'Culturally Significant' Tree Cut down at Highway Site.' *The Sydney Morning Herald,* October 26, 2020. Accessed October 31, 2020. https://www.smh.com.au/environment/conservation/devastated-anger-after-culturally-significant-tree-cut-down-at-highway-site-20201026-p568pm.html.

'Pike.' 1871. 'Angling: The River Hopkins,' *The Australasian,* Saturday 23 December, 11. Accessed August 16, 2021. http://nla.gov.au/nla.news-article138087471.

Powell, J. M. 1970. *The Public Lands of Australia Felix: Settlement and Land Appraisal in Victoria 1834-91 with Special Reference to the Western Plains.* Melbourne: Oxford University Press.

Presland, Gary, editor. 1977. 'Journals of GA Robinson, March-May 1841.' *Records of the Victorian Archaeological Survey* no. 6. Melbourne: Ministry for Conservation Publication.

Proulx, Annie. 2022. *Fen, Bog and Swamp: A Short History of Peatland Destruction and its Role in the Climate Crisis.* New York: Scribner.

Pullin, Ruth. 2011. *Eugene von Guérard: Nature Revealed.* Melbourne: National Gallery of Victoria.

Pullin, Ruth. 2018. *The Artist as Traveller: The Sketchbooks of Eugene von Guérard.* Ballarat: Art Gallery of Ballarat.

Ramsar Convention Bureau. ND. 'The Importance of Wetlands.' Accessed 26 January 2021. http://www.ramsar.org/about/the-importance-of-wetlands

Reid, Nick and David Norton. 2013. *Nature and Farming: Sustaining Native Biodiversity in Agricultural Landscapes.* Clayton South: CSIRO Publishing.

Robinson, George Augustus. 1998. *The Journals of [...] Chief Protector, Port Phillip Aboriginal Protectorate, Volume Two: 1 October 1840 – 31 August 1841.* Edited by Ian D. Clark. Melbourne: Heritage Matters.

Robinson, Joel. 2018. 'Historic Western District station Chatsworth House up for $25 Million.' *Urban.com.au.* Accessed March 28, 2021. https://www.urban.com.au/news/90575-historic-chatsworth-house-up-for-25-million.

Ronald, Heather. 1978. *Wool Past the Winning Post: A History of the Chirnside Family.* South Yarra: Landvale Enterprises.

Ruzicka, Annette. 2020. "Kakadu of the South': 88,000 Hectares of NSW Wetland Handed Back to Nari Nari.' *The Guardian,* April 6. Accessed April 6, 2020. https://www.theguardian.com/australia-news/gallery/2020/apr/06/kakadu-of-the-south-88000-hectares-of-nsw-wetland-handed-back-to-nari-nari.

Ryan, John C. 2020. 'Plant and Swamp: The Biocultural Histories of Five Australian Hydrophytes.' In *Australian Wetland Cultures: Swamps and the Environmental Crisis,* edited by John C. Ryan and Li Chen, 99-138. Lanham, MD: Lexington Books.

Ryan, John C. 2021. 'Toward a Phen(omen)ology of the Seasons: The Emergence of the Indigenous Weather Knowledge Project.' In *The Seasons: Philosophical, Literary, and Environmental Perspectives,* edited by Luke Fischer and David Macauley, 113-139. Albany, NY: State University of New York Press.

Ryan, John C., Danielle Brady and Chris Kueh. 2020. 'Where Fanny Balbuk Walked: Reenvisioning Perth's Wetlands.' In *Australian Wetland Cultures: Swamps and the Environmental Crisis,* edited by John C. Ryan and Li Chen, 163-174. Lanham, MD: Lexington Books.

Ryan, John C. and Li Chen, eds. 2020. *Australian Wetland Cultures: Swamps and the Environmental Crisis.* Lanham, MD: Lexington Books.

Save the Hopkins River - Stop the Quarry Group (STHR-STQG). 2020. *Objection to Planning Application.*

Sayers, Andrew. 1998. 'Eugene von Guérard 1811-1901: 'Tower Hill 1855'.' In *New Worlds from Old: 19th Century Australian and American Landscapes,* edited by Elizabeth Johns, Andrew Sayers and Elizabeth Kornhauser, 154. Canberra: National Gallery of Australia/Hartford, CT: Wadsworth Atheneum.

Schodde, Richard. 1982. *The Fairy Wrens: A Monograph of the Maluriade.* Illustrated by Richard Weatherly. Melbourne: Lansdowne.

Sciolino, Elaine. 2020. *The Seine: The River that Made Paris.* New York: W. W. Norton.

Scott, James C. 2017. *Against the Grain: A Deep History of the Earliest States.* New Haven: Yale University Press.

Sherwood, John. 1982. *An Angler's Map of the Hopkins River Estuary.* Warrnambool: Warrnambool Institute Press.

Short, Daniel. 2020. 'Weatherly's Latest Work Takes Flight.' *The Geelong Times,* October 29. Accessed December 14, 2020. https://timesnewsgroup.com.au/geelongtimes/living/weatherlys-latest-work-takes-flight/

Smyth, R. Brough. 1878. *The Aborigines of Victoria: With Notes Relating to the Habits of the Natives of Other Parts of Australia and Tasmania / Compiled from Various Sources for the Government of Victoria, volume II.* Melbourne: John Ferres, Govt. Printer.

Steffensen, Victor. 2020. *Fire Country: How Indigenous Fire Management Could Help Save Australia.* Richmond, Victoria: Hardie Grant Travel.

Sutter, Paul S. 2021. 'Foreword: Entangled Agencies,' in Emily O'Gorman, *Wetlands in a Dry Land: More-Than-Human-Histories of the Murray-Darling Basin,* Seattle: University of Washington Press, ix-xiii.

Swift, Graham. 1985. *Waterland.* London: Picador.

Thoreau, Henry David. 1962. *The Journal 1837-1861, Volumes I-XIV,* edited by Bradford Torrey and Francis Allen. New York: Dover.

Thoreau, Henry David. 1982. *The Portable Thoreau,* edited by Carl Bode. New York: Viking Penguin.

Thoreau, Henry David. 1988. *The Maine Woods.* New York: Viking Penguin. First published in 1864.

Thoreau, Henry David. 1993. *Faith in a Seed,* edited by Bradley Dean. Washington, D.C.: Island Press/Covelo, California: Shearwater Books.

Thoreau, Henry David. 1998. *A Week on the Concord and Merrimack Rivers,* edited by H. Daniel Peck. New York: Penguin. First published in 1849.

Thoreau, Henry David. 2001. *Collected Essays and Poems.* New York: Library of America.

Thorson, Robert M. 2014. *Walden's Shore: Henry David Thoreau and Nineteenth-Century Science.* Cambridge, MA: Harvard University Press.

Thorson, Robert M. 2017. *The Boatman: Henry David Thoreau's River Years.* Cambridge, MA: Harvard University Press.

Thorson, Robert. 2018. *The Guide to Walden Pond.* Boston: Houghton Mifflin.

Tuck, J. and L. Farrington. 2016. *Wetland Restoration Options for Mortlake Common Flora Reserve.* Nature Glenelg Trust, Mount Gambier, South Australia. Accessed July 21 2021. https://www.google.com/search?client=safari&rls=en&q=Tuck,+J.+%26+Farrington, +L.+(2016)+Wetland+restoration+options+for+Mortlake+Common+Flora+Reserve. +Nature+Glenelg+Trust,+Mount+Gambier,+South+Australia&ie=UTF-8&oe=UTF-8

Victorian Places, NDA. *Ararat.* Accessed March 12, 2021. https://www.victorianplaces.com.au/ararat

Victorian Places, NDB. *Ellerslie.* Accessed March 12, 2021. https://www.victorianplaces.com.au/ellerslie.

Victorian Places, NDC. *Framlingham.* Accessed September 13, 2021. https://www.victorianplaces.com.au/framlingham.

Victorian Places. NDD. *Hexham.* Accessed March 12, 2021. https://www.victorianplaces.com.au/hexham.

Victorian Places. NDE. *Mortlake and Mortlake Shire.* Accessed February 7, 2021. https://www.victorianplaces.com.au/mortlake-and-mortlake-shire.

Victorian Places. NDF. *Wickliffe.* Accessed March 12, 2021. https://www.victorianplaces.com.au/wickliffe

Victorian Fishers Authority. ND. *Hopkins River: Successful Fishing.* Accessed June 22 2021. https://vfa.vic.gov.au/recreational-fishing/fishing-locations/hopkins-river

Victorian State Government Department of Environment, Land, Water and Planning. ND. 'Victorian Volcanic Plains.' *Bioregions and EVC Benchmarks.* Accessed 26 January 2021. https://www.environment.vic.gov.au/biodiversity/bioregions-and-evc-benchmarks.

Victorian Volcanic Plain Biosphere Committee, The. 2017. *Victorian Volcanic Plains*

Conservation Management News. Accessed 26 January 2021. https://victorianvolcanicplain scmn. wordpress.com/2017/04/16/sheep-and-native-grassland-management-on-the-vvp/.

Victorian Volcanic Plain Biosphere Inc. 2020. *Victorian Volcanic Plain Biosphere Project.* Accessed 26 January 2021. https://www.vvpb.com.au/home/.

Wahlquist, Calla. 2021. 'Traditional owners devastated by alleged damage to 1,500-year-old stone arrangement in Victoria.' *The Guardian,* April 6. Accessed 6 April 2021. https://www.theguardian.com/australia-news/2021/apr/06/traditional-owners-devastated-by-alleged-damage-to-1500-year-old-stone-arrangement-in-victoria

Walton, Izaak and Charles Cotton. 2016. *The Compleat Angler.* Oxford: Oxford University Press. First published in 1676.

Ward, Maya. 2011. *The Comfort of Water: A River Pilgrimage.* Yarraville: Transit Lounge.

Warrnambool Art Gallery. 2021. 'Mirteetch Meering (Sea Country).' Accessed 13 June 2021. https://www.thewag.com.au/exhibition/mirteetch-meering-sea-country

Waup, Lisa. 2021. 'Seaing Land.' *Warrnambool Art Gallery January-June 2021,* Exhibition Catalogue, 1 and 24.

Weatherly, Richard. 2020. *A Brush with Birds: Paintings and Stories from the Wild.* Richmond, Victoria: Hardie Grant Travel.

Webb, Hugh 1996. 'Aboriginal Country: Not a Construction, A Way of Being.' In *Western Australian Wetlands: The Kimberley and South-West,* edited by Rod Giblett and Hugh Webb, 61-76. Perth, Western Australia: Black Swan Press/Wetlands Conservation Society.

Wettenhall, Gib. 1999. *The People of Gariwerd: The Grampians' Aboriginal Heritage.* Melbourne: Aboriginal Affairs Victoria.

Wheelwright, Horace. 1861. *Bush Wanderings of a Naturalist; or, Notes on the Field Sports and Fauna of Australia Felix.* London: Routledge, Warne, and Routledge.

Whitlock, Fiona, 1982. 'Wildlife Artist's Eight-Year Pursuit of the Fairy Wren.' *The Australian Women's Weekly,* July 28, 22-23. Accessed November 30, 2020. https://trove.nla.gov.au/newspaper/article/51760659?searchTerm=Connewarran.

Wilkie, Benjamin. 2020. *Gariwerd: An Environmental History of the Grampians.* Clayton South, Victoria: CSIRO.

Williams, Nicholas S.G., Adrian Marshall and John W. Morgan (editors). 2015. *Land of Sweeping Plains: Managing and Restoring the Native Temperate Grasslands of South-Eastern Australia.* Clayton South, Victoria: CSIRO Publishing.

Williams, Raymond. 1973. *The Country and the City.* London: Chatto & Windus.

Williams, Raymond. 1977. *Marxism and Literature.* Oxford: Oxford University Press.

Williams, Raymond. 1985. *Towards 2000.* Harmondsworth: Penguin.

Williams, Raymond. 1989. *Resources of Hope: Culture, Democracy, Socialism,* edited by Robin Gable. London: Verso.

Wilson, Alexander. 1992. *The Culture of Nature: North American Landscape From Disney to the Exxon Valdez.* Cambridge, Massachusetts: Blackwell.

Wilson, Ben. 2020. *Metropolis: A History of the City, Humankind's Greatest Invention.* New York: Doubleday.

Winchester, Simon. 2021. *Land: How the Hunger for Ownership Shaped the World.* London: William Collins.

NOTES:

Introduction:

[1] For the wetlands of the Murray-Darling Basin, see O'Gorman (2021, esp. 7). See also her extensive 'Notes' (199-242) and brief 'Selected Bibliography' (243-250) for references on the Murray-Darling Basin compared to the few books and chapters in books about the Hopkins River Basin mentioned in the references to the present volume.

[2] See Crampton's (2019) extensive 'Select Bibliography' (289-297) of books about the Thames. For a brief discussion of "the new nature writing," see Cowley (2008). For my own "new nature writing" about the wetland next to which I lived for 28 years, see Giblett (2013). Like the Thames, the Hopkins has many artists (as we will see in the present volume). For the cultural and natural history of the Yarra River, see Giblett (2020b, chapter 8) and its references.

[3] Banfield (1986, 3) concurs that Hopkins was "a military friend." Alan E. J. Andrews (1986, 192) gives him the rank of Captain. McKenzie (2011, 15) concurs that Hopkins was a friend, but promotes him to Major.

[4] For Leopold as "the patron saint of marshes," see Giblett (2020c, chapter 7).

[5] It follows in the footsteps of *New Lives of the Saints* (Giblett 2020c) and *Black Swan Song* (Giblett 2021a, parts II and III). The former is about twelve environmental apostles (including Thoreau as the patron saint of swamps and Leopold as the patron saint of marshes), and the latter is about these twelve "major" environmental apostles and the twelve minor prophets of the old testament of the bible, as well as about a further twelve "minor" environmental apostles. I discuss the biblical books of *Genesis* and *the Psalms* in *Environmental Humanities and Theologies* (Giblett 2018, chapters 1 and 5).

[6] This difference has not been noticed nor commented upon by Paul Carter (1987, chapter 4) in his long discussion based on archival research and published sources of Mitchell's extensive body of work. Carter also overlooks that for Mitchell 'Australia Felix' was in part a sublime country, or more precisely, some aspects of it were, and so does not comment on the differences between Mitchell's and Stapylton's accounts of it in aesthetic terms (as we will see in chapter 3 of the present volume).

[7] Despite a recent shift in acknowledging the importance of wetlands for ancient Mesopotamia and "the invention of the city," some writers on the topic persist in calling this time and place the birth, or dawn, of civilization *per se* as signalled in the title of their books; see Wilson (2020, 401-402, n1). "The first cities" were not only, as Ackroyd (2009, 182) puts it, "created by the rivers" of Mesopotamia (in both senses for him of being created beside them with the rivers as the agent of creation), but also created by the marshes of Mesopotamia literally *between* the rivers. London is also the creation of the Thames River and its marshes.

[8] For a brief discussion and illustrations of Aboriginal eel traps and "game nets" in "well-watered areas" of Australia (such as mid-western Victoria) with no mention and mapping of wetlands here (nor anywhere else in Australia for that matter), see *The Macquarie Atlas of Indigenous Australia* (Arthur and Morphy, eds 2019, 27-28, 53, 66, 148-149), yet another disappointing instance of wetlands being written out of geography, history and cartography, of an atlas being an instrument of colonization and neo-colonization, and of aquaterracide (the genocide of wetlands). For further discussion of wetlands being written out of geography, history and cartography, maps as an instrument of colonization and neo-colonization, and proposals for the decolonization of wetlands, especially in relation to Perth and Melbourne, see Giblett (1996, chapter 3; 2020b, chapter 5). For decolonization of nature and deconstruction of the nature-culture binary, see Giblett (2011), aquaterracide, see Giblett (1996) and paludiculture, see Giblett (2021).

[9] This is a Marxist economic theory of value and critique of political economy. Both 'land and labour' are the creators of value and wealth. This theory respects and values that the economic base has an environmental foundation. For further discussion, see Giblett (2011, chapters 1 and 2).

[10] For the history and politics of improvement in England, especially the creation of 'pleasing prospects' in English rural landscapes, see Williams (1973, esp. 122-123; see also Giblett 2020c, chapter 10). For the history and politics of the enclosure of traditional wetland commons into private property in the English Fens, see Giblett (2021, chapter 3). For the history and politics of the colonial clearance of the traditional Aboriginal clan estates with their wetlands in mid-western Victoria, see chapter 5 of the present volume. For "the Australian gentleman's park is Aboriginal country," see Giblett (2011, 91-94). For "the biggest estate on earth," see Gammage (2011). For the economics and politics of "the commons" and recent proposals for "commoning land" and "decolonizing nature," see Obeng-Odoom (2021).

[11] For further discussion of decolonizing nature in general and wetlands in particular, first proposed in the early/mid 1990s, see Giblett (1996, 74-76).

[12] Flooded rice paddies are, as O'Gorman (2021, 16, 100, 105, 118) points out on several occasions, "a kind of wetland," certainly as far as ducks and other species are concerned. The boundary between the two is permeable, as she relates later with birds, frogs, insects and plants crossing it in the case of a couple

of swamps and a rice-growing irrigation area in the Murray-Darling Basin (O'Gorman 2021, 97-119). For a review of O'Gorman (2021), see Appendix 1 of the present volume.

[13] For further discussion of living bio- and psycho-symbiotic livelihoods in bioregional home habitats of the living earth, see Giblett (2011, chapter 12).

[14] Including from its source as traced by Sciolino (2020). The wetlands along the course of the Seine includes those of Paris in the past when it was "Lutece" or "Lutetia," meaning "filthy marsh." Sciolino (2020) touches on this periodically. For Paris as a marsh metropolis, see Giblett (2016, chapter 2).

Chapter 1:

[15] For Thoreau as the patron saint of swamps, see Giblett (1996, 229-239; 2020c, chapter 4; 2021c, chapter 8).

[16] For Leopold as the patron saint of marshes, see Giblett (2020c, chapter 7).

[17] For Massey as the patron saint of regenerative farming, see Giblett (2021a, chapter 41).

[18] *The Boatman* follows Thorson's earlier and similar *Walden's Shore* (Thorson 2014) and was followed by his *Guide to Walden Pond* (Thorson 2018), all indispensable to Thoreauvians. Thorson is the patron saint of Thoreauvian saunterers and students.

[19] For Carson as the patron saint of American conservation, see Giblett (2020c, chapter 8) and Leopold as the patron saint of marshes, see Giblett (2020c, chapter 7).

[20] Trump's fascination or obsession with the uncanny and swampy city of Washington, D.C. (literally and figuratively) prompted me to dub him "the uncanny Trumpster" and to engage in a piece of satirical invective on his inauguration as the 45th President of the US. For the history of Washington DC as a wetland city, see Giblett (2016, chapter 13); for "the uncanny Trumpster," see Giblett (2020d, chapters 5 and 6).

[21] For a critique and call for the decolonization of the egregious nature/culture opposition, see Giblett (2011, especially chapters 1 and 2); for wetlands as wombs and abstraction of water bodies into water, see Giblett (1996, 146-147; 2016, 13). Tom Blass (2022, 6 n2) quotes my discussion of wetlands as wombs from *Cities and Wetlands* (Giblett 2016, 13) and suggests that I should have been "reined in." I can only reply that I am not a horse! Equally Blass's overuse of commas in *Swamp Songs* should have been curbed by an astute copy editor getting him to write shorter sentences.

[22] Proulx (2022, 133-134) acknowledges that "Thoreau has been called the patron saint of swamps because in them he found the deepest kind of beauty and interest." Thoreau also found in swamps the deepest kind of religion of love for a place (more than the mere "fondness" for them she goes on to ascribe to him). Proulx avoids Thoreau's religion of swamps, the theology of the Fens and Seamus Heaney's heretical counter-Catholic Irish bogism in her discussion of his poetry (Proulx 2022, 102, 110-111). For Heaney as the patron saint of bogs, see Giblett (2020c, chapter 11). For Thoreau as the patron saint of swamps, see Giblett (1996, 229-239), the first such naming (see also Giblett 2020c, chapter 4; 2021c, chapter 8).

[23] Each of these aspects receives an extensive, often chapter-by-chapter, treatment in Giblett (1996).

[24] For Burton, Bunyan and beyond, such as E. M. Cioran and muddy melancholy, see Giblett (2021c, chapter 2).

[25] The word "melancholy" appears 32 times in *Middlemarch*. The counter to melancholy is "ardent," or "ardor," Eliot's favourite word, that appears 57 times in total. For further discussion of melancholy as loss of oneself and the psycho(eco)logy of wetlands, see Giblett (2021c, chapter 2).

Chapter 2:

[26] In the seventeenth century William Dugdale (1662) wilfully misquoted this verse to justify after the fact the large-scale drainage of the English Fens as a God-given task when he wrote as the opening gambit of his history "that works of Drayning are most antient, and of divine institution, we have the testimony of holy Scripture. "In the beginning God said, let the waters be gathered together, and let the dry land appear; and it was so"." In the beginning God created wetlands. In order to separate land and water, they were not separated in the beginning. In separating land and water, God did not drain water from the land. Ash (2017) gives a detailed historical account of the draining of the Fens in the seventeenth century, including a discussion of Dugdale's role in documenting and legitimising it. Ash states in passing that "draining the Fens [...] was God's manifest will" and later that "the first drainage projector in his [Dugdale's] account was God, who had had separated the earth from the water at the Creation" (Ash 2017, 182-183, 291). At the creation, on the first day, God did not separate earth and water; that was on the second day, after the first creation of the heavens and the earth. Arguably separation is not creation, but destruction. In an earlier article Ash (2016, 456) argued that "a few projectors and their supporters viewed fen drainage as [having] a divine mandate." Dugdale was among the supporters who misquoted the bible and used it to legitimise the projectors' own capitalist, political and economic power and profit-

making, a not uncommon practice then and since. Yet this was all justification after the fact as earlier royals, royalists and republicans alike generally did not reach for their bibles to legitimise their own capitalist, political and economic power and profit-making in draining the Fens. The enclosure of the commons into private property was "a plain enough case of class robbery," as the late, great E. P. Thompson said. Ash neglects Thompson's critique and the class politics and capitalist economics of the draining of the fens and enclosing of commons into private property, opting instead for euphemistic "propertied elites," etc., including royalty. Charles I played a decisive and deleterious role in the draining of the Fens and enclosing commons, a fact not lost on some Fenlanders. Ash relates how the Epworth rioters in 1628 "identified King Charles as the main source and target of their discontent" as he "had personally concluded the agreement with [Cornellius] Vermuyden to drain *their lands*" (my emphasis; Ash 2017, 142). Ash later argues that "draining the Fens, Charles [I] believed, was an intrinsic good that would benefit the commonwealth and boost royal revenues through improvement" (Ash 2017, 175). The result was that "virtually all the major English projects undertaken in the seventeenth century were begun after Charles came to the throne in 1625" (Ash 2017, 175). In November 1641 the Commons presented to Charles I a set of grievances known as "the Grand Remonstrance", including the complaint that "large quantities of common [...] grounds hath been taken [...] by colour of the Statue of Improvement" (Ash 2017, p.205). The long battle over its passage in parliament between divided royalists and parliamentarians led to the Civil War and the execution of Charles as a tyrant in 1649 (Ash 2017, 205-206, 215). Aquaterracide led to regicide. Yet killing off the king did not lead to the cessation of draining the Fens. The Civil War, Ash goes on to argue, "had wrought many changes on England's political landscape, but it had not altered the plight or fate of the Fens. [...] The new Commonwealth regime was just as enthusiastic about draining the Fens and profiting from the enclosure of [common wetlands into] improved [dry]land [and private property] as the Crown had been" (Ash 2017, 217, 219). The aquaterracide led by Charles I from 1625 to 1649 was perpetuated by the Commonwealth of 1649-1660. Especially galling for many Fenlanders was the fact that they had fought on the parliamentarians' side against the royalists in the Civil War in the mistaken belief that the parliament would support and prosecute their resistance to the draining of the Fens. The aquaterracide led by Charles I and continued by the Commonwealth was perpetuated in the British empire, including Australia. Could Charles III right some of the historical wrongs of Charles I and make some amends for them by instituting a program rehabilitating wetlands in the UK and Commonwealth countries along the lines of "the Queen's Green Canopy" in the UK and "the Queen's Commonwealth Canopy" that plants trees? 'The King's Commonwealth Wetlands'? For further discussion of paludiculture, see Giblett (2021, introduction). For further discussion of the theology of wetlands and its role in draining, including the Fens, see Giblett (1996) and (2021c, chapters 2 and 4). For discussion of the draining of the Fens without mentioning theology, see Proulx (2022, chapter 2).

[27] Clark (1990, figure 4, table 7, 108-109) does not record an Aboriginal name for the mountain.

[28] For the cultural and natural history of Perth and the black Swan River, see Giblett (2013, chapter 15).

[29] For the cultural and natural history of the black swan, see Giblett (2013, chapters 13 and 14).

[30] For photographs of the yam daisy, see Clarke (2018d, 275) and Wettenhall (1999, 36 and 39).

[31] For further discussion of taxonomy in relation to wetlands, see Giblett (1996, 3-4). For further discussion of taxonomy in relation to nature and natural history drawing on the work of Michel Foucault, see Giblett (2011, 24-26).

[32] For a review of this book, see Appendix 2 of the present volume.

[33] For a recent discussion of Hannah Arendt's concept/metaphor of natality, or "being born," in relation to the womb of wetlands and in contrast and counter to Martin Heidegger's morbid, solipsistic philosophy of "being towards death," see Giblett (2021c, 17, 132-133). For further discussion of the Rainbow Serpent and Rainbow Spirit, see Giblett (2020e, chapter 9).

Chapter 3:

[34] For the history of a Scottish/Latin name of a portion of the Scottish Highlands being applied to mountain ranges in western Victoria in Australia, see Wilkie (2020, 45).

[35] For a map showing some Grampians wetlands, such as Brady's Swamp, Bryan Swamp and Lake Muirhead, and other water bodies, all depicted in blue, and not showing some Grampians wetlands, such as Mt William (or Big) Swamp, Walker Swamp and others, see Parks Victoria (2018). For a discussion of the mapping convention of depicting wetlands and other water bodies in blue, see Giblett (2021c, chapter 9).

[36] For black water as a blot both on the landscape of the pleasing pastoral prospect and in the English landed gentleman's ledger, see Giblett (1996, chapter 1) drawing on Wilkie Collins' *The Woman in White*.

[37] It's worth quoting at length Milton's longer description of Eden in book 4 of *Paradise Lost* (lines 223-268) in order to highlight the parallels that Mitchell might easily have drawn in his mind's eye between it

and 'Australia Felix' (though the Hopkins is certainly not a large river and was a typical disappointment for many early European explorers of Australia trying to find one):

> Southward through Eden went a river large
> Nor changed his course, but through the shaggy hill
> Pass'd underneath ingulf'd; for God had thrown
> That mountain as his garden-mound high-raised
> Upon the rapid current, which through veins
> Of porous earth with kindly thirst up-drawn,
> Rose a fresh fountain, and with many a rill
> Water'd the garden; thence united fell
> Down the steep glade, and met the nether flood,
> Which from his darksome passage now appears,
> And, now divided into four main streams,
> Runs diverse, wandering many a famous realm
> And country, whereof here needs no account;
> But rather to tell how, if art could tell,
> How from that sapphire fount the crisped brooks,
> Rolling on orient pearl and sands of gold,
> With mazy error under pendent shades
> Ran nectar, visiting each plant, and fed
> Flowers worthy of Paradise, which not nice art
> In beds and curious knots, but nature boon
> Pour'd forth profuse on hill, and dale, and plain,
> Both where the morning sun first warmly smote
> The open field, and where the unpierced shade
> Imbrown'd the noontide bowers: thus was this place
> A happy rural seat of various view;
> Groves whose rich trees wept odorous gums and balm;
> Others whose fruit, burnish'd with golden rind,
> Hung amiable, Hesperian fables true,
> If true, here only, and of delicious taste:
> Betwixt them lawns, or level downs, and flocks
> Grazing the tender herb, were interposed,
> Or palmy hillock; or the flowery lap
> Of some irriguous valley spread her store,
> Flowers of all hue, and without thorn the rose:
> Another side, umbrageous grots and caves
> Of cool recess, o'er which the mantling vine
> Lays forth her purple grape, and gently creeps
> Luxuriant; meanwhile murmuring waters fall
> Down the slope hills, dispersed, or in a lake,
> That to the fringed bank with myrtle crown'd
> Her crystal mirror holds, unite their streams.
> The birds their quire apply; airs, vernal airs,
> Breathing the smell of field and grove, attune
> The trembling leaves, while universal Pan,
> Knit with the Graces and the Hours in dance,
> Led on the eternal Spring.

If one substituted Bunjil for God, and the Rainbow Serpent for Pan in Milton's Eden (and made some other adjustments), one might come close to describing Mitchell's Eden of the Hopkins Basin as 'a Happy Pastural Estate of Aboriginal Ownership':

> Southward through Eden went a river small
> Nor changed its serpentine course, but through the shaggy hill
> Pass'd underneath ingulf'd; for Bunjil had thrown
> Those mountains as his garden-mound high-raised
> Upon the sluggish current, which through veins
> Of porous earth with kindly thirst up-drawn,
> Rose chained lagoons, and with many a rill
> Water'd the garden; thence united fell
> Down the steep glade, and met the nether flood,

Which from his darksome passage now appears,
And, now converged from three main creeks,
Runs diverse, wandering many a famous realm
And country, whereof here needs no account
For explorers had waxed lyrical on its behalf;
But rather to tell how, if art could tell,
How from that sapphire fount the crisped brooks,
Rolling on orient pearl and sands of gold,
With mazy error under pendent shades
Ran nectar, visiting each plant, and fed
Flowers worthy of Paradise, which not nice art
In beds and curious knots, but nurture's boon
Of native people's care for country
Pour'd forth profuse on hill, and dale, and plain,
Both where the morning sun first warmly smote
The open field, and where the unpierced shade
Imbrown'd the noontide bowers: thus was this place
A happy pastural estate of Aboriginal country;
Groves whose rich gum trees wept odorous oils;
Others whose fruit, burnish'd with golden rind,
Grew amiable, ancient fables true,
If true, here only, and of delicious taste:
Betwixt them lawns, or level downs, and mobs
Grazing the tender herb, were interposed,
Of some irriguous valley spread her store,
Flowers of all hue, and without the thorny rose:
Another side, umbrageous grots and caves
Of cool recess, with painted walls of stories eld

Seeping colours into older rock
Meanwhile murmuring waters fall
Down the slope hills, dispersed, or in a lake,
That to the fringed bank with rushes crown'd
Her crystal mirror holds, unite their streams.
The birds their quire apply; airs, vernal airs,
Breathing the smell of field and grove, attune
The trembling leaves, while the Rainbow Serpent,
Knit with the Graces and the Hours in dance,
Led on the eternal now of cyclic seasons.

More than mere parody — the specular and merely amusing paralleling of one text in another for idle entertainment — the rewritten poem aspires to carnivalesque subversion, cultural and environmental decolonization and progressive politics. The distinction between parodic inversion and carnivalesque subversion comes from Bakhtin (1984).

[38] For writing as inscription and as an instrument of power as distinct from writing as trace and as a performance of inhabitation, see Giblett (1996, chapter 3).

[39] For native and feral quaking zones, see Giblett (2009, Chapter 1).

Chapter 4:

[40] For further discussion of the aesthetics of wetlandscapes, see Giblett (1996, chapters 1 and 2). Annie Proulx (2022, 88-89) claims that Albrecht Dürer's 1497 exquisite watercolour *Der Weiher im Walde (The Small Pond in a Wood)* is "the first known artist's representation of a natural wetland." Or precisely, it is arguably the first known *European* artist's *landscape* representation of a natural wetland as Aboriginal rock paintings of the Rainbow Serpent are at least 6000 years old.

[41] This painting is reproduced as the cover image for *Swamp Deaths: Collected Cold Cases and Other Marshy Mysteries* (Giblett 2022). It is also included in a 'Missing' poster in the fourth detective story of *Swamp Deaths* and is the basis for the story. *Swamp Deaths* introduces Inspector Colin 'Alan' Thorow in his meta-detective memoirs (including his quest for "the Benjamin code" to unlock the secret of swamps and cities):

Death in a Swamp Two mysterious deaths occur in two separate swamps in Victoria on the same day. The coroners in both cases deliver an open verdict, but the two cases must be connected in some way, as Thorow quickly finds out and solves both mysteries.

Rebirth in a Swamp Concerns a swamp in the United States, the beginnings of Thorow's quest for the Benjamin code to unlock the secret of swamps, and a bog in Ireland with its mysterious, secret stories.

Death in the Fens, England's most famous wetland with a rich natural and cultural history. Thorow gets involved in the case of the death of a local brewer. Was his death accidental, suicide or murder? He solves the mystery with a twist in the tail of the tale.

Death of a Swamp An old man reports that a beautiful swamp in western Victoria is missing and possibly dead. It was depicted in an old painting by a famous colonial painter in the nineteenth century, but no one is sure where it is and if it still exists. Thorow solves this mystery, and ends up investigating a death in a swamp, and solving that too.

Death of Venice, Swamp City Central Thorow encounters a strange figure living in a book-lined apartment down the smelly canals of Venice who teaches him about the history of Venice built in swamps and compares it to Paris built in marshes.

Death in Paris, Major Marsh Metropolis Thorow goes to Paris to investigate Walter Benjamin's mysterious death and the equally mysterious disappearance of Benjamin's valise with the manuscript of his highly prized last masterpiece. Thorow travels on to Spain where Benjamin died (or did he?) and where Thorow solves both mysteries.

Death at Black Swan Swamp The case has a literary bent, a swampy slant and international implications that means it needs to be handled sensitively. Thorow is the man for the job on all three counts.

Death of the Swamp World Thorow investigates this death, solves the mystery and discovers the Benjamin code in the process with the help of a guide in Melbourne, a city of ghost swamps.

Death of the Swamp Lady An actual cold case that involves the death of "the swamp lady" or "the lady of the swamp," Margaret Clements. Thorow does not solve it, but helps solves another death in a swamp.

Death of the Swamp Man The well-known death of an Australian writer killed in the crash of a plane shot down over Ukraine by a missile fired by pro-Russian militia also involved the loss of his last novel set in a swamp in Victoria.

With its rich blend of fiction and faction ('non-fiction') crossing between history and philosophy, and combining memoir and biography, *Swamp Deaths* is a unique series of detective stories written by a swamp ghost writer/ghost swamp writer. It mixes different types of texts and creates new and intriguing ways of environmental storytelling that will fascinate and delight rusted-on readers of detective fiction and attract new ones. As *Swamp Deaths* does not include any acknowledgements, I would like to take this opportunity to record in print my gratitude to Anne Bennett for alerting me to the true crime story of the death of the swamp lady.

[42] For the cultural and natural history of the black swan, see Giblett (2013, chapters 13 and 14), and of alligators and crocodiles, see Giblett (2009, chapter 2; 2018, chapter 4; 2019a, chapter 2; 2019b, chapter 3).

Chapter 5:

[43] These details of the Weatherly family history are taken from Ronald (1978, 75-76, 104-106) and Weatherly (2020, 74).

[44] Williams was a socialist, anti-nuclear campaigner, one of the founders of cultural studies and eco-criticism, and the patron saint of ecocultural studies. For a brief introduction to his life and work, see Giblett (2020c, chapter 10).

[45] Or 114 on William's list and 141 on Lionel's; see Weatherly (2020, 74-75).

[46] For thinking, feeling and acting in concert, see also Massy (2020, 363, 365, 369). For Massy as the patron saint of regenerative farming, see Giblett (2021a, chapter 41).

[47] Massy proceeds from the micro to the macro scales, from the practical to the paradigmatic. Compare his inductive and scientific preference and procedure with my arts/humanities ones in *People and Places of Nature and Culture* (Giblett 2011, chapter 1) of going in the opposite direction by beginning with outlining two paradigms (cognate with Massy's; Giblett 2011, figure 2, 32-34), arguing for a paradigm shift from one to the other upfront, and finally concluding with a more practical discussion of symbiosis, bioregions and livelihoods (Giblett 2011, chapter 12).

Chapter 6:

[48] For further discussion of the seasons and the weather in Aboriginal, European and Australian colonial cultures, see Giblett (2021b).

[49] For further discussion of the greed of mining, drawing in part on Aldo Leopold's concept of land pathology, see Giblett (2019b, chapter 5).

Chapter 7:

[50] In the sense of being made by the side of, or set beside, the Hopkins. Warrnambool and the Hopkins

are unlike the Seine, "the river that made Paris" (Sciolino 2020) in the sense of creating the (is)lands and the wetlands on and by which Paris was founded and built (touched on periodically by Sciolino 2020). For Paris as a wetland city, see Giblett (2016, chapter 2). Warrnambool and the Hopkins are also unlike the Thames, the river that "fashioned London" (Ackroyd 2009, 9; see also 71: "London was the creation of the river"), as did the marshes along its course on and by which London was founded and built (touched on periodically by Ackroyd 2009). For London as a wetland city, see Giblett (2016, chapter 3).

[51] For the Brisbane River, its city and wetlands, see Cook (2019) and Leardini, Ozgun and Mouils (2019); for Melbourne, its wetlands and the Yarra and Maribyrnong Rivers, see Bertram and Murphy (2019, 79-153) and Giblett (2020b, chapters 2-5 and 8; 2021c, chapter 7); for the Swan River, Perth/Fremantle and their wetlands, see Brady and Murray (2020); Giblett (1996, chapter 3; 2013, chapter 15); Martin and London (2019); Ryan, Brady and Kueh (2020); for Sydney and its wetlands, see Giblett (2021c, chapter 6); for London and the Thames, as well as other European and North American cities and their wetlands, see Giblett (2016). The largest Australian, European and North American cities, and all the iconic cities of modernity (including Sydney and Melbourne), were founded in ancient or modern times in or next to wetlands derived from land drainage and modified by civil engineering, such as embanking, and landscape architecture, such as landscaping into lakes, gardens and parklands. The drainage in these cities is natural and cultural with the lie of the land and the flow of the water modified by colonial civil engineering and occasionally overloaded by floods with devastating consequences. The classic case of embankment is the Thames in London in which land was "reclaimed" from water in a feat of engineering considered to be "akin to a form of creation" (see Ackroyd 2009, 207-209). More precisely, it was a reversal of God's first and best work of creation in which land and water were mixed and a continuation of God's subsequent act of creation of separating land and water (as we saw in the first chapter of the present volume).

[52] For the cultural and natural history of the Thames Estuary, including the downriver outsourcing of sewage and other wastes into the "black holes" of marshes or "Black Deep" (the ultimate denigration, or 'blackening'), see Ackroyd (2009, 393-398); Crampton (2019) and Lichtenstein (2017); for specific wetland sites in the estuary, such as: the present-day conservation of the Rainham Marshes, see Crampton (2919, 162), Giblett (2021c, 170-171), and Lichtenstein (2017, 24); the current development threats to the Dickensian "marsh country" of Hoo Peninsula and the campaign to conserve it, see Crampton (2019, 229, 233, 237-238, 241-242) and Lichtenstein (2017, 44-45, 221-228); and the rehabilitation of the Shell Haven oil refinery as the Stanford Wharf Nature Reserve, see Lichtenstein (2017, 45) and Crampton (2019, 213). As Ackroyd (2009, 397) writes, "this has been one of the dark places of the earth" reprising Conrad whose heart of darkness of upstream colonial rivers, such as the Thames, ends up in the cloaca of darkness of the black waters of polluted downstream estuarine marshes. The Thames Estuary must be the world capital for the oxymoronic rehabilitation of rubbish tips and other toxic sites as "nature reserves," or as Crampton (2019, 26) puts it, "landfill heaps transformed into wildlife reserves." It is an irony of history that the first national parks were industrially useless or worthless lands (as we saw in chapter 3 of the present volume), whereas nowadays industrially polluted wet wastelands in the Thames Estuary with which "there is nothing else to do" are being rehabilitated as "nature reserves." See, for instance, Two Tree Island polluted with PCBs and DDT (Lichtenstein 2017, 109-110, 239-240).

[53] For a review of O'Gorman (2021), see Appendix 1 of the present volume.

INDEX

platypus 35, 120-121
pleasing prospects 7, 91, 98, 203 n10
Powell, J. M. 83, 200
Presland, Gary 90, 200
Proulx, Annie 200, 204 n22, 205 n26, 207 n40
psychoanalytic ecology 8, 190, 192, 197

Rainbow Serpent, the 3, 13, 29-30, 36, 42, 58, 73, 75, 174, 195, 197, 205 n35, 206 n37, 207 n40
Rainbow Spirit, the 3, 29, 73, 197, 205 n35
Robertson, John G. 88
Robinson, George A. 18, 59, 64, 69, 80, 83, 85-87, 90, 200
Rollinson, Geoff 11, 161
Rossbridge 4, 42-43, 103
Ryan, John C. 3, 5-7, 9, 11, 68, 189-191, 197, 198, 200, 209 n51

salmon 172-174
Salt Creek 17, 31, 65-66, 105, 111-112
Seine River 14, 30, 50, 149, 201, 204 n14, 209 n50
Sciolino, Elaine 14, 30, 50, 201, 204 n14, 209 n50
Scott, James C. 23, 201
Sherwood, John 11, 14, 17, 33, 39, 168-172, 178-182, 193, 201
Staplyton, Granville W. C. 19-21, 89-90, 193
Steffensen, Victor 67, 70, 71, 201
sublime, the 19, 21-22, 78, 82-84, 89-93, 98, 203 n6

Thames River and Estuary 14-15, 30, 50, 72, 103, 168-169, 193, 196, 198, 203 n2, n7, 209 n50, n 51, n52
Thoreau, Henry David 3, 15, 31, 35, 39-55, 107-108, 112-113, 120, 135, 151, 152, 173-176, 194, 197, 199, 201, 203

n5, 204 n15, n22
Thorson, Robert M. 40-41, 201, 204 n18

Victorian Volcanic Plains (VVP) 9, 13, 62, 110, 119, 145, 164, 202

Walker Swamp 96, 205 n35
Walton, Izaak 157, 172-174, 202
Ward, Maya 15, 202
Warrnambool 4, 6, 10-11, 13, 16, 30, 33, 36-39, 54, 91, 105-106, 112, 147-149, 150, 154, 167-169, 172, 176, 179-180, 182-184
Wartook, Lake and Wartook Reservoir 81, 90, 197
Waup, Lisa 182-183, 202
Weatherly, Hamish 10, 135
Weatherly, Richard and Jenny 5-6, 10, 32, 37, 62, 75, 105-106, 111-112, 114-115, 117, 123, 125-126, 132-145, 172, 194, 200, 201, 202, 208 n43, n45
Webb, Hugh 6, 183, 197, 202
wetland humanities 7, 11, 192
Wettenhall, Gib 24, 28, 66, 69, 81-84, 88, 90-91, 96, 197, 202, 205 n30
Wheelwright, Horace 58, 64, 104-107, 112-115, 120-121, 178, 202
Wickliffe 4-5, 10, 17, 32, 38, 103, 105, 106, 112-113, 118-119, 201
Wilkie, Benjamin 19, 77-82, 84, 87-88, 90, 95, 202, 205 n34,
Willaura 3-5, 37-38, 80, 95, 98, 103, 113-115, 121
Williams, Raymond 7, 136, 189-191, 202, 203 n10, 208 n44
Wills, Horatio 57-58
Winchester, Simon 25, 72, 202
Woorndoo 105, 111

yam daisy 9, 35, 68-69, 205 n30
Yarra River 14-15, 30, 48, 176, 203 n2, 209 n51

www.ingramcontent.com/pod-product-compliance
Lightning Source LLC
Chambersburg PA
CBHW071741270326
41928CB00013B/2757